Jazz Now, published in association with
The Jazz Centre Society, is the first book to reflect fully
the vigorous and exciting world of jazz as it is now. It is a
unique combination of up-to-date reference section and
articles by eminent jazz writers and musicians.

The reference section includes a listing of almost 250
jazz musicians currently active. It also lists clubs,
societies and promoters, as well as jazz record labels,
books, films and specialist shops. In all, an invaluable
guide for the enthusiast.

The articles, ranging from the blues and folk roots to
the avant garde, from profiles of individuals to more
general surveys of the scene, are as diverse as the music
itself. Each of t⎯⎯⎯⎯⎯⎯⎯⎯⎯⎯⎯⎯ sad, is
part of the wo⎯⎯⎯⎯⎯

Jim Dvorak
Photo: Jak Kilby

JAZZ NOW

The Jazz Centre Society Guide

Edited by
Roger Cotterrell
Preface by Spike Milligan

Q QUARTET BOOKS LONDON

First published by Quartet Books Limited 1976
27 Goodge Street, London W1P 1FD
in association with The Jazz Centre Society Limited

Copyright © 1976 by The Jazz Centre Society Limited
and Quartet Books Limited and individual contributors
Reference section copyright © 1976
by The Jazz Centre Society Limited

ISBN 0 7043 3097 0

Typesetting by Bedford Typesetters Ltd

Printed by Anchor Press Ltd, Tiptree, Essex

Art Theman
Photo: David Weale

Contents

WITHDRAWN

1 4 JUN 2023

Keith Tippett
Photo: Jak Kilby

Preface

BEING asked to write a preface on a book about jazz is the same as being asked to write a foreword to the Bible; the prospect is massive, the material unending, and the work would last a lifetime. Well, I'm going in for brevity.

The reason why I accepted the commission to write it is my complete obsession with jazz music. It was a rare chance of fate that I was born and finding my feet in life at the same time that jazz music was. The music itself is of freak-political origin; that is, but for the African slave trade, it would never have happened, and, out of the agony and inhumanity of transported African slaves – slaves with no education, no books, no money – out of all that they actually gave birth to a unique art form, an art form that no one dreamed could happen. It was an art form that fell into place of its own accord; it was a successful mistake; it could be called the Penicillin of Music. Its initial use was one of part entertainment, part emotional release for the protagonists; its use, for once, was not frowned upon by the slave owners. In fact, as it developed, rich planters, after dinner, would summon the slaves to perform their 'Jazz Music' for the entertainment of their friends.

With the collapse of the slave system, freed slaves took their music with them into the cities, travelling illegally on railroads, with the resultant train and boogie rhythms coming into the new music. With the age of industrial affluence, negro groups were hired by steamboat companies, bars, taverns, dance halls, etc. and the rest is history we all know.

The interesting part of jazz since then is the incredible diversification of styles and combinations and the technical progress that has now been reached in which many many jazz musicians exceed their brother classical musicians. And it is *still* diversifying. It has been a boon to man. It was of course working-class in origin, and frowned upon by the classical world at a time when it needed support; nevertheless

I

the infant survived. But – now the bad news – whereas there are still a great number of jazz musicians, the commercial popularity they enjoyed between the Wars has, with the coming of Pop, vanished. Very fine musicians like Stan Tracey find it hard to make a living and this is a sad reflection on our times, for here we have an exciting music, a music that throws off the troubles of both listener and protagonist alike. That is why I am delighted that the Jazz Centre Society are publishing a long overdue Jazz Guide. I wish it my warmest regards and hope it is a success. With me it already is.

SPIKE MILLIGAN

Introduction

LAST year the Jazz Centre Society decided it was about time it held an annual dinner. After all, that's what most august and respectable bodies seem to do. So the event was held and was a great success. The esteemed writer of our preface was on hand and several other famous faces could be spotted at strategic points around the dinner table. One of them was that of critic Charles Fox. The country's most eminent jazz writer was just about to begin his paté when the attractive young lady next to him suddenly landed the ultimate bombshell on a hungry jazz authority. I forget exactly what led up to it but, with a winning smile, she simply asked 'What *is* jazz?' The *New Statesman*'s music critic, who is nothing if not patient, put down his knife and fork, went back to West Africa, the slaves, New Orleans and Congo Square, up to Chicago and then on out to all points north, south, east and west. A little later the young lady, who had hardly expected to hear an excellent pocket history of jazz from one of the people best qualified to give it, turned to me and said, with some awe, 'He's an expert, isn't he?'

People have been asking 'What is Jazz?' for the past fifty years and more. And as the years go by the answer has to get longer and more complicated and more and more hedged around with qualifications. Today jazz covers so many different areas of music from traditional and New Orleans styles through to the European avant-garde that it is hard to offer any generalizations about the word. One cause and effect of the immense variety of music which traces itself back into the jazz tradition, is the spread of jazz throughout the world. So that, now, probably the majority of countries either have a jazz scene of sorts or have produced jazz musicians. Britain, of course, has a jazz tradition stretching back to the visit of the Original Dixieland Jazz Band in 1919 and, after a long period when imitation rather than originality was the norm, the local product gradually began to take on

3

an identity of its own. So that today this country boasts some of the world's finest contemporary jazz musicians and the British jazz scene covers every conceivable area of musical activity which falls under the jazz umbrella.

Some time ago I felt that more should be done to document the jazz scene in Britain than was in fact the case. Although it is very easy to find out almost anything you want to know about famous American stars, the bright names on the British scene are still far too often, just names. Their backgrounds, careers and recorded work are not publicized in a way that befits creative artists, many of whom are making significant contributions to modern music. When I became involved with the Jazz Centre Society I found that similar ideas were being bandied around there. What seemed to be needed was some kind of guide to the British jazz scene that would do something to draw it together and make it perhaps more accessible to those who find the huge variety of activity somewhat bewildering.

This book – JAZZ NOW – is the result of these ideas. It is not a yearbook, nor – as you can see – is it a five volume encyclopedia. It is an attempt to set down in compact form enough information to give a reasonably clear and accurate view of jazz activity in Britain today. Although it focuses on the jazz scene here and now, a glance at the reference section will show that the information contained in it covers much more than the events, personalities, record releases and publications of any one year.

This is, in fact, the first book ever to attempt to look systematically at the British jazz scene and provide a reasonably complete picture of who's who and what's what in the music. The main part of its reference section lists information about the careers and records of nearly two hundred and fifty of the most important musicians active in jazz in Britain today. It aims to give a picture of their musical backgrounds and some of their main achievements and musical activity over the past few years. We hope that it will provide a source of reference that will be of interest and value for some time to come.

The reference part of the book also contains information about jazz record labels available in Britain and the musicians represented on them; it also lists recent jazz books, jazz and blues films, societies and promoters. Not least, the information here should make it much easier for clubs and promoters wishing to book musicians to contact them and conversely for musicians to become aware of venues throughout the country regularly presenting jazz music. In short we hope that this book will meet a real need for better communication within the jazz world and will provide a great deal of interesting information for those who enjoy jazz music.

Although the reference section concentrates on jazz in Britain the ten articles in the first part of the book reflect many aspects of the jazz world at large. I have chosen them to try to reflect a wide variety of viewpoints and many aspects of the music and its personalities today. All have been written specially for this book except the Phil Seamen piece which appeared in a slightly different version in *Cream* magazine and is reprinted here with permission.

Jazz today is not a music with rigid, clearly defined lines around it, or fixed unchangeable rules about what belongs in the jazz world and what does not. The healthiest aspect of jazz now is its openness to new ideas from many musical sources. The old insularity which set it apart and made it, for many people, an incomprehensible world of hip cool aliens is fast disappearing. Jazz is being recognized more and more widely as an open music that has the capacity today to mix its traditions with an infinite range of experimental ideas covering the whole musical spectrum from rock to contemporary European classical music.

Consequently, although for reasons of space the reference section has had to be restricted to entries that seem to fall clearly within generally accepted notions of what jazz is, the articles in the book are wider in scope. They include pieces on ragtime and the blues today and on the ways in which jazz has mingled and interacted with some of the world's folk music. Some pieces are portraits of musicians or behind the scenes stories that tell something about the jazz life as well as the music. They are a collection with many themes and deliberately so. Hopefully together they convey something of the immense variety of personalities and musical activity that makes up the jazz scene.

Many people have helped in various ways in producing this book. The most important debt is to my wife, Ann Cotterrell, who helped extensively with work on most sections of it and acted as a much valued constructive critic. Charles Alexander, the Jazz Centre Society's full-time

5

administrator, helped in many aspects of the project including the initial planning. He also helped to check part of the musicians section and compiled part of the listing of addresses within it. The JCS office handled the distribution of questionnaires, replies to which provided some of the material used in the musicians listing and a major part of that contained in the clubs and promoters section. Charles Fox and Victor Schonfield answered a number of my queries on the musicians listing, and Tony Wills helped in organizing part of the typing. Finally, the enthusiasm, support and expertise of Brian Thompson of Quartet has made this book a reality.

The international jazz world is livelier, more varied and holds more promise that at any time previously. We hope that this book conveys something of the vitality of the music today and makes entertaining and informative reading for everyone attracted by the 'sound of surprise'.

ROGER COTTERRELL

Travels with a tape
Peter Clayton

*Broadcaster and author Peter Clayton knows all about the
problems of getting the world's finest and most famous
jazz musicians to talk about themselves on tape. He's lugged
his tape recorder around the most unlikely places to
catch interviews for his BBC Radio 'Jazznotes' and 'Sounds
of Jazz' programmes and the results have brought the words
and thoughts of jazzmen to listeners in the direct, immediate
and personal way that only broadcasting can. But the stories
behind the interviews are sometimes as fascinating as those
captured by the tape machine. Clayton tells a few of them
here – strictly off the record.*

ALTHOUGH the odd form of parasitism
I practise requires me to do it, there's something fundamentally wrong about expecting a musician to talk as well as play.
Nobody in his right mind asks a writer to get up from his
table and sing; likewise once the musician has put his horn
back in its case, that should be the end of it.

It applies especially to jazz musicians who all – to some
extent or other – have chosen their improbable way of life
as a means of expression. For the academic performer, the
craftsman-interpreter-recreator, it may be different. Not
required to carve slices off himself each time he plays, he
may have something left to say in ordinary words. But the
jazzman, with his highly evolved musical language – what
need has he of further utterance?

Probably none. It's the listeners, the historians and the
journalists who want the stories that go with the music, and
so the essay declines while the interviews proliferate. They
proliferate in particular on thousands and thousands of
miles of recording tape, most of which seems to have found
its way into my workroom, where five years of chat, bottled
for various radio programmes, waits to be uncorked. I never

7

Sonny Rollins
Photo: Jak Kilby

intended to assemble such an archive; it simply began to accumulate when, after a programme called 'Jazznotes' had been running about six weeks, I thought it might be an idea to keep the interview tapes for future reference. The interview spot itself was an indirect descendant of the 'Hear Me Talking' feature, which first appeared under that name in 1963, though it had run for three months before that as 'Trad Talk' (*that* dates its origins if nothing else can). BBC producer Steve Allen used to do these with a microphone in one hand and a razor blade in the other, ruthlessly editing himself out to create the illusion of a continuous flow from the subject, or victim. I do all the ones we use in 'Sounds of Jazz' at the moment, and although I aim to remove as much of me as possible – preferably from those hesitant, ill-constructed questions during which I fumble my way through the English dictionary, and the interviewee fidgets to know what the hell is coming – there's enough left in to warrant my calling them 'conversations'.

The prime object, of course, unlike that of the printed interview, is not to elicit hard, factual information so much as to arrive at workable cues for playing music, for the great advantage of the audible interview with a musician is that it can be illustrated. The records are pictures, if you like, with the speech between acting as extended captions. An inherent danger is that it encourages superficiality, for often the deeper springs that drive a thoughtful musician are not revealed in two- and three-minute bursts of speech, nor would they lend themselves to glib illustration. But these are limitations you accept, knowing full well that the result will go out over an entertainment network, and that you are – in spite of the idea being unfashionable in jazz circles – an entertainer.

The Oxford Dictionary of Quotations reveals that nobody actually wrote 'First catch your hare', and that the nearest anyone came to it was a Hannah Glasse, with 'Take your hare when it is cased', meaning, as far as I can see, after it has been skinned. A pity, because First Catch Your Jazz Musician is Rule 1. You have to catch him both physically and on tape, and furthermore in a technical state good enough to broadcast, remembering that possibly fifty percent of the audience are going to be listening on transistor sets with speakers no bigger than bath plug-holes. Indeed, many of them will probably actually be in the bath at the time.

It's at this point that the intrusive nature of what you're trying to do comes home to you. Kai Winding is in London very briefly. You know that you owe it to the programme to try and get him. Over the hotel telephone he makes it very plain that he's going out with friends in a few minutes; somehow you have to persuade him to give up those few minutes to talk into your microphone. As things turn out, he's fine, and it never shows on the tape that he's glancing at his watch all the time, but it means that you start in a one-down position, a great disadvantage for an interviewer. Catching your musician also involves checking the mechanical state of your equipment. John Lewis has agreed to talk to you backstage at the Fairfield Hall. You're a bit new to it all and rather excited and nervous; you realize there's not much time so you lace up the tape recorder in the taxi on the way there. You rush in and start, and he talks a whole reel's worth, interesting stuff suggesting that lack of success is often a musician's own fault. Later that night you discover that you've got 15 minutes silence because the tape wasn't passing over the recording head properly. You forgot Rule 2: Test Everything Every Time.

The next consideration is: Your place or mine? If it's a visiting American musician you're talking to, acoustically the best place is liable to be his hotel bedroom. But that, temporarily, is his *home*, for God's sake. That open case and the strewn shirts and the scotch bottle and the after shave are the trappings of the nearest thing he's likely to get to privacy. You're not even a chick with a warm body and a brief welcome, but a man with a microphone.

Hence all those interviews done to the accompaniment of the opposite attraction at Ronnie Scott's. That they could ever have been held there is due to Ronnie's unfailing hospitality, his patient tolerance of those of us who troop about late at night with tape recorders. The greatest privilege I've ever been accorded in connection with jazz took place in Ronnie's back office. It was an interview with Sonny Rollins. In my eyes Rollins is a giant of such magnitude that it's presumptuous to hope that he'll talk at all. Coleman Hawkins didn't ('Bean ain't gonna talk', Ben Webster would say, accurately) so why should Rollins. But he submitted to my ham-fisted questioning with a dignity and humility that only the truly great can afford. I'd hate to guess how many times he's been asked about his occasional retreats from active playing into solitude, but once more he dealt courteously with what for him must now be a tedious subject. He told me it's not always the music he's withdrawing from, but the business; yes, these sabbaticals are a calculated risk in that the audience might not be there when he comes back, that he might find eventually that he'd nothing more to say on his instrument. No, such absences from the scene wouldn't necessarily be a good thing for all musicians, for some of whom the inactivity might produce demoralization rather than replenishment. He tried very hard to work out the intricate musical and verbal connections in his mind that enable him apparently to think on two levels simultaneously – in the middle of a complex improvisation based on one tune, he will not only throw in a quote from another which is right musically, but which is appropriate verbally. It's not simply a matter of associating titles and say, working *Flamingo* into *Nightingale*, but of using, in one of those bird-titles, a few notes from *It might as well be spring*, precisely those which fit the words 'like a nightingale without a song to sing'. We never did get round to finding out how he's had time in his life to hear so much music, how, for instance, he came to be familiar with *To a wild rose*, a drawing room ballad written before he was born but now the basis of one of his most beautiful series of variations. Maybe next time, though the chances of a next time are never very good. As Ronnie says: 'The only way of getting Rollins here is to chain him to your wrist.'

The exact opposite of Sonny Rollins was Eddie Harris. 'I want to be known as the Charlie Parker of the electric saxophone,' he said, modestly. Well, he certainly makes more of that octave dividing device and the various other attachments (none of which appeal to me, incidentally) than Sonny Stitt seems to, but the electric Parker? I don't think so.

One of the most enjoyable encounters was with Dizzy Gillespie. He was happy to be recorded away from the club, but insisted that we do it at tea time in the foyer lounge of the Mayfair Hotel. I came away with some tapes which were about sixty per cent sound effects – Mayfair Hotel waiters saying 'Indian or China?', cups rattling, jaws champing, little knives being tinkled against little plates, Mr Zapadopopolis being paged, American ladies laughing for no particular reason. And somewhere in among it, absolute gems from a high-spirited Dizzy, who ate my sandwiches and cakes as well as his own, because one thing you can't do is handle a microphone and convey food to your lips at the same time. 'I was one of the Lindy Hoppers', he announced through a shower of crumbs. 'I was a natural dancer long before I was a musician.' But he was nonetheless very aware of his contribution as a musician, and stung by what he thought (correctly, I believe) were Ross Russell's faintly knocking comments on himself in Russell's book on Bird*, which had just appeared.

' "Let's have a copy of your book, man", I said to Ross, when I met him on the street. "Well", he says, "this is the only copy I've got with me, and I'm just on my way to a TV studio to be interviewed about it." "Well, give me one some other time", I told him. But he never did. You know why? He knew what he'd written about me and he knew I wasn't going to like it. I suppose in playing down my part in the music he thought he was protecting Parker. But he didn't have to. Parker's safe, and people know what *I* did, too.'

Neither boastfulness nor indignation; just the voice of a man absolutely sure of himself as an artist.

The hubbub in the background of the Gillespie conversation was perhaps exceptional, but public eating does seem to be the most common setting – after Ronnie's back room, that is – for these meetings. Half-past-nine in the morning, in the unbelievably noisy coffee shop of the White House (not Mr Ford's pad, but the hostel for well-heeled transients near Regent's Park) was the only time and place Bob Wilber and I could get together. The band, the World's Greatest Jazz Band, whose name makes everybody shudder, was setting off for some outpost like Bolton. This was before the rebuilding, and every surface was hard down there – the floor, the walls, the seats, the toast – and the din was deafening. But this is where it helps to have a together, practical man like Bob Wilber with you. Rollins, shy, retiring, perhaps only totally at ease when that tenor is in his hands, would have recoiled from a microphone placed practically at his lips. Bob accepted the fact that if his voice was to be recorded at all, he was to regard the thing as a kind of toffee apple, and get close. The result could hardly have been better if we'd worked for hours to produce the

* *Bird Lives*, Quartet Books, London, 1973.

effect, for a radio play, of two people talking in a crowded restaurant.

On the whole I rather like those conditions. God gave us battery operated tape recorders so that we should be mobile, and it seems no more than just that the interviewing mountain should go to the musical Mohammed. Don Rendell was recorded in a car parked in the East End; Alan Skidmore's car became a studio for a conversation between him, Mike Osborne and myself. Acoustically there were no problems, but we clearly worried a traffic warden who was alarmed at the sight of three men plotting in a large Volkswagen. Humphrey Lyttelton was recorded in Eamonn Andrews' dressing room at Thames Television; that doesn't sound odd until you understand that the interview was destined to be used in a BBC programme.

Editing is usually a matter of cutting out coughs, sniffs (which sound like the tearing of calico) and the word 'y'know'. Except with Milt Buckner. He laughs all the time, and the chuckle is not the easiest thing to get a razor blade round. You have to do it, though, because with all that mirth going on, it takes him twice as long as anybody else to say anything.

The lady singers form a special little group of subjects. First of all, some of them are 'stars' in a way that musicians seldom are, and can be that much harder to get to. They are sometimes touchy; I never felt at ease with Anita O'Day, for instance, while Carmen McRae grumbled (unjustly) about her British accompanying musicians. Peggy Lee, from whom I'd been prepared to take, at best, some star-like condescension, proved charming and even more intelligent than her witty lyric writing suggests. The best moments with Miss Lee, though, came after the tape machine had been put away, when quite suddenly she began talking about her first husband, Dave Barbour, who was Benny Goodman's guitarist when Peggy was with the band. It wasn't much, as I recall, just some stuff about her making curtains for their first apartment, but Dave Barbour and her early marriage were subjects I'd been told you didn't bring up, yet here she was bringing them up herself. It was an enormous delight to talk recently to Helen Merrill, who likes staying, when in London, in a dowdily opulent hotel within a precious stone's throw of Harrods, full of dull green paintwork and not-quite-ugly works of art and magnificent old fashioned service, recommended to her by John Lewis. Why Miss Merrill is so little known is a mystery to me, and I'm glad we were able to broadcast that little conversation, for the number of people who wrote or telephoned the following week to find out more about her was really gratifying.

My attitude to the whole idea of the recorded interview is ambivalent. I don't actually like doing it, because, as I have said, of the intrusive nature of the thing. Yet the moment the victim begins to speak, I'm utterly absorbed in him. Even, or perhaps especially, Bobby Hutcherson, who I think of, perhaps unfairly, as a hostile witness. And I also wish I had begun sooner. I was in time to get Cap'n. John Handy ('A big band I had was rehoislin' one day, and when one of the fellers saw me comin' he shouts out: "Look out; here's comes the Captain." That's how I git that name'). But I was too late to meet Billy Strayhorn. I was in time to reach gentle, beautiful Harry Carney, in one of those brick cells that pass as dressing rooms at the Odeon, Hammersmith, but Johnny Hodges had gone before there was a chance to talk to him.

Unless you were part of that charmed circle, it wasn't too easy to get to Duke Ellington himself. The one occasion when I did, backstage and completely alone at the de Montfort Hall, Leicester, when he talked of the ethics of performing to quarter-full houses, and of Strayhorn's long illness, the tape-recorder had not yet become part of my life. Later, there was always that hedge of people around him, those hip descendants of medieval courtiers, and the atmosphere was never the same.

It was at an Ellington press conference, at Southport, that I acquired my most moving, saddest piece of recorded speech. Not from Duke; whatever sadness he may have had was not for the public. It was from Paul Gonsalves, suffering from hospitality thoughtlessly poured into him by people who considered they wished him well. He'd been five weeks in Russia; after the British tour, the band's day off would be spent in the air between Europe and South America. There would be concerts there, then more somewhere else. Then one day he would go home, and he began to remember another occasion, when he arrived to find that his wife and family had had enough of it and that the house was empty. That time they came back, but he was trying to prepare himself for the day when they wouldn't. 'She doesn't understand,' he said in a blurred way as he pointed to his saxophone. 'I'm married to that piece of steel there.' It was only after he died that I realized that was almost literally true, when someone told me that his next of kin, on his passport, was the Ellington band. Quite apart from its awful technical quality, that's one tape I can't play.

Keith Nichols,
British ragtime musician

Raggedy but right
Charles Fox

Who would have thought it? Scott Joplin in the bestseller
charts more than seventy years after he wrote the MAPLE
LEAF RAG. *And Joplin's wild pipe-dream come true; his music*
presented on the concert platform with all the reverence
and respectability that European so-called 'art music'
attracts. The wide popularity of ragtime in the Seventies
is a strange and thought-provoking phenomenon. In this
piece, broadcaster and author Charles Fox looks at various
phases in the acceptance of ragtime and at the potential
of the music today.

THE fact that centenaries have not
loomed at all largely in jazz has really been because of their
shortage. Buddy Bolden's was celebrated, by the erudite
minority which realized it was happening, in 1968. Alphonse
Picou's lies only a short distance ahead – 1978 – while the
first big ones, Jelly Roll Morton's and King Oliver's, come
up in 1985. Which makes it all the more curious that the
centenary of a man born in the same year as Buddy Bolden,
yet whose music remains as substantial as Bolden's seems
mythical, was allowed to slide past without special comment.
In 1968, however, Scott Joplin was, for the majority of jazz
fans, just a name on the cover of *Maple Leaf Rag*, while
ragtime was looked on either as jolly, knockabout music or
else a kind of nostalgic corridor, full of tinkling bead curtains
and the whiff of patchouli, leading up to jazz. But since then
the ragtime phenomenon has taken place. Juke-boxes everywhere have hammered out the theme from *The Sting*;
Joshua Rifkin has persuaded concert hall audiences to listen
intently to *Euphonic Sounds* and *Easy Winners* and *The
Ragtime Dance*, sometimes with scores in hands as well.
And this present day ragtime boom stays faithful to the
classic rags; not at all like the boom which Britain experien-

ced just before World War I, a boom revolving around Tin Pan Alley's pseudo-ragtime songs – and most notably of all, *Alexander's Ragtime Band*.

Early in 1913, *The Era*, a theatrical trade-paper, announced that 130 American ragtime acts were shortly expected to be touring British music halls. (One of those, a coloured group, the Royal Poinciana Quintet, direct from Reisenweber's Restaurant in New York, concluded their routine by ragging the sextet from Donizetti's *Lucia di Lammermoor*.) Yet local performers were not slow to take up the challenge. *The Era* is filled with references to the Fourteen Ragtime Tromboniers, Cola Robinson and his Chinese Ragtimers, the Eight Ragtime Sisters ('A charming and refined English ragtime act', runs their advertisement, 'with music arranged by Arthur W. Ketelbey'), and, most tantalizing of all, Miss Olive Tempest and 'her clever and astonishing thought-reading Ragtimers'. It was in 1913 too that a music critic in *The Times*, anticipating by half a century the rapturous analysis which the Beatles were to receive in the same columns, declared that these Tin Pan Alley ragtime songs contained 'rhythmical subtleties (that could) only be paralleled in the motets of the early contrapuntalists'. Cultural acclaim of a different sort had been provided the year before by Sir Arthur Conan Doyle in a poem recording his admiration of the behaviour of the ship's orchestra aboard the *Titanic*:

'Ragtime! Ragtime! Keep it going still!
'Let them hear the ragtime! Play it with a will!
'Women in the life-boats, men upon the wreck,
'Take heart to hear the ragtime lilting down the deck . . .

'There's glowing hell beneath us where the shattered
     boilers roar,
'The ship is listing and awash, the boats will hold no
     more!
'There's nothing more that you can do, and nothing
     you can mend,
'Only keep the ragtime playing to the end.'

Whether classic piano rags or Tin Pan Alley songs, ragtime, just before World War I, not only revealed the *zeitgeist* but confirmed how totally Afro-American popular music was taking over all round the world. The Versatile

Four, a black American instrumental group, earned £200 a week playing at Murray's Club in Beak Street, London, where, in 1916, it was possible to dine and dance to the newest ragtime for six shillings. By 1917, however, 'jazz' had become the latest craze and ragtime groups were busy metamorphosing into jazz bands. (This was partially a matter of transferring the emphasis from the banjo to the drum-kit; 'Frying-pan' music was one writer's description of the clattering that resulted.)

The earliest jazz bands – authentic American jazz bands that is, not the fashion-conscious turncoats of 1917 – seem, in any case, to have started out playing ragtime. (It's significant that Bunk Johnson's finest LP – and certainly the only one made exactly as he wished it to be – was of fairly straightforward performances of rags.) And rags remained part of the repertoire of the bands; not just of groups like the Original Dixieland Jazz Band, who either originated or collected a good deal of their material (after all, the band's pianist, J. Russel Robinson, was the composer of *Eccentric*), but, for example, of King Oliver's Creole Jazz Band, who at the Lincoln Gardens in Chicago would play *High Society* as a rag, to be danced rather than marched to. Jelly Roll Morton, a one-time 'ragtime professor' in New Orleans, devised his personal variant upon the form, pulling the music closer to jazz. (For instance, an early Morton piano rag, *The Pearls*, later got transformed by Morton's Red Hot Peppers into a genuinely orchestral jazz composition – but within the traditions of ragtime.) And several classic piano rags by Joplin, James Scott and Joseph Lamb simply entered the repertoire of the jazz bands, even if some strains were lopped off to make improvising easier, or their lilting rhythms got replaced by the more insistent pulse of jazz. What happened can be glimpsed by listening to the 1934 recording of *Maple Leaf Rag* by Earl Hines and his Orchestra, very much a vehicle for Hines's virtuosity, or the treatment given the same tune two years earlier by Sidney Bechet and the New Orleans Feetwarmers, an even more remarkable example of a soloist upstaging a theme.

But whatever has been extremely fashionable always suffers the indignity of descending to the nadir of popularity. And throughout the 1930s the form and rhythms of authentic ragtime occupied that dolorous situation. It was a decade when young musicians and fans took pride in the fact that jazz was progressing harmonically and rhythmically, moving away from what they chose to regard as its crude, illiterate beginnings. In Britain the music's name even got discarded for a time, *aficionados* preferring to talk about 'modern rhythm' and, later, 'swing music'. Curiously enough, the piano playing of Duke Ellington, who as a composer and bandleader was a symbol of the sought-after sophistication, tended merely to be tolerated if not actually criticized, probably because it was rooted in ragtime and conveyed an old-fashioned stance.

In 1939 Muggsy Spanier won critical and popular acclaim with a band he called his Ragtimers, but that was a precursor of the New Orleans revival more than anything else. And it was to be that revival, with its delving into the music's historical background, which really started the rehabilitation of the classic ragtime composers. Brun Campbell's memories of Joplin and other ragtime pioneers were printed in the American collectors' magazine, *The Record Changer*, where Roy Carew also reminisced about the piano players of New Orleans. In Britain, Charles Wilford searched for sheet music in the British Museum; he revealed his findings in the magazine, *Jazz Music*, and even arranged a broadcast of Joplin compositions. 1950 saw the appearance of the first full-scale history, *They All Played Ragtime*, by Rudi Blesh and Harriet Janis. And meanwhile the rags had begun to be performed again, even if most jazzmen could not resist adding their own decorations and shifting the rhythmic tilt. In war-time America there were groups such as Lu Watters's Yerba Buena Jazz Band and pianists like Wally Rose specializing in rags. And the British got involved quickly. Billy Jones, a Chelsea publican who had replaced J. Russel Robinson as pianist with the Original Dixieland Jazz Band when they arrived in London in 1919, was rediscovered and played in a concert with George Webb's Dixielanders. By the end of the 1940s ragtime piano contests were being held in London. Later on, both the Ken Colyer and Chris Barber bands were to make excellent recordings of classic rags.

Ragtime, in the broader sense, had always been a part of commercial British dance music. Harry Roy's Orchestra, in particular, exploited the word a great deal, even featuring a small group, the Ragamuffins. (As late as 1949 Harry Roy had a hit record with his *Leicester Square Rag*, its theme based, according to Chris Ellis, on Roy's recollection of a clarinet break that Larry Shields used to play in the Original Dixieland Jazz Band's version of *Jazz Me Blues*.) One of Ambrose's most successful recordings of 1935 was Sid Phillips's arrangement of *Hors d'Oeuvres*, written twenty years earlier by the British pianist, Dave Comer, who at that time worked in Murray's Ragtime Trio. (Phillips later used the piece as his own signature tune.) And in 1952 Winifred Atwell, a West Indian who came to Britain with visions of becoming a concert performer, made a recording of George Botsford's *Black And White Rag* which started a vogue for jangling pianos.

Following in the wake of the New Orleans jazz revival of the 1940s and 1950s came the folk revival, a bit later in Britain than in America but pursuing similar aims. The young guitarists who surfaced during the 1960s found the rags – and they transcribed classic rags as well as writing their own and using more ethnic varieties – a technical challenge as well as an aesthetic delight. There was nothing anachronistic about the situation. Ragtime has always had a foothold in white American country music ('Grand Ol' Opry' still presents banjo pickers syncopating in the approved fashion). In any case, the classic rags may have been composed for the piano, but they sprang out of a background where rags had been performed on banjos and guitars. And they reflected this fact, just as boogie woogie piano relates to blues guitar playing, or, to burrow a lot further back, as many 17th century keyboard compositions can be viewed as extensions of lute music.

Both the jazz and folk musicians' revivals of ragtime represented a scholarly attitude, even if liberties were often taken with the material. But the revival of classic piano rags for their own sake, and their elevation to a respectable position in the pantheon of American music, has been very much a latterday activity. The idea of recording a collection of Scott Joplin rags got mooted in 1951 but did not come about until Ann Charters, the wife of the American musicologist, Samuel Charters, did so seven years later. Meanwhile propagandizing on behalf of ragtime – on TV and radio as well as in clubs – was being carried on by Max Morath, who had learned to play the music from his mother, a pianist in a silent movie theatre. Morath sang and played ragtime songs as well as classic rags, his approach not at all pedantic and exhibiting a vigour which some devotees find lacking in the work of later, more correct performers. Yet it was those later performers, and most notably Joshua Rifkin and William Bolcom, both academics, genuine Doctors of Music rather than self-styled Ragtime Professors, who brought jazz to the attention of concert audiences.

Contrary to popular notions, Joshua Rifkin began playing jazz on the piano – 'more or less in the style of Jelly Roll Morton' – when he was ten. At a very early age he found himself sitting in with musicians such as Zutty Singleton and Red Allen. The decision to perform Scott Joplin as, he was convinced, Joplin would have wished his rags to sound came very much later. His achievement has been to make the Joplin rags a part of the piano repertoire, capable of being fitted into a programme alongside Chopin and Debussy. It has been brought about by Rifkin's emphasis upon the pieces as compositions rather than as functional works, intended as a background for drinking or dancing. Maybe the romanticizing was sometimes taken too far (Charles Wilford has suggested that Rifkin makes Joplin sound like Schumann) but undoubtedly the pieces have found a new and attentive audience among listeners with a classical background. (That it was this category of listeners, rather than hard-core jazz fans, who became enthusiastic about the classic rags, was borne out by the letters sent to the present writer when he presented a series of broadcasts about ragtime on BBC Radio Three.)

The limits of ragtime seem to have been roughly coincident with Scott Joplin's own experience and career. *Treemonisha*, the folk opera by which the composer set so much store, contains delightful passages (if very little ragtime) but reveals Joplin's inability to handle material on this scale (George Gershwin was to do so much more successfully in *Porgy and Bess*). What Joplin excelled at was making his melodies float within the tight disciplines of the four- or five-strain rag. As Joshua Rifkin has pointed out: 'Ragtime is a small-scale form. And that is not a value judgement. The waltz remained a short form too, and Chopin wisely kept his waltzes to relatively small dimensions. Any form of this nature, built on closed phraseology, on an instantly and perpetually reiterated basic rhythmic framework, obviously is not going to be suitable for the large-scale development typical of the symphony. But the important thing is the way Joplin constantly refined and made more intricate his work, so that the last piano rags may be straightforward but they're far from simple.'

Magnetic Rag, a five-strain rag with a suggestion of development in the third and fourth strains, is an example of Joplin bringing introspection to the form; endeavouring, perhaps, to make it carry more than it could manage. It was also, significantly, the last rag he published. During the 1920s the piano rag tradition moved in two directions: Harlem jazz pianists such as James P. Johnson and Fats Waller turned it into an open-ended music, a performer's idiom, based upon improvisation rather than the formal relationship of contrasting strains; composers of novelty piano solos either exploited pyrotechnics, like Zez Confrey, or leaned more heavily on harmonic sophistication, like Rube Bloom. Classic piano rags did not cease to be written (James Scott went on composing rags until his death in 1938, although none got published); the market for them simply dried up. The current revival, of course, has encouraged some performers to try their hands at composition. William Bolcom's *Graceful Ghost* possesses something of the wistful melancholy of Louis Chauvin. And several of the British ragtime pianists – Hugh Crozier, Neville Dickie, Ray Foxley, Keith Nichols, Ray Smith, Ron Weatherburn Roger Quentin Williams – have written rags as well. But their greatest contribution has been in the reviving of classic rags and the way most of them have continued to adventure along the lines laid down by Waller and Johnson and Jelly Roll Morton. Music needs to be played to be kept alive.

For modern jazz musicians, ragtime offers an example, more than anything else – and a useful set of exercises. (Jaki Byard once pointed out, before the ragtime boom, that he required all his pupils to analyse as well as perform *Maple Leaf Rag*.) Ragtime's rhythmic conservatism, as well as its hermetic structure, makes it difficult for any adaptation to be made without the sacrifice of identity. Yet at a moment when jazz – understandably, frequently with admirable results – has been going through a period of excessive looseness, ragtime demonstrates, just like bebop, the virtues of a tight set of disciplines, and how these can squeeze the imagination rather than frustrate it. The important thing, however, is that the best rags justify themselves simply through being fine compositions. That, and the fact that they also helped to transform the world's popular music, is reason enough for honouring their creators.

Phil Seamen
Photo: Valerie Wilmer

I remember Phil . . .
Brian Blain

Phil Seamen was someone very special in jazz in Britain;
a musicians' musician, a drumming man who knew how to
stoke a fire under any group he played with, a talent
big enough to cut Stan Getz – and live! Brian Blain's
warm portrait of one of the great characters of jazz
touches on a whole cross-section of the scene and reflects
the strange mixture of tragedy and triumph that somehow
characterized Phil Seamen's life.

'PHIL SEAMEN lived here.' I don't
remember exactly when that statement, sprayed in black
aerosol paint, appeared on the wall of the end-terrace house
in London's Kentish Town, but there it remained, for weeks
on end, until the outside was painted in readiness for 'The
Great Property Boom'. By which time, Phil had moved on
to the next resting place, taking his few possessions and his
beloved drums with him, and yet another phone number had
to be found for the address book, to mark the passage of
this remarkable musician.

'Phil Seamen lived here' – everyday I used to pass that
proclamation on my way to the tube station and wonder
how on earth it could be that, in the years of superstars and
rock idols, someone, almost certainly young, could be so
moved by a man whose prospects at that time seemed to
reach no further than a gig in the pub across the road – the
Tally Ho; 'Jazz Nightly, no charge for admission'.

Now that Phil is dead – he died on Friday, October 13th,
1972 at the age of 46, his thin, frail body giving up the
unequal struggle against close on 20 years of excess and the
lack of even the most minimal care – there seems to be
nothing remarkable about the fact of that slogan appearing.
It was a spontaneous demonstration of the quality which,
on looking back, seems strongest about him: he had the

power to move people. By his music, by his personality, and his vast reserves of sheer inner strength; no matter how down he was or how insignificant a gig appeared to be, and even if he was playing badly, as far as his music was concerned his commitment was nothing less than total.

For Phil, there was a sense in which it was always 1951 or 1952. Those were the days when I first met him, when he was touring the ballrooms, doing concerts, making records (still 78s) with the Jack Parnell Band. Parnell was the drummer-leader, Phil was the actual drummer, of one of the most exciting bands this country has ever seen. The high spot of the evening was the drum duet between the two men and every night the crowds went wild. In my prissy jazz fan's way, this was the part of the evening I liked least and it was this image of Phil Seamen, playing to the crowd, revelling in being the notorious big-bad jazzman, which stuck with me for years; even after I got to know him and began to find out that his approach to music was in fact deeply serious. So serious that, right at the heart of the matter, it killed him.

But the show with Parnell was no aberration. Like most of us, Phil was at least two people; the extrovert, and the introvert. Inside, there was a deep and genuine modesty about his ability. Outside he was the extrovert; making people laugh, lashing the foolish with his tongue and, when the demons were up, sometimes capable of great cruelty to young players and even his friends, converting every situation to theatrical advantage. Even at the lowest point of his career, to himself, he was still the man on the concert stage or on the ballroom bandstand: the star that the people had come to see. And so, when he was late for a gig, the door would burst open and he would almost literally fall into the room yelling his familiar cry of 'Nurse!' to the barmaid, before proceeding to set up his kit, all lurches and staggers, dry asides and sarcasms; as much a part of the performance as the music which was to come. And the people loved him for it. Phil was doing his turn, being outrageous, being what they expected him to be; turning his personal problems to his public advantage.

And yet there was a side of this which always worried and disturbed. Like the time when I actually heard some hooray say, several years ago when the Old Place was still Ronnie Scott's, 'I say, isn't that the fellow who was asleep on the chairs all night – that drummer chap?' Really. 'That drummer chap' – is that all he was to them? The one who might fall down or the one who might make you laugh? One day I imagine someone might produce a book about Phil Seamen and in it the Phil Seamen stories, the Phil Seamen legend will loom large . . . 'do you remember that time?' For the stories, hundreds of them, do exist; he *was* larger than life, he *did* do all the outrageous things that people talk about, he *was* fearless, and he *was* a rebel, totally unafraid of the fat cats of the music business. And he went through life his own way.

But what interests me now, at this moment, is to put it down that Phil Seamen was not just all of these things but that primarily he was a musician: probably a great one. He was certainly a great jazz musician and it was his tragedy to be born into a country where *great* jazz musicians were not supposed to exist.

I said earlier that Phil was two people; musically, he was several. He learned his craft in the popular bands of the day at the end of the Forties. As a very young musician he played with all kinds of dance bands, graduating to names like Nat Gonella (very jazz conscious in a traditional kind of way for the time) and Billy Ternent, Britain's own Guy Lombardo. It was with Ternent that he learned to read. Ternent was quite a task master and you either read or got out of the job. So Phil learned. It was an attribute that was never considered very necessary for mere jazz musicians in those days.

His roots then were popularly based but the music which grabbed him wasn't. It was, in some ways, the most demandingly narrow and self destructive the world has ever known – bebop. The first drummers in Britain to catch hold of its techniques were Laurie Morgan and Tony Crombie. I was only young at the time and living in Manchester, so with hindsight I suppose it would be fair to guess that these two mopped up most of the gigs that were going for music which, while it had a brief popular burst, had no lasting demand.

Phil therefore came to our attention with the big bands – which he loved. And maybe here was a source of some inner conflict. Throughout the Fifties and even into the early Sixties whenever his name appeared on a sleeve, the cryptic comment 'Britain's leading studio and big band drummer' was frequently all that was said about him. He was that certainly, but, unlike most others who are great in that field

– Buddy Rich and Kenny Clare for example – he was also a supreme small band drummer too. He could play big and he could play small. 'Tiny' as another drummer, John Stevens, puts it. 'Tiny' but with that inner power.

A few days ago I listened with John to an album which came out in 1960, Joe Harriott's *Free Form* (Jazzland JLP49). Even as late as that, the same sleeve note cliché appeared 'Britain's greatest big band, etc.' and yet here was the music complementing that information in a way that demanded eulogies about Seamen. But that's how it always seemed to be in those days. In its day, the *Free Form* album and Joe Harriott's Quintet were considered to be very advanced, and although there were associations with the music of Ornette Coleman, really, in retrospect, they seem to have had little in common. What was odd, listening to the album, was not only how good Phil Seamen was then, but how his playing has stood up to the test of time. It's probable that throughout the Fifties he was in advance of the others. Maybe that's why he didn't get the small band acclaim which seemed to be his due. And now, as another decade has rolled by, his music achieves a kind of eternal quality which is the hallmark of all the great jazz musicians.

Listening to that album was a stunning experience. Seamen doesn't play fast – I expect lots of young rock drummers hearing of his associations with Ginger Baker and hearing the grapevine of chat would be disappointed if they heard it, first time off. They can always readily see the point of Buddy Rich and Tony Williams, for example, because their playing *is* fast, even though their styles are completely different. But it wasn't Phil's hands that his contemporaries dug – hundreds of drummers could play rudimental paradiddles faster than he. It was his mind, a mind open to music.

Why was James Blades, O.B.E. at his funeral? There were many drummers there but why Jimmy, the grand old man of British percussion, veteran of a hundred music halls, theatres, musical associate of Benjamin Britten for many years and author of one of the definitive histories of percussion and percussion instruments? James Blades is no raver, but he's a wonderful old man and he loves music. He recognized and responded to a natural percussion man when he heard one, someone who thought of sounds and beautiful silences, variations of pitch and timbre, as well as the jazz and the swing of it all.

To Phil, swing, time, call it what you will, and differing layers of sound were what playing drums was about. And sometimes excitement, and vulgarity, and bawdiness and lovely bad taste as well; everything you can think of in music that makes your hair creep up the back of your neck – Phil was something to do with that.

Maybe Jim was responding to the man who, before anyone else in Britain, was being called into the studio to play the jazz percussion parts. He was the man who held down the *West Side Story* chair. 1958 does now seem a very long time ago but when that show opened, it was as revolutionary in its time as *Hair* and *J.C. Superstar* were to be later on. And it probably made more demands upon the musicians as well, for the book is terrifically hard and, for once, a theatre orchestra was studded with some of the finest talents in British popular and classical music. Phil was asked to fill the drum chair. It's said that he looked at the book, memorized it, forgot it and got on with playing the music. He was absolutely superb, and possibly for the first time orchestral musicians in Britain were beginning to get a glimpse of musical talent and minds other than their own, and to be impressed. He was also outrageous, too, but that would take us into the realms of the stories again, and the temptation must be resisted.

It was about this time, I suppose, that I used to meet Phil socially. He was the first professional musician that I ever got to know and our contact arose from mutual friends rather than from the fact that I was interested in music. We'd see each other from time to time, not very often, possibly spending the night just talking and listening to records.

It was a funny relationship. I suppose dozens of people knew him better than I, but somehow he always seemed glad to talk to someone 'outside'. It always seemed to me that the 'modern jazz set' were tough and self-protective. They didn't seem to take too kindly to the world of 'straights'. But Phil, on the other hand, seemed to want to communicate with people outside as well. I think he was always a bit surprised that there were others who really cared about *his* music, and by that I mean the music which he represented and not just what he was doing.

Had I never met him under these conditions, I would have

said that he was an arrogant man – machine gunning people down with his tongue. But in these exchanges he really seemed to want to know what you thought and this was what I meant about the introvert side of him. I'll never forget the almost shy way in which he reminded me of the fact that it was he who Kenny Clarke used to call to Paris for his deps. It was as if he could never really believe that he was on that level but somehow felt the need to communicate what it meant to him to others. And then I remember the evening when he pulled out a Stan Tracey album, *Little Klunk*, a beautiful thing, on which there is Phil, Stan Tracey and bassist Kenny Napper. I listened, I enjoyed it; but I must confess I didn't get all that much out of it then, because for quite a long while I had not been listening to any music for all kinds of reasons. What did I think of it? he asked. I couldn't really believe that he cared all that much, but he really wanted to know. 'You know, I think that's the first time we've done something as good as them.' He meant the Americans – the leaders, the heavyweights, the ones the world looked up to as the jazz champions.

In recent years there's been more enlightenment, if not employment, on the question of British jazz musicians, but back in the Fifties and early Sixties it was axiomatic that our lot were well out of it. I didn't realize it at the time but pressures on the British modernists of the day must have been enormous. There must have been something almost intolerably depressing about knowing how good the local musicians were, how well they could play and because there was a scene of sorts they could make a living; but somehow no one really *believed* it and the kind of serious critical articles which appeared in the next decade for such musicians as John Surman, Chris MacGregor and all the rest never seemed to come their way. Someone wrote once in a *Down Beat* article that Phil Seamen was playing in 1953 what Philly Joe Jones did later in 1957. And Philly Joe, remember, was called by Miles Davis to play with Coltrane and Paul Chambers – the very, very best. I think it was Phil Woods who said that. This was the kind of reputation that Seamen already had among the American musicians. But by this time the scuffle was on.

Studio time was becoming more precious than ever and producers, however sympathetic, could no longer afford to take a chance on Phil's unreliability. For 'the old evil', as he called it, was well and truly upon him.

I must admit that I didn't really rate Phil's playing as much as that of certain other drummers. And I suspect that as a jazz fan, I was not alone in this. In the big-band things you could always catch the thrill, the power and the excitement; but the way that Phil, already, in those days was breaking up the time, keeping the beat flowing but disguising it by playing figures all around it was quite unique in Britain. If you hadn't had a great deal of experience listening to live music, all that seemed to be rather overpowering and busy, even though the volume level wasn't too great. But just from records your habits were such that you were conditioned to listening to the horn players only. How many times did the critics admonish players for not being content with their role as time-keepers? Phil was the first of the British drummers to want to play an equal and complementary musical role. Drummers were musicians too.

It was in the early Sixties when he had a flat near the school where I was teaching that he started to explain something about his preoccupation with African music. Unlike Art Blakey, who had been to Ghana at the end of the Fifties, Phil had to rely on records and these he studied with immense care, using what he could find to solve, as he put it, his own 'musical problems'. I remember him playing an album of Senegal drums. The *music* from the drums made his face light up with that curious Beelzebub-like expression. With a twisted smile, eyes closed, head slightly back and then a slight snort of satisfaction, he would lurch forward to slap the knee and make the point he wanted you to grasp. I found it hard to believe such musical dedication in one who, in every other way, seemed to be falling apart.

But why should he put me on? We weren't doing an interview for anybody; he was just talking to a friend who was interested, that was all. It seemed obvious to me even then that there could be nowhere for him to go with the knowledge that he was so carefully acquiring. There was no British jazz scene to speak of, his run-in with the immigration authorities in 1957 for possession of heroin had effectively barred him from the possibility of the successful American career which, I am convinced, could have been his, and unless he straightened himself out the studio doors would be forever closed in his face. It didn't seem that he was even 'reliable' enough to be the house-drummer at Ronnie Scott's.

And yet there was never any doubt about his abilities. Even though they always seemed to be threatened with extinction he could pull out of the bag, when the occasion demanded, such a display as to leave those who were lucky enough to be there in no doubt as to who was King. Like the time he played with Stan Getz on, I think, his first visit. As I remember it, he wasn't booked for the job but somehow on this particular evening at Scott's little club in Gerrard Street, he was in the drum chair alongside Stan Tracey and the bassist, probably Rick Laird. According to those who *were* there Phil played like an absolute angel, at the top of his powers. Not overwhelming, or blustering, not drawing attention to himself by physical volume and power. That wasn't his way. But because of the sheer force of his music, for once, Getz was not the star. And he was not the man to take such thunder stealing lightly.

Apparently, Getz became more and more needled by what was happening and so he produced, for the final set, some new tunes, handing the music round with no little show of spite, in a kind of 'now let's see what you can do with this' way. Phil looked at it, as he had done with the complexities of *West Side Story* a few years earlier, mouthed some obscenity or other, put the music to one side and told Getz to get on with it. Whatever it is that amounts to near genius, the side of his mind that never became engulfed had committed enough to memory to feed him all the cues he needed; his musical imagination could take care of the rest. And it did. It didn't please the Great White Chief any the more, and orders were given that he was not to fill the drum chair again. Any safe time-keeper would have been preferable.

I tell this story not to unleash a flood of Phil Seamen yarns but because it has a musical point. Getz is one of the finest musicians that jazz has produced. He's famous for a style which, superficially, is renowned for delicacy and even charm, although in point of fact Getz has got plenty of muscle power as well. And yet here was Phil Seamen 'Britain's greatest big-band drummer . . .', the only British drummer whose music had that indefinable 'black' quality, able to complement and match him at his own game.

But this was the period of isolated flashes. A later booking, when he was booked to play with Freddie Hubbard, was a different story. By then, working three sets night after night was just too much for Phil to manage at full pressure and Hubbard, a young trumpeter with prodigious technique and speed, was plainly contemptuous of the house drummer's playing. The night I was there was almost painful. Hubbard, playing the fashionably arrogant young black cat, made no secret on the stand of what he thought of Phil. At one point, he drawled to the audience to enquire if there was a drummer in the house who could play 'real fast'. In another decade he wouldn't have survived that crack, but Phil desperately needed that job and so he took the punishment and tried to make the remarks into some kind of comedy banter routine. No one in the audience was very amused.

Maybe Hubbard was drunk that night, I don't know, but it wasn't a pretty sight and even if it didn't happen again, by the end of the tour when they were to play in Manchester at Club 43, Phil just couldn't make the gig and it was another case of 'Isn't that the drummer chap lying on the floor?' and a quick phone round to Liverpool for a dep. More raw material for the Phil Seamen fun-book.

There are jazz musicians and there are jazz fans – I suppose I should say freaks nowadays. And there are some jazz musicians who are jazz fans as well. Phil was a jazz fan. He never seemed to be less than enthusiastic about the music. He knew all about its past as well as its present and I think he genuinely tried to come to terms with some aspects of its future.

In a period when it was not the normal practice, he would enthuse about those things which were supposed to be a little un-hip. Like the time he talked me into going to see Lionel Hampton. This was in 1956 and we were just being hit by rock and roll and everyone in jazz hated it. 'Now there's a real rock and roll band', he said, 'the best there is.' He loved the vulgarity, the showmanship, the earthy sweat and balls of what was going on out there at Olympia. It was the love of a man who didn't have to strike self-conscious critical poses or worry about bad taste. 'Swing the blues, you can't miss' said Hamp. If such things had been said at the time, Phil might just have replied 'Right on'.

He had enough showbiz roots to take a very broad view of popular music. I remember how much he adored the film musical *Carmen Jones*, not just for Max Roach's scene in it but for all of it; he loved Judy Garland, maybe empathizing in a way that never struck me at the time; and I remember when he and a crowd of the heavies burst into applause in a West End cinema when Ella Fitzgerald had finished 'Hard Hearted Hannah' in *Pete Kelly's Blues*. He was the first one to turn me on to Ray Charles, and to my surprise, as early as 1957 he was enthusing to me about Duke Ellington. Modernists weren't supposed to do that sort of thing in those days.

He really did seem to love all music, as well as the music around the fringes of jazz, and he never tired of listening, talking about it and trying to widen the scope of his own playing. Why then with all this love and devotion, talent and skill did he seem bent on his own destruction?

There have been times in the past when to see him was a painful, saddening experience. Degradation is not pleasant, and to see him sometimes as low as it is possible to imagine any human being to be could be a very sad, and sometimes a frightening experience. But, each time, when you imagined that he was not going to come up again he would re-appear and somehow hold on, and the really strange thing is that, despite everything, he was *never a pathetic figure*. This, more than anything else, would have been impossible to bear.

He worked with Dick Morrissey for a while, and Alexis Korner regularly for about a year; these groups kept him going. His association with Ginger Baker gave him another lease of life, introducing him to a new public. Maybe our slogan painter had seen him at one of those festivals organized by the NJF where a duet between the two had climaxed the whole weekend, and the large rock audience went wild for Phil.

Not that he ever got involved with rock in any strong way. He was involved with Ginger because Baker was another drummer who had turned to him for help and he had things to tell musically. Ginger was grateful for the knowledge, and when he was in a position to do so, he did what he could to help bring Phil to the attention of another public; a public which might not otherwise have known of his existence.

But there is no point in trying to create the impression that he was all that excited about rock music, although he loved the basic swing and earthy feel of the Blues shouters and people like Ray Charles and Louis Jordan. According to Alexis, when he was in his band for almost a year he would never play that heavy back beat which was supposed to be essential. 'Everybody knows where the fucking off-beat is, what's the point of playing that?' was his stock response to any criticism. He didn't think much of Baker's Air Force either – 'too fucking loud' – but, to be fair, most observers agree that that was a better band after he had left. Phil was not God after all, and he could be wrong about some things.

During the last months of his life he had begun to develop some kind of working relationship with John Stevens, although frequently in print over the past decade he had castigated free music in fairly vituperative terms. John, who has soldiered on for ten years with the various permutations of musicians known as the Spontaneous Music Ensemble, somehow was able to divine the peculiar essence of Phil. As a young teenager, he had followed him from gig to gig, learning something very basic about the music from his playing. Now, as a more mature musician himself, he felt emboldened to approach him to talk, not as an equal, but at least as someone who might be prepared to play and to exchange ideas together.

Only four days before Phil died, John was talking to me at length about the weekly 'plays' they were having, as if, having sized him up with deep suspicion, Phil was now prepared to hand over some of his knowledge to someone who he knew could be trusted to keep the faith. For he could see that Stevens, whose life style was so totally different to his own, was just as dedicated to the music.

During 1972, Stevens organized two jam sessions between musicians of different persuasions and generations; himself and Trevor Watts from the free end of things, Jeff Clyne and Kenny Wheeler, second generation modernists who have played in almost every kind of musical environment, and three of the heaviest musicians that Britain has ever produced – Stan Tracey, Tubby Hayes and Phil. I saw the second gig at Grass Roots, the South London Co-operative organized by the Musicians' Action Group wives, Hazel Miller and Jackie Tracey. The place was packed to the point of unpleasantness and the music was wildly exhilarating. Phil looked as if he was enjoying himself enormously, and I think he probably was, but possibly more because of the occasion – the excitement and the crowd giving him a taste of the old days of star status that he and Tubby had always assumed to be part of the business of being a jazz musician.

But musically – we'll never know. A few weeks prior to this, Stan Tracey was depping at Phil's regular pub gig in South London at the Jolly Cockney. As the drummer lurched and stumbled about, disguising the enormous care which he always took in tuning his drums and setting up, his mouth twisted into its familiar leering grin, his eyelids drooped and he produced one of those looks that seemed to be probing deep down into the soul. The croaking Cockney voice rasped, 'I hear you've gone over to the other side'. (A reference to Tracey's movements in recent months with a different crowd of younger musicians of different persuasions to the boppers that he had grown up with.) 'Well, let's see if you can still play.'

And so I come back to the question, why? Why did such a great talent do what he did to himself? Once, a few years ago, I would have had a pat answer: society rejected him and his music, even though I knew that he would have laughed at the idea. Now I am not so sure that the answer is so simple.

For in those early years he wasn't rejected at all in conventional terms. With Parnell and Tommy Sampson, he was the idol of the crowds; in the studios he made a great deal of money for the time, and could have gone on doing so. But he chose to blow it. And he knew he was blowing it. When asked if he would do the same again his answer was always an unequivocal 'Yes'.

When he was young, because of what was going on in New York, with Bird and everyone else, he believed that drugs could make him play bebop, the 'speediest' music ever, even better. Just like all the romantic tales used to say and all the jazz socio-apologists have spent years in denying. The state of mind among the early modernists, of course, produced a secondary condition, a kind of jazz mafia. 'Old evil' would get you to play with musicians who otherwise wouldn't look at you. And that kind of jazz freemasonry was a very very strong and powerful feature of the music in those days. Whether being high was or was not a precondition of playing the music, one of the most difficult things for a certain kind of personality to face up to was the downer at the end of the gig. Regardless of whether the habit would make you play better or not, it certainly helped you to face the let-down when the music was over. Even as a listener, I have found many an occasion when one has never wanted the music to finish. To someone as involved and as creative as Phil, I can well imagine how impossibly grey and dull the straight life could appear to be from the other side of the fence. As he himself often put it, 'I was born under the star of Rave-o. That's all there is to it.'

But it isn't. Ever since the mid-Sixties we have heard a lot about love. The thing the rock revolution was supposed to have brought, if nothing else, was plenty of that. By comparison, the heavy team of Fifties modernists were hard men indeed. They were all touched by Mailer's White Hipster thing in one way or another and a kind of self-defensive emotional armour plate seemed to be part of their uniform. But despite the hard look of the Fifties, the crew hair cuts and the suits, which Phil never forsook, his whole life was one of love measured by what he did and what he gave, rather than what he said. Love for his drums, for his cymbals, for the tradition of the music.

The double tragedy is that in the last few months, all the signs were that he was coming out of the tunnel. There was a buzz going round about his playing and his modest pub gigs were in front of packed audiences. Lots of them, too, were young people who could know little of his past.

At about the beginning of this last period I asked him how he faced up to the prospects – because then, after years of falling down, there seemed no hope of a revival. His reply was as honest as I like to believe it always was when we were talking. 'When you get to my stage all you have is the music and a few good friends. I am doing three, four gigs a week. I am working. If I get *one* good one, I mean a really good one, a week then that's enough. That's all I can expect – and it's as much as Miles probably gets.' He was, of course, talking about musical satisfaction, not bread.

'Phil Seaman lived here.' Yes he did, and in so doing he touched thousands in ways that we shall never know. He lived in a style that he never tried to pass on and his warnings on the perils of the habits which finally extinguished his life were dire and awful to anyone impressionable enough to want to follow in his path.

But when the stories are forgotten, luckily some small part of his music will remain with us.

There are times, . . . those rare and powerful moments of deep emotion which revolve around the question of the death of those we care about when I really wish I had that belief in the afterlife to fall back on. Because if it does exist, Bird, Brownie and Bud were waiting for someone to fill the drum chair for long enough. That's how good Phil was. He really was.

Burbles and squeaks – reflections on the British avant garde

Ronald Atkins

The battle still goes on though it's quieter now. The old trad/mod feud – Seventies style – is a matter of bewildered looks and much head scratching from the outsiders countered by the determined and very serious music making of the free improvising avant-garde. In spite of the secret or not so secret hopes of its detractors, free improvised music shows no signs whatsoever of quietly slinking away to die. Its select but expanding group of British exponents are steadily making an increasingly significant contribution to the improvised music scene. Here, Ronald Atkins, music critic of the GUARDIAN, picks his way around AMM and SME territory and reports back, apparently unscathed.

THROUGHOUT the twenty or so years that I've been a cast-iron jazz fan, there have always been arguments about the avant garde. The names and the music change, but the arguments remain much the same. Rights and wrongs of bebop were being hammered out as late as the early 1950s; then came the rarefied experiments of the West Coast, followed by the introduction of triple time and other alleged innovations all the way down to the 1960s, when the avant garde was everywhere.

In this article, I intend to look at the current British avant garde. My views have been formed largely by hearing the music in person, which is probably how most enthusiasts have come to it, rather than on record. No one can doubt that a new music is with us. Here is an excerpt from a review

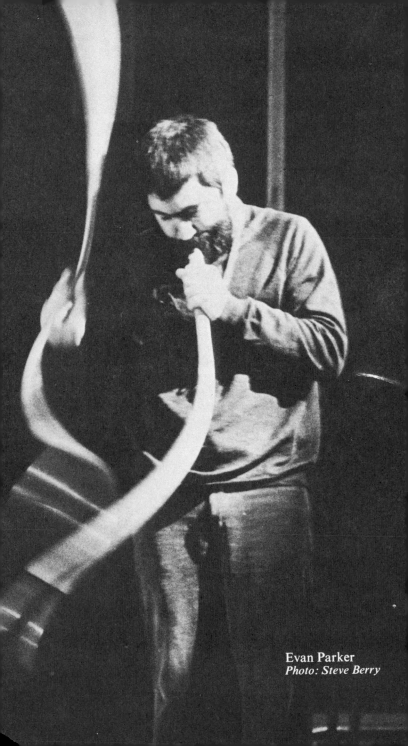

Evan Parker
Photo: Steve Berry

of a Wigmore Hall concert which featured several young free improvisors: 'Solomon's drumming walks a tightrope between a situation where it doesn't matter if he misses a cymbal and one where it does – i.e. between primary energy and energy mediated through technique. That uncertainty produced a tension which was exciting, if lacking in resolution.' (Peter Riley, *Jazz Journal*, June 1975.)

Riley explains the missed cymbals by invoking the now popular concept of energy, and it seems that energy has taken the place of what we older buffs still call swing. The difference is that swing can be roughly defined. Energy, once you get away from glorifying the honk-at-all-costs musicians, seems a vague term by comparison and, because of this vagueness, one that lacks the fine gradations (insistent, relaxed, etc.) of swing.

The hint that precision does not matter goes against tradition. From Armstrong to Coltrane, jazz has been a music for virtuosi in which even collective styles have been founded on the prowess of the individuals concerned. We'll examine the collective idea later on, as that is claimed in some quarters to be the cornerstone of the new music. Meanwhile, it's worth noting that very inexperienced musicians can in some cases 'sit-in' with the greats without any problems. John Stevens has often put together ensembles in which learners are able to join. Of course this is a welcome move, recommended on social and many other grounds, but can anyone imagine a raw beginner finding his way round a Parker blues or being able to read-off a Gil Evans score after maybe one rehearsal?

Just as the avant garde has always been there, so have its critics. In putting together these modest strictures I'm conscious of the pitfalls, especially of the dangers of accusing people of wilful esotericism. Take, for example, the attack on bop by Henry Pleasants in his *Serious Music – And All That Jazz* (Gollancz), an attack admittedly tortuous enough and hedged around with enough qualifications to disappear down its own throat. To put it kindly, the chapter 'Bop and the new jazz' is the work of someone generalizing on a subject of which he is insufficiently informed. Just two quick quotes: first, 'a good part of the trouble may be traced to the jazz musician's preoccupation with harmony'. This pearl appears ten lines after the author has cited Miles Davis, Charles Mingus and Thelonious Monk, with the implication that here are your harmony addicts. Then we learn that the modern jazzman has 'a tendency to think instrumentally rather than vocally . . . an instrument . . . is not a vocal substitute but a horn'. We barely have time to think of more than fifty exceptions to this ruling before we come across a slighting reference to Ornette Coleman and to his, wait for it, 'singular noises'.

Writing at about the same time Philip Larkin, in the introduction to his collected record reviews *All What Jazz?* (Faber & Faber), took much the same line. And, unlike Pleasants, he did not stint from identifying his bogeymen: Charlie Parker ('couldn't play four bars without resorting to a peculiarly irritating four-note cliché'); Gillespie; Monk ('a not-very-successful comic'); Coltrane ('deliberate ugliness'), and others.

Larkin eagerly lays bare his long-standing aversion to modernism in art, which he unashamedly defines as anything he doesn't understand. 'It will divert us so long as we are prepared to be mystified or outraged, but maintains its hold only by being more mystifying and more outrageous.' Applied to the music of Parker, Monk, Rollins, the MJQ or Gil Evans this is clearly arrant nonsense. All Parker's music, for instance, was based on structures with unvarying numbers of bars and of beats to each bar. Harmonic sequences were often similar to those of a popular song or of a pre-war standard. As for deliberate obscuranticism, well, you can orchestrate his solos, you can whistle them, you can tap your feet to them, you can buy records on which people sing them.

These precedents suggest that one must be careful when blaming musicians for not communicating. New guidelines may be needed, however, because a fair proportion of the music aimed at the jazz audience over the past fifteen years has no longer been played according to the old conventions. First to go was the bar-line. In the late 1950s the music of Miles Davis, Coltrane and Mingus often included long passages where the chords never changed. The breakthrough came with Ornette Coleman. Several of his written melodies fell roughly into the old pattern. His solos, though, got right away from the round of eight-bar phrases and the tempos, constant enough most of the time, tended to change subtly at odd moments.

A good Coleman solo may develop one or more motifs

from the theme. It will have an overall melodic shape. You will in most cases be tempted to beat time to it (making the occasional adjustment). It will often stay close enough to the old order of regular beat and regular bar structure for Coleman to exploit the melodic-rhythmic relationship – phrasing across the beat, playing phrases that momentarily seem out of sequence – to set up the kind of tension/release that Charlie Parker could achieve. Most of what happened in the 1960s was based on Coleman's precepts. Out-of-tempo incantations over free rhythm, spontaneous collective improvising, headlong blasts of noise (called 'energy music' or 'freaking out', according to taste) and other disparate fashions of the decade could all be traced back, though they have naturally been modified in several ways.

British jazz at first imitated and was influenced. The early editions of the John Stevens–Trevor Watts Spontaneous Music Ensemble adapted Coleman's approach most skilfully, with Watts emulating the American saxophonist's melodic flair. Archie Shepp came and gave us a lesson in programming, mixing popular tunes and march-like tags into his free-blowing concoctions. Most widespread of all was the impact of John Coltrane, Miles Davis and the musicians and musical styles associated with them. What gave an extra distinction to the music here was the number of musicians who demonstrated a flair for organization, for composing music and/or for combining in a collective format. This applied equally to the comparatively conservative Don Rendell–Ian Carr quintet as to the various John Stevens groups. The term 'organization' covers everything from formal composition to the most casual group arrangement, since both were prevalent. Never before had we witnessed this quantity and quality of original (non-American) material.

This was one of the points made in the argument for a distinctly European jazz, written by the German critic Joachim Berendt. He claimed (*Jazz and Blues*, June 1973) that American jazz was based upon individual self-expression, which reflected the aggressively competitive American ethos. Europeans leant more towards cooperation and collectivism, and our jazz was at last forging its own identity by developing these virtues. He added that Europeans were specially suited to adapt the latest techniques of 'straight' music to something which deserved to be called a strictly

European form of improvised jazz.

Let us look first at the area in which premeditation is least encountered. Our leading practitioners here would definitely include Derek Bailey and Evan Parker. Whether or not you enjoy their music, no one can miss their exceptional skill and craftsmanship, the way they have systematically developed their own sounds. They improvise – indeed, they do little else – and they make use of a very wide range of instrumental effects. So far, nothing to upset the jazz fan. Free improvisation in this case, however, means that there are no pre-set structures (bars, keys, chords) nor rhythmic patterns (regular or even semi-regular beat). The European avoids both the propulsive rhythmic energy and the structural relationships that have previously been part of even the most advanced American jazz.*

Neither Parker nor Bailey seem to be interested in composed or even in collective music. They might share the stage with one or two colleagues or sometimes, Bailey in particular, they just appear by themselves. In all cases, the music will be totally improvised. Some of their associates are keener to impose a loose structure around the improvisations. The structure will be sketchy enough – the composer may indicate tonal or emotional areas, or allocate different passages to different instruments. Simply by ordering the bassist to use a bow instead of strumming with his fingers you are influencing the resulting texture, and it doesn't take many similar instructions for a composer to put his stamp on what may seem to be nothing but a round of free improvising.

There have been attempts at more formal composition within the idiom. Examples are the pieces written for the London Jazz Composers Orchestra, a big band (if members will excuse the term) which draws from both wings of the modern movement, combining the ultra-free improvisors with those who prefer at least a pulse or a key-signature. Barry Guy's massive *Ode*, which launched the orchestra, I would now describe as a commendable failure. Later works seem, on a fleeting acquaintance, more rewarding and I hope

* This is implied by Berendt's article; I'm not familiar enough with the continental European scene to comment. The last group I heard in London, the Dutch ICP group, functioned well within the American progressive norm.

the orchestra survives even if only on its present intermittent basis.

We have touched on the new conventions and shown where they differ from earlier approaches to rhythm and melody. Probably the crucial difference is one of time scale. An improvisor of the old school might play for several minutes but he would be confined within a framework which could be, indeed had to be repeated throughout his solo. Everyone knows how the three-minute gramophone record affected jazz, but the repertory itself also influenced the miniaturist scale of the music. As we have seen, the existing structures came under attack until, with Ornette Coleman's arrival, they crumbled. No need to build solos around repeated patterns; the day of the 'chorus phrase', as André Hodeir called it, was over. Passages for improvising on were no longer defined by specific chords nor by the number of beats to the bar.

How have our musicians taken advantage of this new freedom? For all the myriads of sounds and textures, most performances of free improvising fall into two distinct parts. One section we can call 'conflicting', the other 'uniform'. Conflict implies opposition, and this approach is dominated by each musician playing against the other – letting the other fellow lead and then jumping in with the counterpunch. The idea is not to oppose so much as to build, to ensure that your statement makes the greatest impact upon the statements that the others are producing. At its crudest, you get the free-for-all braying which rose to prominence in the 1960s. Today's musicians are thankfully a great deal more subtle: decibel levels often remain low as tension accumulates through the overlapping rhythms. The problem seems to be one of evolving an overall form out of deliberate form-lessness. Take any two minutes of this music and you will find incident galore; a continuous 45-minute set tends to leave one curiously flat.

Instead of developing through conflict, free improvisation can also blossom with each participant in accord. The instruments play together, and it is here that the advantages of extended form are most often exploited. Sometimes the piece develops from quiet to loud, or *vice versa*; sometimes the volume does not change much but the texture alters, perhaps by instruments dropping out. Whereas improvising based on conflict moves in tight, quicksilver clusters, a uniform collective moves leisurely even throughout the climactic passages. The droning can go on and on, though in practice the performers are just as conditioned by the limitations imposed by stamina, intermissions, licensing laws and shared billing as is anyone else. (The group that pioneered this kind of improvising, AMM, used to play two-hour sets at the Royal College of Art. They would start at 9 pm and the janitor would turn them out at about 11 so that he could close the building.) In some of John Stevens's pieces (*Family*, *The source*), an overall design is clear, and Stevens was one of the first to realize that a performer could step out of line and become almost a featured soloist, cushioned by the other instruments blending behind him. The more orthodox saxophone trio SOS (John Surman, Mike Osborne, Alan Skidmore) sometimes impose a regular rhythm via a tape loop; alternatively, two of the saxophones may set up a riff behind the third.

When Ornette Coleman first startled the jazz world, some of his more wary supporters claimed that he had probably discovered something, but that he was musically and instrumentally several years from mastering it. Now, of course, one regards the early Coleman Atlantic LPs as his finest achievements. My main contention about the kind of free improvising heard today in Britain is that it is musically incomplete, but I could be just as wrong. My feelings, anyway, are ambivalent. I would not have forgone the chance of hearing Parker, Bailey and the rest bounce strange noises off each other; yet the music does not seem complete enough for public performance. Free improvisation as a discipline has much to recommend it; but is there not a point at which it becomes a self-indulgent exercise, fun for the practitioners but not for the rest of us?

What pleases me is that Bailey's guitar has grown more expansive and mellifluous over the years, and that a musician like Paul Rutherford obviously enjoys playing in quite conventional settings. (Iskra 1903 – Bailey, Rutherford (trombone) and Barry Guy on bass – were the most lyrical and listenable free improvising group I have yet heard.) The career of John Stevens shows that a man can absorb the most extreme techniques and mannerisms of free improvising and win through to a style closer to the mainstream. After his Coleman period, Stevens formed a duo with Evan Parker that developed an intricate, intense form of improvising. Having mined that vein pretty thoroughly, he gradually moved back to a style based largely on swinging tempos.

Though he can still put together a free-form ensemble, Stevens as a performer has recently been most convincing when closest to old-fashioned drumming. Something similar may have happened to Stan Tracey. Among the most respected established jazzmen, composer of the *Under Milk Wood* suite and a pianist of immense originality, Tracey suddenly took up the cause of free improvising a few years ago. His unaccompanied piano solos exploited the same kind of rhythmic/melodic tension that Ornette Coleman had done – breaking the old rules rather than ignoring them. Tracey also seemed to realize that totally free improvisation is difficult to sustain, and that once you run out of ideas you might as well stop rather than mark time and hope for inspiration.

His first attempts to go back again were inauspicious. At the concert he gave in 1973 to celebrate his thirty years in music, the purely improvised sets took all the honours. Recently this has begun to change, and his playing on regular structures (blues, etc.) has at the least recaptured its old brilliance. No doubt he has been able to transplant several of the ideas which he first evolved as a free improvisor.

The future will probably depend on the type and size of the audience. Flashing lights, funny uniforms and the like have so far been kept at bay, but the temptation to bolster the music's appeal must be strong. The Dutch percussionist, Han Bennink, has attracted an audience by cashing in on his talent as a comedian, and perhaps some of our men might be drawn to the clichés of mixed-media. Meanwhile, many of the older-established free improvisors can occasionally be heard in more straightforward settings, and this with luck is where a part of their future lies. Even within the idiom a move towards American practice, with more emphasis on swing and melody, would be welcomed – by me, at least.*

---

* I remember the Anthony Braxton–Derek Bailey concert of June 1974 as an excellent example of Anglo-American collaboration. Apparently, however, some local enthusiasts were disappointed by Braxton because he played too much melody.

A sound like nobody else
John Chilton

*Jazz has never lacked fine trumpet players and this piece
brings two of them together. Billy Butterfield, the subject
of the article, whose career spans the exciting days of the
big bands, has toured Britain several times recently.
John Chilton – trumpeter and author – leads his own band, the
'Feetwarmers', and has recently published his definitive
biography of Billie Holiday.*

ONE of the blessings of the 1970s for
British middle-of-the-road jazz lovers has been the visits of
Billy Butterfield. His very first trip to Europe (in late 1971)
was as a member of The World's Greatest Jazz Band. On
his second visit to this country (in October 1974) he guested
with the same outfit and recently in June 1975 he played a
series of one-nighters throughout Britain as a solo artist.

He is one of a rare species: a jazz musician whose work is
admired equally by out-and-out jazz fans and by top session
men. On several occasions I've seen some of this country's
leading trumpet players mixing and mingling in with fans in
order to get a chance to speak to Butterfield, a player whose
technique never obscures or over-rides the emotional content
of his work.

These days Billy has more hair than I have but I've been
a great admirer of his playing since I was a schoolboy.
Thirty years ago I used to look at photographs of American
jazz trumpeters in the same way that my sons look at colour-
prints of star footballers. Simultaneously I'd listen to a
musician's recordings and wonder what sort of personality
lay behind the sound. In the ensuing years I've been lucky
enough to meet many of my boyhood heroes and occasionally I've found that my photo-analyses were accurate – but

48

Billy Butterfield

my assessment of Billy Butterfield, the man, was totally wrong.

Billy's playing has never been flashy but somehow I pictured him as the biggest extrovert of them all; a round-faced, fast-talking wisecracker – the life and soul of every party. Now, Billy is marvellous company, but he is actually a quiet, thoughtful man, almost shy and retiring amongst strangers. He speaks in slow, soft sentences, occasionally hesitating until he finds the exact word to make his meaning crystal clear. He talks quietly and informatively on a wide range of subjects and, though he is always courteous and friendly to well-wishers, one can almost hear him sigh when he gets penned into a discussion that revolves around and around discographical queries relating to a record he made thirty years ago. He never loses his patience but sometimes those bright china-blue eyes seem to be gazing out to a distant horizon whilst he's being asked for the middle name of a third trombonist who played on an evening session in May 1947.

For Billy the important day is today and, although he looks back on his lifetime of music with pleasure, endless discussions about his own recordings wouldn't rate high on a list of his favourite activities. However, he never bites a discographer for, as he explains, he can still remember his own days as an admiring jazz fan. His boyhood heroes were Louis Armstrong, Jack Teagarden, Bunny Berigan, and Eddie Miller; by the time Butterfield was 20 he was working alongside Eddie Miller in the Bob Crosby Band.

Billy, born in Ohio in January 1917, comes from a musical family. His father, a keen amateur musician, had been to school with the American cornet virtuoso Frank Simon; he arranged for Billy to go to Simon for lessons. Billy stayed with the same teacher for almost two years before being offered the chance of a place at Transylvania College. Billy was coerced into studying medicine but as the College had an excellent band, Billy's chances of qualifying as a doctor diminished in ratio to the enjoyment he got from playing local gigs. Bill also gigged with local bands. Eventually he was persuaded to work regularly in Lexington, Kentucky, with a band led by Andy Anderson, a fairly non-musical former All-American Basketball player. A trick of fate occurred during Billy's stay with this band that altered his entire career. Bob Crosby and his musical adviser, bassist

Bob Haggart, were travelling by car to a succession of one-nighters when their vehicle broke down in Lexington. Immediate repairs were out of the question; they wired details of their predicament to the rest of the band and then settled down to take in the not too expansive night life of Lexington. At a local club they heard Butterfield, who was instantly picked out by Haggart's keen ears as a most promising trumpet-player. He and Bob Crosby approached Billy during the band's interval and asked if he had ever considered touring with a professional band. Billy could hardly believe his ears – all thoughts of returning to college to finish a course disappeared immediately – and he eagerly gave Bob Crosby his name and address.

The months passed, and Billy reluctantly came to the conclusion that Bob Crosby's interest was simply encouragingly polite praise. He and several other musicians from Andy Anderson's Band joined up with Austin Wylie's Band in Pittsburgh. However, almost six months to the day after Haggart and Crosby's visit, Billy received a telegram asking him to join Bob Crosby's Band as soon as possible, at a salary of 75 dollars a week. The money offered to Billy was little more than he would have got playing regularly in local bands. However, the chance to play alongside the fine musicians who worked in the Crosby Band, particularly reedman Eddie Miller, meant there was no hesitation. Billy immediately packed his bags and joined the band in Cleveland, Ohio. Recently Billy said, 'What Crosby didn't realize was that I would have worked for much less, I was so keen to join the band.' As soon as the new trumpeter had settled in, the co-operative committee which ran the band passed a resolution that Billy's wages be increased.

'That band was a very special band,' says Billy, 'a true fraternity, and so many of the guys who I worked with there became life-long friends of mine.' The band was based in New York for several years but occasionally everyone, including wives and families, moved on to another city, such as Chicago, when the band played a long residency. Billy left the band in 1940, and travelled to Hollywood to play on the soundtrack of the film *Second Chorus* as a member of Artie Shaw's Band. From the West Coast he moved to Chicago to work as a featured soloist with a big band led by clarinettist Bob Strong. All the work with Strong was in-and-around Chicago, but plans for the band included nationwide touring. Billy was well aware that the band had a big following in Illinois through its regular radio programmes, but he was uncertain about its prospects on the road. His hunch was right; Strong went on the one-night stand roundabout but lost a lot of money during the ride. However, Billy wasn't aboard. After six weeks with the band he received a very good offer to work with Artie Shaw on a permanent basis. Bill stayed with Shaw from September 1940 until February 1941. His memories of those five months seem less than joyous and it is apparent that he does not rate Artie Shaw very highly as a person or as a jazz musician.

As a member of Shaw's band, Billy still remembers his own astonishment at reading in a music magazine that a critic regarded Shaw as America's foremost jazz clarinettist, since Billy didn't consider Shaw an improviser at all. He well remembers the famous series of Gramercy Five recordings that he made with Shaw, 'We must have spent about four hours rehearsing each number before we ever got to the studio. All of the guys in the group were experienced musicians, and it took us about 20 or 30 minutes to get one of the small band arrangements off as near perfect as could be. However, we then had to sit around and run the same number over and over again whilst Shaw perfected his "improvised" solo. Nothing was left to chance, and when that business was all over he might get around to running through another carefully worked-out solo for a second take!'

In Billy's mind, there was no comparison between Shaw's talent and that of Benny Goodman. Butterfield has worked for B.G. on many different occasions, the first time being in 1941, the most recent in 1975. Billy is full of praise for Goodman's playing. He regards him as a wonderful musician, but surprisingly enough does not think of him as a great bandleader. 'He has always been practically incoherent when talking to his sidemen. Benny has a great ear, and can immediately spot a wrong note in an arrangement, but sorting it out was something else. The way out of this problem was solved by having the tune's arranger take the rehearsal, otherwise it meant we sometimes spent four hours rehearsing one arrangement which never got played in public.

'With Benny, you always made good money. Even though he was only paying union scale, you'd earn a lot because there were so many extras like radio, recordings, etc., and he always has good musicians working for him.' During Billy's first spell with the band he worked alongside Cootie Williams, which he describes as 'a great experience'. Goodman has no racial prejudice whatsoever, but some of the hotel-owners that the band met up with on tour were less liberally minded. Once, in Toronto, when Cootie was openly refused a room, Butterfield immediately insisted that he shared his room, much to the hotel-manager's annoyance.

Over the years, I've found that most ex-Benny Goodman sidemen just shrug their shoulders when asked about the clarinettist; some go as far as to say enigmatically, 'Well B.G. is B.G.'. Butterfield is an exception. He has carefully analysed his reasons for returning again and again to work with Goodman. 'I always think that, if I return once more, I will actually end up understanding the man, but I never have done. He is a perpetual enigma.

'Only a few months ago I worked with Benny again. The band sounded good. With guys like Urbie Green and Hank Jones in it I guess it had to be. I enjoyed playing with these musicians and it seemed to go down well with the audience, but even now after all these years I wasn't sure whether the intrigued look that Benny kept giving me was because he was mad or glad that I was getting some applause.'

Billy's very first stint with Goodman lasted for almost a year. He left early in 1942 to join the up-and-coming Les Brown Band. 'That was really Joe Glaser's idea. He had signed Les Brown and was really trying to build the band up. It was Glaser who actually paid my salary.' Billy was only with Les Brown briefly before he came to the conclusion that the time was right to take up the offers of studio work that he was regularly getting. His ability as a soloist, both sweet and hot, his sight-reading capabilities, his adaptability and temperament made him an ideal session man and he was just settling into lucrative grooves at CBS and NBC when the US Government sent him an offer he couldn't refuse. As a result he spent three years in the Army.

For many musicians, conscription into the services meant immediate drafting into a big service band with very few military duties to perform. Billy was an exception. He was posted to an Infantry Regiment and did his full share of square-bashing, marching and rifle drill. Billy remembers it all philosophically. 'There were consolations. I could carry my mouthpiece anywhere. I've always believed in pushing that into my chops when there were no facilities for practice. Even today I'll be sitting watching television and grinding that mouthpiece cup into my lips to keep them in shape. I met one of my life-long friends whilst I was stationed in Arkansas. I was cleaning my rifle one Saturday afternoon, confined to camp. A full sergeant, who happened to be a swing-band fan, came and looked me up and whisked me out of camp for a great week-end. His name was Howard Cockerel and he has since become a Judge in the States. We've always kept in touch ever since.'

In the immediate post-war period many star soloists were tempted into becoming leaders of big bands and Billy was no exception. To this day, he regards that experiment as one of the big mistakes of his life. 'I suppose it cost me about 35,000 dollars which in the 1940s was a lot of money. The bottom was falling out of the big band market. We just couldn't get that big breakthrough. Our last tour ended fairly abruptly out in Indiana. Being stranded is a band-leader's nightmare and it happened to me. We had to wire RCA for the money to get back to New York. I was forced to have all the arrangements in the library re-written for a smaller band. Out of it I did learn an important lesson; it's better to pay 25 per cent commission on regular well-paid work than to pay 10 per cent on occasional dates.'

Late in 1947, Billy joined the house-band at Nick's, the famous New York club named after its founder Nick Rongetti, a jazz-loving restaurant owner who only introduced a discord to the musicians when he sat-in on piano. Billy did countless residencies at Nick's. Sometimes he'd work there for weeks at a time, sometimes for months on end, dovetailing the night-work with daytime sessions. 'After Nick died his wife ran the place. She really objected to our schedule of also playing at Eddie Condon's Club but as she was only paying out around 40 dollars a week we used to shrug it off. For quite a while I played regularly in turn Nick's, Condon's and Ryan's. Most of the bands at these clubs were formed up from the same pool of musicians. I think Jimmy Ryan's was one of the most tiring gigs ever. We had some good times there but those long hours were tough; on Saturdays and Sundays there was live music from 5 pm until 4 am. Old Joe Grauso, the drummer, actually used to doze off to sleep whilst he was playing. He kept going right up to the moment of sound sleep, then we would have to nudge him to set him swinging again.'

Fortunately most of the phases of Billy's career have been recorded, as have the many aspects of his instrumental versatility; his fine solo and lead playing in small dixieland ensembles, his biting ride-outs over big swing bands, his warm-toned ballad playing, and the wily give-and-take of his jam-session work. The man is a consummate musician able to play anything in any key at any tempo. Some of my own particular favourite examples of his work were recorded live on a college campus tour in 1955. Bill, leading a sextet, is in wonderful form and precedes his version of *West End Blues* with a heartfelt tribute to Louis Armstrong. Louis was connected with some of Billy's happiest memories of free-lancing in New York when Billy was working in a radio studio band which did occasional broadcasts backing Louis. The programme schedule called for a broadcast to the East Coast of America to be played live and there was then a three-hour break before the cast returned to the studio to play another live session beamed at the West Coast. Billy, Louis and some of the other musicians would spend those three hours relaxing in Hurley's Bar and the net result was, as Billy says, 'that the West Coast got some of the swingingest shows going'.

Anyone attempting to compile a discography of Billy's recordings would have their work cut out trying to track down the many many studio dates on which he has played. Some of the dates were very interesting for Billy, some totally run-of-the-mill, but, as he points out, it isn't always possible for a professional jazz musician to choose an ideal set-up. Occasionally he played gigs for a well-known American 'society' band-leader who had total belief in the theory that 'the customer is always right'. At one important inauguration ball a very heavy customer of great importance accidentally stepped on the bandleader's tender big toe. The leader turned a violent shade of purple and rose two feet in the air. On the downward journey he heard the famous trampler apologize. Choking back the tears, he gave a low, obsequious bow and said 'It was my pleasure, Sir'. Billy said that, while he and all the other 'deps' in the band curled up with laughter, those musicians on the regular payroll looked stonily ahead. This and dozens of other small incidents made Billy realize that there were more and more musicians in New York City seeking fewer and fewer jobs. He had long felt that he wanted a rest from the clique-like attitudes that are even more prevalent in New York than in other cities. Billy decided to move out to Maryland with his wife and two daughters and there he organized his own territory band. His wife Dotty, who has sung with several name bands, often worked with Billy's new band; the group's work area was comparatively widespread and they also played residencies in Richmond, Virginia, and Atlanta, Georgia.

During the mid-1960s Billy and his family were on the move again, this time to Florida, where Billy again led his own band. He also played many dates alongside Flip Phillips, whom Billy describes as one of his greatest buddies. Billy has great admiration for Flip's tenor-playing. 'He is one of the finest jazzmen I've ever worked with. Great though Coleman Hawkins was, I do believe that Flip has taken that particular style a stage further.'

In addition to his work in Florida, Billy was being sought after for jazz festival dates throughout the US and he played on many of the reunion dates that were a regular feature of the 1960s jazz scene. A Bob Crosby alumni get-together led to a band, later to be called 'The World's Greatest Jazz Band' being formed. Co-led by Bob Haggart and Yank Lawson, the band's original personnel was like a jazz all-star listing. Billy's work alongside Yank Lawson produced some wonderfully exciting trumpet duets. Yank has always been one of Billy's greatest fans, which is an unusual situation when two musicians work so often together. However, Butterfield's talent stands up to the closest scrutiny and another of Billy's ex-Bob Crosby Band colleagues clarinettist Matty Matlock told me that he considered Billy to be the greatest all-round trumpeter that there has ever been in jazz.

Butterfield was a full-time member of the W.G.J.B. for over four years and, although he left the band early in 1973, he has 'guested' with them on many occasions since. During the past two years Billy led his own band at the Bahama Hotel in Fort Lauderdale (with Dotty on vocals) and continued to play many successful solo dates throughout America and in Germany and Holland (where he recorded a fine album with the Dutch Swing College Band). Billy returned to Europe in June 1975 to play a series of one-nighters throughout Britain, usually guesting with local bands, all of whom gained pleasure and experience working alongside him. His three-night 'season' at the 100 Club in London brought out the trumpeters in droves and various generations of brassmen including Tommy McQuater, John McLeavy, Kenny Ball, Colin Smith, Alan Littlejohn and Digby Fairweather stood side by side listening with obvious admiration to Butterfield's skills on trumpet and fluegel horn. Each of them realized they were listening to a player whose musical concepts are too expansive for any particular jazz pigeonhole. Let's hope that all of us have the pleasure of listening to his great sound again very soon.

Dick Sudhalter with the
'New Paul Whiteman Orchestra'
Photo: Dennis Austin

Yesterday's men:
the generation gap
in British jazz

Richard M. Sudhalter

*Good old days! The nostalgia of one musical generation
is ancient history for a later one. But the past is
sometimes too easily forgotten, as jazz cornettist and
Bix biographer Richard Sudhalter shows in this piece.
His 'Yesterday's Men' are musicians whose jazz is
generations away from the present frontiers of the music.
But they keep their ears and eyes open, observing today's
youngbloods perhaps a little wistfully and a little amusedly.
And in their quiet, stay-at-home way they have some
interesting things to say, not only about the past but also
about the present scene.*

RON MATTHEWSON was making little
attempt to hide his incredulity. 'I mean, I've been on the
scene awhile now, and I know most of the jazz players – but
watching those guys file in was a hell of an experience. I
hardly knew a single one of them . . .'

'Those guys' were an assemblage of twenty-eight musicians
recording at the BBC one January day as the 'New Paul
Whiteman Orchestra'. Most have spent long careers in radio,
television and recording studios and are from ten to thirty
years older than Ron Matthewson's generation. What is
perhaps ironic is that several made their earliest and perhaps
most enduring reputations as jazzmen.

They are a few of many whose faces – and in many cases
whose names – are all but unknown to Britain's jazz community today. Even the most outstanding and accomplished
of the younger musicians, Matthewson among them, remain
at best only vaguely aware of their accomplishments.

Beginning in the 1920s and continuing through the dark

of World War II, home-grown jazz talent flourished in Britain, often in a social climate anything but conducive to its growth. Derivative of precedents set in the United States – America's role in those years as the fount of jazz creativity was unquestioned – but good and accomplished nonetheless, and occasionally distinctly individual.

Many pioneer British jazzmen are gone, unavoidable passengers of the years. But others remain: some, like trombonist George Chisholm, still make their presence felt, playing jazz with undiminished strength and creativity. Many are out of music altogether but still interested and aware, memories and sensibilities intact.

There is a third group, perhaps the largest of the three. It includes musicians edged by economic necessity and other, related factors into careers outside jazz, usually as studio or pit orchestra freelancers, hired guns in the increasingly demanding and complex world of popular music-making. They retain a love for, and often passionate playing interest in, jazz of a variety of styles.

In a sense they are forgotten men. Their names mean less to British jazz followers today than do those of the legions of amateur musicians spawned by the traditional jazz 'revival' of post-war days. Even 78 rpm record collectors, a breed normally only too eager to beatify the most obscure of New Orleans street drummers or American dance band section players, hastily dismiss their efforts as mere pallid imitation of 'the real jazz'.

But research and objective, informed listening seem to tell another story and indicate that London in the late 1920s and throughout much of the following decade was as much a centre of jazz activity as many of the lesser US cities. Since the visit of the Original Dixieland Jazz Band in 1919 there had been steady exposure to American musicians and bands. Some came only briefly, for concert appearances; others stayed longer and left influences: an American, the saxophonist Bert L. Ralton, founded the band later to become known as the Savoy Orpheans. The three Starita brothers and pianist Carroll Gibbons, all Bostonians, became important names; The Original Capitol Orchestra, many of whose members had worked the Streckfus steamers with the young Bix Beiderbecke, left some excellent records.

The turning point came in 1927, with the arrival from New York of the bass saxophone virtuoso Adrian Rollini and a contingent of first-rank American hot musicians. The all-star band Rollini had organized to play the Club New Yorker had folded with that establishment after less than a month of operation. Bix and saxophonist Frank Trumbauer had gone off to join Paul Whiteman's Orchestra. Rollini, altoist Bobby Davis and trumpeter Chelsea Quealey sailed for England. Here they joined Fred Elizalde, Cambridge-educated son of a wealthy Philippine family, in an ambitious and jazz-flavoured dance orchestra opening at the Savoy Hotel.*

Most of those who entered the music business here in the years 1927–34 reflected the influences of these 'modern' white Americans of the day: Bix, Trumbauer, Rollini, cornettist Red Nichols, trombonist Miff Mole, violinist Joe Venuti, guitarist Eddie Lang, the Dorsey brothers and many more. Few were aware until later of the significance of the black pioneers, with the exception of Louis Armstrong.

Recently a group of pre-war British jazzmen got together to talk about the old days – and to tackle one central question: why Britain appears to have its own jazz 'generation gap'. If New Yorkers in their early twenties can blow side-by-side with sexagenarian veterans with no lack of mutual appreciation, why doesn't it happen here?

The participants:

NORMAN PAYNE, AGE 64: Chelsea Quealey's trumpet sectionmate in the Elizalde orchestra. Gave up trumpet in 1940 and went into artist management. Possessor of a lyrical and gently melodic style highly influenced by Bix and Red Nichols. Recorded prolifically throughout his entire career with Ray Noble, Spike Hughes, Freddy Gardner, and other British jazz notables. Thought by many to have been his country's finest trumpet stylist of the early years.

GEORGE HURLEY, AGE 68: Violinist with the Elizalde orchestra, a self-confessed devotee of Joe Venuti and a musician long respected for versatility and unflagging good taste. A close friend of Manny Klein, Matty Malneck and other US veterans, Hurley has been out of jazz for many

* The history of that band and of most others in Britain at the time has been well chronicled in Albert McCarthy's outstanding *The Dance Band Era*, Studio Vista, London, 1971.

years, making his living in studios and theatre pits. But the love still lingers.

GEORGE ELLIOTT, AGE 62: Elliott entered professional music in the early 1930s. Yet his guitar style still reflects strongly the influences of Eddie Lang, Dick McDonough and Carl Kress. His career has been mainly in the studios, and it is many years since he played jazz regularly; but during the 1930s he was a regular associate of the late saxophone virtuoso Freddy Gardner and a respected jazzman.

HARRY GOLD, AGE 68: Though known chiefly as the leader of the 'Pieces of Eight', which recorded and broadcast extensively in a dixieland style during the post-war years, Harry Gold has been a life-long disciple of Adrian Rollini. He is perhaps the only British jazzman since the late Arthur Lally to have played the bass saxophone regularly in jazz – in a style clearly pioneered by Rollini. Harry still works freelance today, though he makes his living in music publishing.

PHILIP BUCHEL, AGE 69: Like Norman Payne, Buchel is no longer an active musician; but during the late 1920s and early 30s he recorded extensively, often in company with Payne, for Spike Hughes and others. He quickly became known as one of the premier alto sax stylists of his era, with a tone and approach firmly rooted in those of his idols, Jimmy Dorsey and Frank Trumbauer, yet distinctly his own.

JOCK CUMMINGS, AGE 60: The junior of the group, in that his career began in the middle 1930s and peaked during the war years. The original drummer with the RAF dance band, the Squadronaires, which also included such outstanding younger jazzmen as George Chisholm, trumpeter Tommy McQuater and saxophonist Andy McDevitt. Today he is a busy freelance musician, constantly in demand for a wide variety of ensembles. But his heart remains with jazz.

To begin, then: Why, gentlemen, do you think Britain's jazz community – both musicians and listeners – has developed a kind of cultural amnesia about its own past?

Payne: I think it's the attitude of the British way of life – whatever they've got they don't seem to get it across to anybody else. After all, the Americans did a lot to advertise or make known to the British public – and the public at large, all over the world – their famous musicians through records and what have you. But not us: like everything else we seem to do things in dribs and drabs – if we do anything at all.

Cummings: Also don't forget how people used to think years ago: whatever happened in America was just the greatest, and we all walked about with this inferiority complex. I for one could never see any further than an American drummer. Lots of guys kept making excuses for themselves, rather than approach the thing with confidence and courage. It was just awful.

Elliott: Well, wasn't British jazz basically just a copy of the American in those days? It wasn't until after the war that you got a skipping of the imitators and they went back again to the originals. They wouldn't have imitated the early British musicians, who were already imitating or copying the originators.

Cummings: Yeah. There sure wasn't any question of going down to listen to somebody English in a club. Anyone who did go was only there to listen to 'em to knock 'em. It was very hard to get a guy to say, 'Christ, he's good'. Had to knock 'em for something. It was all sour grapes.

Hurley: I don't remember it that way at all. Right from the start, I think the influx of American bands with the players we were able to hear was like a shot in the arm. At first they mainly worked in the Kit Kat Club or did shows like Paul Whiteman did, but after they finished the players would inevitably come into the nightclubs where they would sit in with the bands – and the feeling was always good.

Buchel: It was tremendous incentive. And we were learning all the time. What difference if we were imitating? Everyone learns that way at first.

Hurley: The Americans were virtually being teachers without knowing it. They were enjoying themselves and we were learning because this was entirely new. We had nobody here then to learn from, and they were bringing us everything that was newest and best in jazz of that era. I'm not saying they were even the best jazz players in America, but they were pretty near the best.

Gold: You know, all this talk about imitators and imitation – perhaps we ought to have a rethink about it. In the States at that time there were a lot of players who were listening to Bix and the others and absorbing what they heard. You might say they too were imitators. I've been sitting here wondering at what point one ceases to be an imitator and begins just being influenced by someone instead.

Elliott: There had to have been a higher degree of imitation here, just because jazz didn't grow up in this country. The Americans, even the secondary players, were at least there – they heard it all at first hand and were part of it. They weren't learning at a remove.

Yet how do you explain someone like Norman here, who developed a very personal and individual style, regardless of what it was based on – sufficiently to prompt Adrian Rollini to invite him back to New York when he left Elizalde's orchestra?

Payne: Funny thing is that although I was heavily influenced by Red Nichols and Chelsea Quealey and later tremendously by Bix, the guy who first knocked me out on trumpet was British: Max Goldberg. I listened to Max and loved what he was doing at that time, and the sound of the instrument.

Gold: It seems to me that the very act of being a jazz musician means that you're giving something of yourself. Sure, when I play bass sax I can only think of one person, Rollini, though of course there have been other bass sax players on records from time to time. But Rollini made the impression – on them as on me. And yet I don't think I'm just being an imitator when I play. At least I hope I'm not.

Hurley: I think if you're just an imitator it shows; if you're under somebody's influence it shows too, but in a different way. An imitator is someone whose music, when you listen to it, always seems to start from here, from the head. Other people – well you know it's starting from way inside: you know they've got something to say and they're saying it in sound, through the medium of the instrument.

This is taking us a bit afield. I'd like for a moment to concentrate on the fact that people today don't seem to know or care what went on in the old days.

Elliott: I think you've got to face the fact that hardly any of the older musicians we've been talking about are actually playing jazz anywhere on any regular basis. Where would anybody hear any of us playing jazz as such?

Buchel: Well, there aren't really any places, are there? No place you can go. When I was in it, there were always night clubs where you could go to escape from the commercial side of things. There was a big distinction between 'hot' playing and the rest then, too. I think that alone was capable of enhancing the appeal of the jazz, the feeling that it was something special. We let ourselves open up and do what we wanted.

Elliott: You can also be overwhelmed by fashions in style. Nobody's going to book or engage musicians who play in a style other than the current one, the one that's trendy and that sells. If you're not doing that you're not playing, because you're not being asked to play. I could say that's true particularly as far as the guitar is concerned. Style has absolutely overwhelmed and bent my instrument in about fifteen different ways over the years, and it hasn't stopped yet.

Hurley: And let's not forget the real basic point: there's no living to be made in jazz nowadays other than for a very tiny handful.

Buchel: I think, too, that the pop field has had a very damaging effect on jazz over here. Some of it, awful stuff, has just closed people's minds, especially the young, to jazz. They don't want to know about it, let alone hear it.

Gold: Well there's been a resurgence of jazz playing in pubs. There's one over at the Old Bailey where my brother Laurie and I go sometimes on Sunday mornings, he with his tenor and I with the bass. We play jazz there, and it's fun. But if you don't have time for sitting in like that, if you're involved with lots of sessions in the profession, earning money, perhaps you don't feel like going out and playing.

Hurley: On consideration I think we're forgetting an important point, and that's the sociological side of this. Back when I was with Elizalde at the Savoy – I joined on April Fool's Day, 1928 – the people who came in there were all from – well, you could draw a line across society at one point and go up: nobody from below that ever came near the place.

Elliott (chuckles): Except if you were a working musician.

Hurley: Right you are, George. But it was true, you know. The only person who would have thought to break that might have been someone who had come into some money – and then might have been frightened to go there because he felt out of place. Everybody turned out in tails, mostly. I'll tell you what we had to wear for the tea dances: we wore black jackets and vests and striped trousers and a grey cravat and grey spats. This is how we had to dress because we were playing to the cream. I say cream only to express myself in this way: *I* didn't think they were the cream.

Buchel: But *they* did.

Hurley: Oh, indeed. This was the cream of the population, the people who could afford to go to these places and be entertained by and played to by musicians who were considered the best available for their entertainment.

Buchel: In fact they didn't really appreciate jazz at all, though. To tell the truth, many of them actually hated it.

Payne: You know who were the real jazz fans then? It was the university people – they were the ones who were keen on the jazz. It's extraordinary, but most of my friends today, who have the greatest collections of records and more of what I've done and what every other musician has done, are doctors. Surgeons. Jazz enthusiasts from Cambridge, back when the Elizalde brothers were there.

Cummings: Those Oxford and Cambridge seasons used to feature all the best bands. Great jazz balls – the biggest bands and the best bands.

Payne: The university lads were the followers all right. Even after they left university and came down they still followed the jazz and kept collections of it, very religiously.

Hurley: If the Savoy and places like it had been accessible – if all those swank hotels and night clubs had been accessible to the complete strata of society as it is today, the kids would have been able to come in; they would have heard the few places where individual musicians were given a chance to show themselves off as we did with Elizalde. Ambrose too featured certain players. But before the war, in the 20s and 30s, no average kid, unless he came from a family which could afford to give him money, could ever think of going to the Savoy, the Dorchester or the Mayfair. Or even the night clubs. If they had – well, they would have got to know the musicians in a way which was much closer than buying a record.

Payne: But nobody really made any importance of music here the way they did in the States, you understand. Here, then, you still had that stupid attitude of a judge saying in court, 'a *sax*ophone? What on *earth* is *that*?' All terribly narrow. I'm always sorry I didn't take up that invitation to go to America. Adrian Rollini asked me to go back with him at the time, in 1929. I was just seventeen when those musicians joined Elizalde – I'd bought every single record I could of those players, mostly of Adrian. And there he was in the same band.

Norman, why did you finally get out of the business, stop playing trumpet?

Payne: Toward the end there, around the beginning of the war, it just got uninteresting. I had quite a bit of work – film work down at Pinewood and Denham and what have you. And a few good records with Ambrose and Ted Heath. But it just didn't add up to anything interesting. I just lost interest in playing and orchestras. I think it had become just a question of living then, earning money.

Cummings: He's right. Things musically were really diabolical just before and in the early days of the war. No place much to play any more – not jazz anyway. And there wasn't the freelance scene there is now. Sometimes you worked hotel jobs – though those bands were being knocked down to nothing too. Even the band they had then at the Savoy was down to about ten, which for them was pretty small.

As practitioners yourselves of a vintage jazz style, what did you think when, right after the war, the new generation of 'trad' players came along with a rigid imitation of far more primitive music than you had ever thought of emulating?

Hurley: A lot of these people – at least some of them – may play pretty well technically, but it can never have any meaning other than as a copy. They can never create, because everything that had to be said about that particular era was said first and better by the people who played it then.

Cummings: When all that started some of the bands were so bad.

Payne: One or two of them sounded as though they were just running scales. No feeling. Nothing at all to it. Just notes. Colourless notes, as I called them. Irritating. Such fumbling, getting from one phrase to another, as though they didn't know what they were doing. Like a kid running across a room and falling on the floor. No continuity. No theoretical knowledge.

Gold: Oh my – I'm afraid I don't agree with that at all. To some extent I always welcome this kind of musical development. You have to start somewhere, and I don't see any harm – never did – in starting back at the beginning. I'm not going to suggest that they were inventive, but some of those trad musicians developed into very fine players. I can think of Bruce Turner, for one, who played in a trad band at the beginning of the revival.

Elliott: A lot of it sounded hopelessly commercial to me, like playing for the market.

Hurley: I think a jazz musician particularly should reflect the era in which he lives. I feel that a young musician today with a desire and a bent to play jazz will make his greatest contribution from being part of the environment of jazz today – and I'm not talking about rock or any of those things. They're all just funny names without meaning. Labels.

Is jazz that sociological? Is it invalid for good, technically equipped musicians to come along who are more interested in exploring the earlier styles, without recourse to strict imitation? Can't they be creative too?

Hurley: It's harder. Of course there are exceptions.

Gold: I still think it's possible to be creative within the framework of *any* music. It depends on the individual. It's a question of talent and development and enthusiasm.

Hurley: But, Harry, there's something fundamentally wrong with that. Today individual techniques are better; they've improved enormously. Why, I can remember when if a trumpet player could hit a top C he was – well, a god. Nowadays if a fourth trumpet player can't screech around at least a fifth above that he's no good. So you'd be bringing superior technique to a form which was in many respects defined by its technical limitations.

Buchel: But that's not to say you'd be bringing improvement musically, would you?

Why can't the music be improved through the improved techniques of the players?

Elliott: It's very simple: the advance of technique brings with it new ideas and harmonic thought which it makes possible. The change from the earlier jazz has already happened in history as a result. And not just with individuals, but with the whole musical environment. So as soon as you get more technique and more ideas and a wider harmonic scope you're going to start altering those original basic very ordinary three-chord ideas and spread them out, which has happened.

Payne: There's no reason why you can't pick it all up, absorb it all. I listen to everybody: to Bix and the ones I loved back then, because I still love them. But my favourite is Dizzy Gillespie. He's so amazing – and *he's* learned from the years too. Bobby Hackett. Clifford Brown . . .

So you still listen to jazz and follow it.

Payne: God, yes. I can't resist watching a jazz programme on TV or listening to it on the radio. I love it and I'll always love it.

Cummings: You never lose the enthusiasm for it. Never.

If you didn't have to worry about the economics of it, making a living and the rest, how many of you would welcome the idea of playing jazz again full time?

Elliott: I would love it. But it would have to be under certain conditions: I wouldn't like to travel around the world or the country, for that matter. I'd like to do it peaceably in one place. More or less – I mean, excursions by all means. But basically in one spot. And on my own instrument. My way. Acoustic. Leaving out any question of electronics and all that. But if I could do that I'd jump at the chance.

Gold: To some extent I go along with that, and that's where *anno domini* comes in. I've travelled many years and arrived at a certain situation in life. Home is home, and that's where my roots are and that's where I'd like to be. Given that, I'd love it. Anytime.

Elliott: The sorts of things I'd like to do would be in a salon environment, a sort of chamber music setting. Quiet. This goes back of course to Joe Venuti and Eddie Lang and the Blue Four – that kind of thing, which was the kind of jazz that first took me over. That's the kind of jazz I've always wished to stay with and would still like to belong to. But it doesn't exist. It died out. That kind of chamber music jazz had a very very short run, a very short life, and it's not ever come back. But that's where my sympathies lie, even though there's been no Venuti Blue Four since that period.

Hurley: I'd just like to play jazz again. I love music in all its forms, when it's artistically played. Of course age puts a limit on the extent to which you can travel and the conditions you can put up with; but certainly the biggest thrill I've ever had in my life was to be playing in clubs and playing freely, doing it different every single time – differently in the sense that if I could remember something that I did that I liked and would want to play again I'd attempt to marry it to something else that was just as good and try to make the whole better.

Elliott: I find that similar to my experience as the sort of thing I like to do – and would do if I were playing jazz regularly. I'd probably evolve a kind of definitive chorus on any given piece and then wouldn't be able to do better.

Hurley: All the Americans I worked with in those days did the same. Formulated a routine – so if they didn't feel good on any given night they'd still sound good, no matter what.

Elliott: It gave them a higher level to start from.

Payne: As far as I'm concerned the chance to play jazz again regularly would be like being released from bondage.

Ever feel a compulsion these days to pick up a horn and start practising again?

Payne: Oh yes. Yes indeed. I wish I had one often, but I gave it away. In fact, the only thing I have left of what I call my utensils is my French horn, a Conn, in very good condition. But my kids at some time or other got on to the mouthpiece, and I don't know what they did to it – turned it into a blowgun or whatever. They even destroyed one or two of my good records, the old ones, by making 'shapes' out of them after heating them.

Hurley: How about you, Phil?

Buchel: That's a difficult one. I always think playing the saxophone by yourself is as dreary as could be. You can't, really. I'd love to be able to play with a group but I just couldn't now. It's much too late. But as George says, you get this marvellous feeling if you're in the right mood, and everybody's going like that and you more or less know what the next person is going to do. But after forty years I'm not in a position to say one way or the other – I still get a tremendous kick out of it, perhaps a lot more than I did then. But just to listen to. I couldn't take it up again.

Gold: But why not, Phil?

Buchel: If I *were* able to get back into it I'd probably find myself going back on to what I was doing in those days. So dated! I'd never get a chance to play with anybody.

Hurley: But assuming conditions were right.

Buchel: No. No. I couldn't. I'd have to work so hard: my

embouchure, my sense of pitch – all gone. I'd never know where I was, or where to begin.

Gold: I think the question is really whether you would *want* to do it. When you hear a jazz band playing along beautifully don't you ever think, 'My God, would I love to join in'?

Buchel: Yes, oh yes, I do do that. Often. Because – well, I don't think you can have a feeling in anything in the world such as you get when you get that feeling of playing and improvising on a theme. It's an extraordinary feeling. But it's been forty years, and that's a long time.

There was some difference of opinion earlier about relations among musicians back in the old days. Do you think things are as good – or as bad, depending on your point of view – today?

Hurley: I think the feeling among younger musicians for one another is as good as it ever was amongst us in those days we've been talking about. But there's another factor, too, I think: the competition today is so much more fierce that perhaps people tend to lose a bit of – are devoid of sentiment that they might have otherwise had.

Cummings: Standards are certainly higher now in music. Today standards here sometimes even surpass a lot of American standards. And even the best over there, as marvellous as it is, is no longer out of reach.

Hurley: But the economics of the profession *must* have a bearing on people's feelings for each other. I know one trumpet player who said the other night, 'When I hear some kid who comes out of college and can play rings around me the first thing I want to do is go and kick him in the teeth.'

Surely he was kidding, though. If not, that sort of feeling must be rare . . .

Gold: I can't help it, but this sort of thing is still strange to me. You want to be able to recognize the ability of some-body and if it's good and you love music, give him the credit. Why not go along with it?

Elliott: You can't love all the music you're playing all the time, Harry, can you? I'd say 90 per cent of the work I do is that way: the moment you get outside the studio you forget everything and everybody concerned with it. You're happy to take the money and get out.

Gold: Isn't that the difference between playing music for a living as such and playing jazz, which is what we're supposed to be talking about?

Hurley: Maybe. That's why I'd rather play jazz.

Buchel: It's the feelings which come as a result of playing jazz together – or even just listening.

Gold: That may be the very element that gets lost. I think we should treasure it.

Jimmy and Alan Skidmore are the most famous father and son in the jazz business in Britain. We asked Brian Case, jazz columnist of the NEW MUSICAL EXPRESS, *to talk to these two saxophonists whose combined careers span more than forty years of British jazz. The result is more than just a portrait of two fine jazz musicians. It says some interesting things about the ways and lives of two generations of British jazzmen.*

In the tradition
Alan and Jimmy Skidmore
interviewed by Brian Case

HOW FAR HAS YOUR FATHER'S BEING A TENOR PLAYER INFLUENCED YOU?

Alan: A helluva influence. As far back as I can remember there was jazz in the house, and all his musician mates coming round, falling about. Since I was knee-high to a grasshopper there was all that going on. He didn't press me in any way – it was up to me what I wanted to do – but he gave me a saxophone that he'd disregarded, a Buscher, because he'd bought a new one for himself. I think it was on my twelfth or thirteenth birthday. I didn't touch it – I left it out completely. It stayed under my bed for several years. It wasn't till I was about fifteen that I thought, well, I'll try and give it one on this, you know? I made a terrible mess of it for a few months like most of us do, something awful.

Jimmy: Alan wanted to play the drums at first like all kids do. I was with Eric Delaney at the time and I used to bring him round. He was kinda all eyes at everything going round and glittering and all that. I changed my tenor for a Conn, so I gave him the old one. I said, well, it's yours if you want it and after a year or two he made up his mind that he finally fancied it. He got onto it pretty quick. He used to practise eight hours a day like a good 'un.

A: He didn't actually teach me, like, being so close – like a husband trying to teach his wife to drive sort of thing, it

Alan Skidmore
Photo: Steve Berry

Jimmy Skidmore

doesn't work. So then it was down to scales and things. I did quite a bit of woodshedding. Dad's influence was strong in that I used to go about with him all the time on his gigs. All the years that he was working with people like Delaney and the big band – ironically enough, I was to take over his gig when he left – and Humphrey Lyttleton, I used to sit in the front row and dig him, listen all the time, so he taught me like that in a roundabout way. Just being amongst it all the time, a lot of it rubbed off.

J: I did give him a few pointers – things like alternate fingerings – but I didn't teach him as such. He turned professional when he was sixteen.

There's a fallacy that your generation by-passed the craft apprenticeship. Did you pay the same sort of dues as your father?

A: I worked at the Talk of the Town for four or five years in a quartet, played all the standards, all the changes. I was about twelve years with all kinds of bands. I was two years with the Radio Orchestra, a couple of years with the Eric Delaney band on the road, Alexis Korner – that covered the Blues – so, like, with regard to getting changes together, I have done it. Now I've just reached a stage where I don't care so much whether people dig what I'm doing – I'm doing what I want to do. Luckily most people do like it.

It's a funny thing, this business about not playing on changes and playing free. I'd rather play on changes. I'd rather play something melodic really, although when you're playing in certain bands with certain guys and you hit something, it does go out. It goes out automatically and it's all magic, all lovely. Other guys, you gotta play inside.

How did you get started, Jimmy?

J: My little bit? Well, there were a few nice people about then. Not many. I mean, there was only one jazz record a month at that time, the old 78s. I went semi-professional in 1934, I was about eighteen. My first jazz record was a Benny Goodman Trio, 'Tiger Rag', and 'Sweet Sue' on the other side. Then there was Chu Berry and Coleman Hawkins. Lester hadn't come along then, I don't think. I liked his honking, all that playing about with the one note. Da Da Da Da. Lovely. I play tenor. I don't play nothing else really – oh, I've had a dabble at one or two things. I don't get on very well with clarinet. Flute I'd like to take up even now.

75

If you play flute you get a few sessions, know what I mean?

My first pro. job was around 1940. The Café Society in Dean Street, run by a fella, a Mexican, called Jack Hamilton who was quite a fair trumpet player. Rhythm clubs they called them in those days, 10 till unconscious. Me, Coleridge Goode on bass, Jimmy Benson on drums and Colin Beaton on piano. It didn't last very long because Jack got called up and he got killed in the war. Then I went with Harry Parry and the Radio Rhythm Club Sextet.

What was your first reaction to be-bop?

J: I remember Denis Rose saying, what do you think of this? It was Charlie Parker. We were down in the rehearsal room, in Mac's. 1946. I said 'Cor, bloody hell!' I thought, I'll never play like that . . . and I didn't. All the little chord changes were there, the ones you can't really fit in because normally they're gone before you can do anything about them. Oh yeah, old Charlie. Still the best.

Do you feel that the big bands are a valuable part of the apprenticeship?

J: Good experience. You get the noise all round you. I was with Vic Lewis and the pseudo-Stan Kenton noise – *Come Back To Sorrento* and all that lark.

Alan? Big bands?

A: It was important to me. It's very hard to say about other people. John Warren's Big Band is dynamite.

It doesn't seem to be possible to make a living playing jazz in England. How important is Europe to your finances?

A: I don't think I could make a living totally in this country – I don't think anybody could. There's a lot of people and organizations such as the JCS that are trying their damndest to get it on for jazz guys, but even so, there's not enough venues. There aren't enough people interested, there isn't enough money. For instance, I'm going back to Germany with the John Warren Band tomorrow. It's been to Germany more times in the last couple of years than it's done gigs in this country. That's a fourteen piece band. They've got this thing in Germany and a lot of European countries where you turn up to do a gig, and nine times out of ten, it's recorded by local or national radio -- so, like, that's where the bread comes from. That's how they can afford to do these things. You don't get that in this country. You can't go to Leicester or Liverpool and get the local radio to subsidize it. It doesn't happen. But you play in Stuttgart and it's supported by Sud-West German Radio. There's always a radio lorry outside the gig. Jazz musicians in Germany get very well treated indeed. Your music is an art.

Jimmy? Europe?

J: I went to Sweden with Vic Lewis around 1946. We were the first British band to leave the country to go to foreign parts. It was well received, I'll tell you. They were starved of it. When they clap, they all clap together. Sweden was a very free country. Open to influence. Not 'arf.

I went to the first Jazz Festival run by the French Government in Nice, 1948. That was when I first met Humphrey Lyttelton. He'd just come out of the Guards then. Derek Neville was sent over specifically to meet Coleman Hawkins, Louis, Jack Teagarden and Big Sid Catlett, and he was put in charge of our band. We represented England – Django and Grapelli represented France. It was a big jazz package lasting twelve days – we didn't get any money, but we had the best hotel. Marvellous time!

A lot of musicians have teaching to fall back on. Do you do much of that?

A: I do teach a chosen few. If someone comes up and says, that's lovely, do you give lessons, I'm only too pleased to try and pass it on. There's the school that Jackie Tracey runs, the Lambeth New Music thing, I do that for two weeks every year with Ossie and Surman. I don't do a great deal, but when I do, I quite like it. You get some lovely little cats coming up sometimes, really so keen. It'd be a terrible drag if the tradition wasn't passed on.

J: I did try, but I didn't approach it in the right way. I expected everyone to be a genius. Eddie Harvey is the one – he's got a good teaching job with thirty-odd pupils. They're all brass, and they're all bloody good. It must be a great pleasure for him to be able to say, 'Right, come on lads, put Sheet Number Two up and let's have it.' And that's it . . . there . . . bom. I think he's got the best of both worlds, because he does a lot of writing too. As a long term policy it's a good idea to get into teaching – with the right outlook.

Do you think there's any way of demanding a realistic rate for pub gigs?

77

A: That's where you're fighting. You get a musician who's totally dedicated to his thing, there's nothing you can do about a publican who's only dedicated to his wallet. I quite frequently get calls from guys up and down the country to do a guest appearance with the local quartet. Obviously it's gonna come to the crunch – either I say, OK, what's it worth? – or they say how much is your fee? Now, I don't want to screw anyone for more than they can afford. I end up asking how they're fixed, tell me the truth, how many does the club hold, are you losing, making money, subsidized? All that kinda thing . . . I won't screw a cat for £40 or £50 if he's making like £12.50 on the door.

J: I don't know. I don't think anybody makes a living from jazz really. Take Tommy Whittle. He runs his own club just for a blow. The Hopbine, Wembley. He's even got the backing of the brewery but he can't make a living at it. You used to be able to – there was a nice little circuit all around Manchester and places.

I did a job on Sunday – I won't mention no names – which was governed by the guv'nor of the pub. 'It's getting a bit too modern,' he said, having a dig at me really, 'what about a bit of Trad., the public need it.' Well, let's face it – they don't need it. He had no right to say anything at all.

I did a spate of Clubs in the Fifties, like Club 51. Good days those were. We did a series of concerts in the Fifties, we formed the JATP – not 'Jazz at the Phil', but 'Jazz at the Prom' – we got permission from Norman Granz to use the initials. 1954 I joined Eric Delaney's big band, had a coupla years together, made a lot of records. 1956 Humphrey Lyttleton asked me to join him and I was there till 1961. Oh – before that – where can I squeeze Ralph Sharon in? We opened three of Al Burnett's Stork Clubs. Lovely jazz! Bernard Braden used to like a little tickle on the drums, Bonar Coleano – they're all dead now, you know – and I don't feel so well myself. Well, then after 1961, I just faded away. I was waiting for the phone to go more than anything. I just don't think I'm much of a hustler really. You have to be. You have to go up and see these producers and promoters and things. I never had an agent. I've had a good life though. I haven't made a lot of money out of the business, but I've been all over. Went to America with Humph, met people like Monk, Julius Watkins. I met George Shearing again over there. We used to play together during the war at the

Jamboree Club. The first thing George said to me after all those years was 'Got any bread pudding?' Frances (Jimmy's wife) was a good bread pudding maker and it was quite a find in those days. What a brain though.

Do you see many differences between the generations of Jazzmen? Attitudes?

A: About my Dad's era . . . I can remember like going down to the Bull's Head and it'd be like the drinking and the raving would be much more important than the blowing. Like they'd spend ten minutes in between each number getting a round in and discussing what they were going to play. Nowadays I daren't go on the stand unless it's all worked out and I know what I'm gonna do, and I'll play for an hour without stopping. It's like a business. It's either that or you sink. That's how it should be. No good standing around scratching your arse. I feel guilty if I don't get it on. Cats come several miles to hear me, then I'm gonna work.

J: I never knock the music. It's having a hard enough time as it is. It's much more competitive now, which makes it healthier I suppose.

A: London is up there now – lots of very fine jazz musicians. We really are jazz musicians. I don't think I'll ever be rich – don't want to be particularly – we just chug on in our own sweet way. The most important thing is to play jazz. I think that shows.

Michael Garrick

Spreading the word
Michael Garrick

*Michael Garrick has many interests, not all of them
within the hazy boundaries of jazz. He is well known as a
jazz pianist and composer with a string of successful albums
to his credit. He has long been an important figure in the jazz
and poetry movement in this country, has written extended
compositions allying jazz forms to religious settings (as in
JAZZ PRAISES – first performed in 1967, MR SMITH'S APOCALYPSE
– 1969, and JUDAS KISS – 1971) and has taken Tolkien for
inspiration in his HOBBIT SUITE (1973). Apart from this, he is
profoundly interested in education and spends a great deal of
his time spreading the word about jazz with his trio and
sextet in schools and colleges throughout the country. Quite
simply, he is one of the most interesting characters around
jazz in Britain. Here he writes about himself and some of
the ideas that have led him in the directions he now pursues.*

ONE of the beauties of life is the unexpected. The first time this happened deeply to me was
when I discovered the joy there was in really learning to
study; the richness of things becoming quite suddenly
accessible in imagination despite an otherwise humdrum
existence; the world expanding at last, and, after years of
indifference, smiling back. That moment when the heart and
mind, long estranged perhaps since early childhood or even
further back, come together like two highly charged elec-
trodes – the spark leaps across, and illumination begins. All
this, just for a little mental effort.

The sharing of this illumination is for me what life and
education is about. Its properties are the opposite of envy
or narrow ambition and are instead quite similar to those of
the sun in that it is there for all to enjoy. People long for
such illumination but, except that they are glad when the
sun itself comes out, this longing is rarely conscious. Some

time ago it began to seem to me a worthwhile thing to do what I could to coax people to undertake that not over-whelming mental effort in order to make their world-view, if you like, a bit more open, and their lives more exciting and even happier. I could after all only judge by what had happened to me.

So when I started with concerts of poetry and jazz in 1961 (my first quartet dated from 1958/9 with Peter Shade on vibes) and later taking music to children in schools, these thoughts were very much in my mind. I wrote in programme notes for Jeremy Robson's 'Poetry and Jazz in Concert' that apart from anything else, the form enabled both lovers of poetry and lovers of jazz to meet and appreciate each other's art and emotional values. Exclusiveness tends to lead to narrowness and poverty of being and I had lived through so many years of that both at school and after that I wanted to do everything I could to combat it.

An interest in jazz at the age of twelve was something that neither parents nor Enfield Grammar School staff had the smallest desire to encourage. It was greeted with derision or, at best, a faintly indulgent smile. I learned a few basic chords from a good locally-based pianist called George Rattee, but he had to be trapped into giving lessons. Often in disgrace at school, usually for consistent sabotaging of the system, I left at sixteen and told the Headmasters' Appointments Board that I wanted to be a jazz pianist. Naturally they burst out with gales of laughter. (I give these details in the hope that a boy or girl today may pick up this book and feel they are not alone.)

'You seem qualified best for, let's see, hmm, the Civil Service (clerical grade of course) – that appeal to you? Good pensionable job – er, a shipping company, perhaps an oil company or something where you work with people – how about a department store, that not appeal to you? No. Or bus conducting – you'd deal with people there you know.' They rumbled on unperturbed.

I thanked them and left to spend the next two years within the bracing confines of Harrow Meteorological Office where a personal vendetta was waged against me by the tetchy Yorkshire boss of the Test Room and Radio Sonde Section. 'Yoong mun, yev coom ere ta werk,' he boomed on my arrival. He could tell I was going to love my job.

Two more years of boyish pranks and excruciating bore-

dom in the RAF (aircrew and met. office) and back to
Harrow (Wealdstone actually, not so grand sounding) –
decoding and recoding ships' reports this time – brought me
almost to the end of my endurance. After two more jobs in
Brimsdown factories, I decided to opt for education after all.

I had bought Blavatsky's astonishing book 'The Secret
Doctrine' on my twenty-first birthday (and later some of
Rudolph Steiner's incomparable works) and realized that if
I was ever to even start getting to grips with them I'd have
to equip myself with some basic tools. The Regent Street
Polytechnic Annexe in Balderton Street was in 1954/6 a
haven for lost sheep like me. In our class was a heavily
bearded Midshipman recently discharged from the Navy,
a highly intense mature lady called Mrs Montieff and a
marvellous collection of others at all stages of ignorance
from 17 upwards. It suited me perfectly. We were treated
as adults (I'd never experienced that before) and we in
turn responded as such. For the first time I began to love
my daily work – it was so freshening to hear good sense
talked for one thing – and the impetus I gained there was
to last me a long time. But underneath I was longing to play
and had the first real piano lessons of my life at Ivor
Mairants' Central School of Dance Music. Teachers there
were intermittent and expensive, though that was where I
met Dill Jones and Stan Tracey, who was then modelling
himself on Bud Powell.

I wrote a horrible little poem to sum up the situation. It
went like this:

THE FAMILY ENIGMA

He sets himself apart from us
This strange and awkward lad
Who speaks and acts as though he doesn't
Know what's good from bad
Ignoring all the best advice
Pursues his Aimless Trend
And try we may, we can't
Deter him from that Sticky End

To suit the part he's set himself
He's changed his facial plans
For what was once a boyish chin
Is bearded like a man's

83

Hush quick – no decent man
Of normal type was meant
But the other sort, the waster
And the one on sponging bent

Although he's read peculiar books
And studied for a year
It hardly seems to make his main
Ambition very clear
Poet and Musician eh?
(The words call forth a titter)
He might as well employ himself
By sweeping gutter litter

We don't suppose his silly words
Will come to much at all
Even if he is accepted
In some college hall
And when he fails, events will turn
Exactly as we feared
He'll have no safe profession
But he'll keep his blasted beard

How right they were. Later I ran the London University
Jazz Society for a couple of years and met Don Rendell. I
did part time and supply teaching. Later still I opened the
Highwayman Jazz Room in Camberley which ran for three
years. I wasn't able to break clear and actually become just
a musician till 1965 at the age of 31.*

All this rather dismal prelude seemed to hold the lesson
for me that jazz needed to be seen to have real value and
potential not just within its own special circle but also in
unlimited social situations outside and particularly in
education. Now this demands a great deal of jazz musicians
because they as artists are engaged in a constant inward
search and therefore find outer distractions a hindrance. To
talk or draw attention to the music by any other means than
by just playing is always a step and sometimes several steps
away from the music itself. But sometimes the rewards of
making this effort are unexpected in that one can find one-
self with a really attentive and sympathetic audience where

* When he joined the Don Rendell–Ian Carr Quintet. – Ed.

one least expected it. At eleven o'clock in the morning in a Hampshire village school, for example; in a provincial art gallery at lunchtime with old people free to drift in – and who stay in. Part of the satisfaction is the surprise of acceptance, part of it is the knowledge that there is unmistakably a substantial audience for jazz in the UK which cuts across all generation gaps and social demarcations. When I say the UK it must be clear I don't mean London, Manchester, Glasgow and so on: I also mean Connor's Quay Technical College, Fishguard or Lutterworth Community Centres. Of course it's exactly this diffuseness that makes such an audience so difficult to reach when planning publicity: it *is* so diverse. And the JCS is the first truly conscientious attempt to provide a centre of gravity for all these people.

Despite my strong views about jazz presentation and the way, it might seem, I had carefully worked it all out, I can only approach an explanation of my own work from the spontaneous impulses that came to me at the time. With poetry and jazz it was a genuine love of both that tempted me: the jazz choral works started with an emotional catharsis which I attempted to embody in a piece called *Wedding Hymn* and which led to other music (eucharist settings, psalms and prayers) which seemed to want to combine processional, clamorous or meditative moods with the upsurging fire of jazz improvisation. What musicians like Art Themen, Don Rendell, Norma Winstone, Coleridge Goode, Dave Green, Henry Lowther, Jimmy Philip, Trevor Tomkins, John Marshall, Colin Barnes and Ian Carr have given me towards realizing these demanding pieces cannot be overestimated. They've borne their fair share of enough bone-chilling cathedrals and late-entry pipe organs to deserve instant canonization. Don Rendell always warms the proceedings by quietly leaving a plentiful supply of *Watchtowers* and *Awakes* for the clergy and making sure that, when refreshment time comes, no worthy morsel is wasted. I remember we had a lovely couple of days at Exmouth in 1970 when *Mr Smith's Apocalypse* was chosen for a teachers' summer music course and there were a hundred really good choral singers to work with. The piece has, I hope, been useful to the various secondary school and college choirs and dance groups that have performed it with us. Such occasions have left many delightful memories!

Junior children are lovely to play for and to work with, though in practically all cases country schools tend to be the nicest and greatest fun. A far-seeing gentleman named Victor Fox began writing pieces to combine our Trio with junior singers and players in 1965/6 (*Nature Studies* and *Where is Fred?* for the Havant Music Festival and *A Week of Praise* for Christchurch Priory). He was marvellous with children and achieved something quite unbearable for me with 300 of them on a summer evening in Hamble when their opening of a junior concert with the National Anthem had the tears almost streaming down my cheeks. You wouldn't think it possible? Neither did I, but it taught me volumes about the strange, blinding loveliness that is locked up inside humankind and the wonderful gift some people, like him, have of releasing it. There is much pain, too, that we have to express, but at such moments even that may be totally eclipsed. He ought to be Prime Minister.

Colin Barnes and Trevor Tomkins (drums), Coleridge Goode and Dave Green (bass) shared these early experiences with me and it was interesting to see how we all softened as it gradually dawned on us how great a privilege it was to be doing this kind of work. Soon afterwards I wrote something more specifically on jazz lines; six pieces to do with rhythm called *All God's Children*. I'm now writing a *Norman Gnome and the Rhinoceros* series, which again I hope will give young children a lot of fun – as well as stretching their musical skills.

It's my experience that younger brains have less trouble with the 'unusual' (all life is new to them) – time measures of 5, 7, or 11 for example, and they love things like exchanging fours with the drummer. Also, the great thing about jazz discipline is that it is completely elastic in any direction, permitting extemporization on anything from *Lisa Lân* to *All Things Bright and Beautiful*. So a musician versed in jazz techniques should be able to make anything out of anything.

Some of the hardest criticism I have had is that my music is a thin-blooded commodity hardly worthy of consideration as full-bodied jazz. In the past I might have replied by saying that there were plenty of excellent musicians providing the raw stuff whereas no one was attempting the experiments and social expansions which I saw as important to try and bring about. My answer now would be that any time of tentativeness is gone and while losing nothing of the strength and power proper to jazz, these expansions are, I hope, in a better position to grow. Some of the nicest compliments, on the other hand, run on these lines: 'I haven't heard much (any) jazz (or) I didn't think I liked jazz, but this has made me realize what I've been missing and from now on when someone says the word "jazz", I'll be there.'

I'm sometimes asked if the word 'jazz' isn't outdated, no longer adequate to describe the great variety of music claiming that title. The only answer can be that a musician is a jazz musician because he acknowledges, loves, and feels himself to be part of the tradition that started for all practical purposes with King Oliver, Armstrong and Ellington and goes on via Parker to Coltrane and British geniuses like John Taylor. This alone is the criterion. The word may well be left behind by the end of the century by which time (Armageddon permitting) all jazz techniques will be a required part of every musician's training. But the spirit of jazz, its freedom, its warmth, its closeness to the soul, are here to stay.

I began by talking about illumination. A great artist generates his own by being what he is and doing what he does. This experience can make him humane and wise, but only if he finds a place where he is allowed to shine. It is said that Michelangelo carried with him a testimonial to the Pope when he first went to Rome. It read as follows: 'If this man, Michelangelo the sculptor, be treated with kindness and given encouragement, he will work well. But if he be shown love, he will surely accomplish things that will make the whole world wonder.'

As a sculptor, Michelangelo had an established place in the world-order of his time. This is what we seek.

The blues: revival and survival

Tony Russell

Jazz styles may come and go but the blues goes on – also changing and developing and reflecting new social situations. In this article blues expert Tony Russell looks at the situation of the blues today in terms of popular acceptance and the effects which aspects of the present scene are having on the music of some of the most notable contemporary musicians.

TEN years ago an essay like this would likely have been sunny and optimistic. The blues was thoroughly engaged in a course from the esoteric to the commercially estimable. Dropping a blues name into conversation no longer caused a brisk ripple of uninterest – you were talking about something generally identifiable, the guest on a TV programme or at a college dance, a name familiar from those ubiquitous club posters. Rock groups were singing blues, even naming themselves after them, and were not reluctant to reveal their sources. Blues by actual bluesmen even entered the pop charts.

It was the brightest stage of a progress whose outlines might have been guessed early, for jazz had more than once travelled some of that path. From the esoteric, blues moved first to the status of advanced pop, then popular (Top 30) pop – and this without significant alterations in the music. Arriving at the third stage, however, it faced problems. If blues could get into the charts, something unpredictable was happening, and the record industry has no love for the unpredictable. Either it was time for a drive, making bluesmen household names, generating a solid market, or it was all a flash in the pan, and should be underpromoted until it extinguished itself.

By and large, the second attitude ruled. Bluesmen were

Buddy Guy at Theresa's
Chicago
Photo: Valerie Wilmer

evidently not quite right for Top 30 circles – a mogul had only to spend a few minutes round John Lee Hooker or Sonny Boy Williamson to see that conventional manipulation could do little there. Blues receded to the second-stage status of advanced pop, a position from which two courses could be adopted, the concentrated or the roving. Concentrated meant choosing a few considerable artists, people in regular work who could be relied upon for tours and albums. Roving meant trying anything to see if it would take off and take the rest with it – novelties, American-British collaborations, collector-inspired reissues.

These lines of development were pursued in the late Sixties and early Seventies, and it's possible to see where they have led. The concentrated approach has been successful after a fashion – there are bluesmen with respectable commercial portfolios. Not many, since they are the survivors of a sifting process, and have needed both adaptability and constancy to come through it whole. But at least they have a place they didn't have before, which is more than you can say for the objects of the roving technique. Most of those experiments failed. It was agreeable that a major record company should promote the sort of thing previously confined to limited editions, but many of the collector-inspired productions sold only to the collectors, and the company seeking anything more than the thanks of a few hundreds was wasting its time. So gradually the experiments were relinquished to the independents who could handle them without losing money, and all that area of the blues returned to the status of the esoteric. It had more takers, for the blues boom had not failed to make converts, but in terms of a proportional market it was minor league stuff once more.

Survivors

The index of what has happened to blues in the ten years, more or less, since the blues boom is the small group of 'big' bluesmen, the artists who command assured audiences and record sales. At present these seem to be B. B. King, John Lee Hooker, Freddy King, Albert King, Muddy Waters, Buddy Guy and Junior Wells. Just outside the group are several figures who would qualify on some grounds but not others: Bobby Bland and Little Milton (successful, but mainly outside the norm of old-guard blues), Howlin' Wolf (unsuccessful of late on records), Albert Collins (of uncertain standing, just now) and the still up-and-coming Luther Allison and Jimmy Dawkins. To a follower of the rock scene it may seem an extraordinarily small number of top-level figures, and one that's separated from the next level by a very wide gulf, but it's doubtful whether any musical idiom with a comparable audience can ever maintain a much bigger establishment.

B. B. King seems unshakeably situated at the head of this company. He headlines most blues festivals, or blues segments of jazz festivals, while his singles obtain airplay and sometimes chart places. But there you have the elements of a double life, because B. B. King at a blues festival is a bluesman, singing *Sweet Sixteen* and *Everyday I Have the Blues*, whereas his singles are aimed at an almost MOR audience. For audiences outside the US who see him only occasionally, LPs like 'To Know You Is To Love You' (1973) are puzzling, until it's realized that such stuff is King's key to a mass market it would be pointless to neglect – rather like *Hello Dolly* for Louis. Unless King discards his blues for these orchestral fripperies, which seems psychologically very improbable, there will be no cause for the enthusiast to discard King.

John Lee Hooker is more enigmatic. Ever since the runaway success of the 'Endless Boogie' LP (1970) he has been wringing all there is to be wrung out of that thrumming, hypnotic, boogie format, and old-guard blues enthusiasts have been evenly divided into those who hate it and those who simply ignore it. Yet attentive listening shows that Hooker's current music is not, whatever else it may be, a simple sellout. He has been doing essentially that sort of thing all his life, only now he's relaxing into it and letting a band take some of the workload. If the product is merely dance music, the last and least objection to it can be that it is untrue to the blues tradition. However, most of the blues' present followers look for something other than dance music, and Hooker is unlikely to please them unless – what would be extraordinary – he steps back twenty-five years into his past.

The safety of a tried format protects B. B. King and Hooker – in King's case, of two formats – and it seems to be working quite well too for both Freddy King, whose last few years of record-making and concert appearances have been cooperative exercises with Leon Russell, and Albert King, who has been even longer associated with the Memphis soul label Stax. Format is perhaps too constricting a word for either, but each has worked out his ideas against a consistent background, with few or no experiments. Albert King is an intrinsically unadventurous musician, and has maybe been lucky to have Stax's reliable rhythm and horn sections playing things usually worth hearing, but on the other hand he is a forceful singer, the most downhome in his idiom. Freddy King, by contrast, is agile, and can cope with repertoire from the periphery of the blues, but his records frequently substitute efficiency for vitality, a fault less evident in concert.

Unlike the others in this company, Muddy Waters, Buddy Guy and Junior Wells come from a blues background of immense cohesiveness and constant competition, the Chicago club scene. While B. B. King and John Lee Hooker instantly marked themselves out as individualists, with whom nobody could exactly compete, the Chicago bluesmen were a close-knit community of musicians sharing a great deal of songs and ideas, and facing mutual criticism. To come out pitching from a melee like that requires not just a competent but a committed bluesman – anyone less than that would have given up or gone elsewhere. Muddy Waters is certainly committed – he cares for the blues tradition, and will not easily be led even a short distance away from it. The blues fan who came away shaking his head from B. B. King's 'To Know You Is To Love You' LP would have been able to nod contentedly at Waters' contemporaneous LP, 'Can't Get No Grindin' '.

Wells and Guy are younger men than Waters, and less apt for the elder statesman's role of custodian to the tradition, but their playing experiences – touring with the Stones, recording with rock bands or for conceptualizing producers – have done little to erase their knowledge of or fidelity to mainstream Chicago blues. At their best they convey a more vivid idea of musical cooperation, blues bandmanship, than anyone, while compromising least with rock models they might be expected to imitate.

Platforms

Of course, the successes are not the whole story of what is

happening in, or to, the blues, but they are probably indicative of what will be left of the old blues another ten years hence. Not that these observations should be taken for doomwatching – too often commentators have predicted death or disappearance, or at any rate decadence, only to witness a natural development in the music which ought to be no ground for pessimism. Gloom is appropriate, if at all, not to descriptions of the blues, but to analyses of its opportunities. Here the gains of the blues boom have been scanty. Club and concert tours outside the US are common enough, but they often assemble ill-assorted musicians, or attempt to inflate a reputation awarded according to the special criteria of record-collectors. In Britain, at least, it now seems doubtful whether anyone could set up a prestigious blues concert and clear his expenses. In so far as this puts travelling bluesmen back into the clubs, where they are more sympathetically presented, it is no bad thing, but the economics of small venues rule out visits by first-rank performers.

In the US, where the blues renascence was a steadier affair, and might have eventually attained a more secure place for itself, there was hope that large festivals might provide regular and cost-covering exposure for both the stars and the other luminaries. The latest reports, however, suggest that it is not working out like that. The annual blues festival at Ann Arbor, Michigan, promised a great deal, and in its early years delivered a great deal too, but the 1974 event looks like the death of the experiment. In a detailed and depressing postmortem for the magazine *Living Blues* Steve Tomashefsky outlined the errors: inadequate advertising, ill-judged distribution of the money for artists' fees (three-quarters of the total payout to James Brown, reduced fees or no fees at all for nearly everyone else), tactless handling of the drugs issue. Anyone concerned in festival promotion, whether in blues or jazz or rock, will recognize these as the sort of spanners hardest to keep out of the works, and since the rewards of promoters' speculation in blues events are never likely to be handsome, the future of the blues festival on any but a local scale is dubious.

The musicians affected most by this loss of exposure are, naturally, those to whom any exposure comes as a surprise; B. B. King has not much to lose from the disappearance of a dozen Ann Arbors. The loss of major blues events widens the gap between first- and second-rank bluesmen, so that the enriching, variegating effect of the latter's presence counts for less and less in the total sound-picture of the music. The blues is a story told by many voices, and we cannot afford to have any of the congregation silenced.

One solution of this problem, which seems to be working in the US, though it cannot be applied so easily elsewhere, is a sort of decentralization. Instead of having to look to Ann Arbor, or the blues night of the Newport Jazz Festival, artists can more and more often find places open to them at local – state or county – festivals. The growth of the heterogeneous 'folklore' or 'heritage' festival, which is sure to be accelerated by the bicentennial, has been beneficial to the blues. One significant function of this kind of festival is its juxtaposing blues with jazz and bluegrass and 'ethnic' musics (cajun, Mexican and such), so that bluesmen find themselves preaching, for once, to the unconverted. The challenge is not likely to do the blues any harm, and it may be that the local emphasis of these events will discover or encourage musicians whom all the brouhaha of the blues boom never reached. Perhaps a closing note of sunny optimism *is* appropriate, after all.

Back to the folkways
Roger Cotterrell

With folk-rock, Afro-rock, Afro-jazz, jazz-rock,
latin-jazz, Afro-Cuban and the rest, labels start to get pretty
confusing. One thing seems clear: a lot of musical barriers
which have isolated jazz are coming down – and not before
time. This piece discusses some aspects of the way jazz has
expanded its frontiers both geographically and musically in
recent years and looks at ways in which it has drawn on and
been influenced by folk sources from different parts of the
world as both the music and the attitudes that go with it have
undergone some important changes.

STRANGE things have been happening
in jazz over the past few years. Some of them went un-
noticed at the time or were just shrugged off as the kind of
odd activities of odd characters that the music ought to be
able to take in its stride by now. But put a few of these
strange things together and it becomes clear that change
is in the air.

Take, for example, Don Cherry, the diminutive trumpeter
who helped Ornette Coleman map out a new language for
jazz in the late fifties. Cherry still plays trumpet but his
recent records show him also grappling with such curiosities
as Tibetan bells, ancient wheezy sounding harmoniums,
Chinese ceramic bowl flutes and primitive twangy stringed
instruments from distant parts of the world. And, although
Cherry hasn't completely forsaken jazz, his music now
ranges over the folk music of a dozen or more cultures.
Bernt Rosengren, an excellent Swedish tenor player and
one of the finest jazzmen in Europe, has taken to playing
the taragot, a Rumanian folk instrument apparently tradi-
tionally used for wedding ceremonies. In America, Ornette
Coleman has been heard playing the shehnai, a shawm-like
wind instrument, and, by all accounts, producing sounds

remarkably like the bellowing drone of the zurma of traditional Turkish dance music. The very different 'Third
World Music' of Gato Barbieri – one of the most publicized
figures in American contemporary jazz at present – draws
on the music of his native Argentina. In London, South
African expatriate Julian Bahula can be heard playing (with
immense gusto) the Malombo drums of the Venda tribe of
North Transvaal alongside British musicians who make do
with the less exotic instruments of the Selmer and Boosey &
Hawkes families. And, in the same city, a soft-spoken
Cypriot pianist named Arman Ratip combines a strange and
unique blend of Turkish folk music, jazz and Western
classical influences in his own playing and composing.

Does all this mean that folk music has suddenly bowled
over the contemporary jazz world? In a sense there is
nothing completely new in any of these isolated cases. Since
the Fifties Detroit tenorman Yusef Lateef has been doing
battle with argols and shehnais and bassist Ahmed Abdul-
Malik has doubled on the oud. And, from the time of
Django Reinhardt, non-American musicians have coloured
their jazz with elements drawn from their own culture.
'Spanish tinges', 'latin-jazz', 'Creole Echoes' and 'Afro-
Cuba' are part of jazz history. Attempted fusions with folk
or classical sources seem to come and go. Bossa Nova hjt
big in the Sixties and declined almost before anyone had a
chance to go back to the original recordings of Bud Shank
and Laurindo Almeida to see what a *real* fusion of jazz and
Brazilian music could achieve. The high hopes of a jazz-
classical 'Third Stream' seemed to come to nothing in the
same decade. Similarly Indo-jazz, with its incongruous
juxtaposition of sitars, tambouras, tablas and jazz drums,
rose to the trendy heights of fashionability in the Sixties but,
after a period when jazz-Indian recordings seemed as
normal as rock groups with symphony orchestras, the steam
seemed to go out of the whole experiment.

What really is new about the present interaction between
jazz and folk music of many kinds is the scale of it and the
degree of genuine fusion which is taking place. It seems
clear that over a period of time a number of factors, musical
and otherwise, have come together in the jazz world to make
the music far more widely receptive than in the past to the
influence of other musical forms. Complementing this, it has
gradually become possible for more and more musicians to

bring to jazz new musical elements frequently derived from folk sources. The result is that the face of jazz is changing because of these new factors. Folk elements are no longer important merely as exotic colouring – a kind of garnish to spice up the old jazz mix; 'jungle sounds', the optional conga drummer, a stray sitar. Genuine musical fusions are taking place in a manner which can only be beneficial to jazz in many ways.

None of these changes could have occurred without a gradual but crucial adjustment of attitude on the part of many jazz musicians. It is dangerous to generalize too widely but there does seem to be a new kind of musical open-mindedness among many contemporary jazz musicians which is in sharp contrast to the old insularity and restrictiveness which used to keep the jazz world a rigidly enclosed place – socially and musically. Perhaps the change is most clearly symbolized by the way the word 'hip', that label which clearly draws the line between insiders and outsiders, is slowly disappearing from jazz argot.

A decade or more ago all this started with the at first heretical idea that jazz might be able to learn from rock music – that those untutored kids might even have something after all. And, even though in strictly musical terms jazz had more to offer rock than vice versa, jazz musicians began to shed some of their pomposity, their stultifying superiority complexes and their distrust of simplicity and musical directness. This change of approach was bound to affect attitudes to folk music along with all other forms of 'non-art' music.

If most jazz musicians and enthusiasts had not taken folk music very seriously in the past there was certainly some excuse for the neglect. As Benny Green once remarked, 'a large quantity of what masquerades as folk music is a ghastly grinding cacophony which may very possibly have flourished in times when the manufacture of instruments was not the scientific and comparatively economic process it is today'. But, if in the West folk music has suffered all manner of mutilations, through commercialization and the decline of folk traditions, that is not necessarily true of other cultures. Genuine folk music possesses a strength and timelessness which much jazz lacks and which springs from the fact that it only survives because of its capacity to express the feelings and experiences of generation after generation in the same basic form. Its vitality is in its closeness to the people and their culture. As contemporary jazz has groped in many directions with varying degrees of success these qualities of stability have come to take on more and more importance. As the horizons of jazz musicians have broadened some of them have come to look on the combination of musical integrity and popular roots in the genuine folk music of the world with something almost approaching envy.

Two other factors have helped to widen jazz horizons immeasurably. One is the comparatively recent loosening of its strict musical rules and the other is the long term effect of the dissemination of jazz around the world through records, the media and concert tours. Ornette Coleman – so the story goes – blew on his white and gold plastic alto and the old jazz order began to crumble, like the walls of Jericho, in 1958. In fact a good many other musicians had been chipping at the structure in various ways before then. But after Coleman and Coltrane, free improvisation and modal improvisation put the emphasis on melody and complicated harmonic patterns no longer seemed necessary. Simple forms suddenly seemed to be as good a basis for blowing as complex ones. The biggest single factor which isolated jazz – the rigidity of its musical rules – began to disappear. If you could play a solo over just one chord, then why not over the drone of a tamboura or the accompaniment of an African drum choir.

So jazz, over the last decade and more, has prepared itself musically and emotionally to meet the outside world on something like equal terms. But nothing really fruitful could have occurred without the worldwide spread of jazz music and the feedback from it. Dizzy Gillespie's 1956 US State Department tour of the Far East is still remembered as something of a breakthrough even though jazz musicians were wandering the earth well before that. But Gillespie's immensely successful trip set a trend and the US Government began to treat jazz as a good ambassador for winning friends and influencing people abroad. Charlie Byrd came back from his 1961 South American tour with a souvenir – Bossa Nova – which set the American music world alight the following year. Dave Brubeck's trip to Europe, India and the Middle East in 1958 produced a string of compositions using folk elements from the countries visited and spurring Brubeck's attempts to incorporate then unusual time signatures into jazz. In 1963 the German Goethe Institute sponsored a Far East tour by the Albert Mangelsdorff Quintet, one of the most important European contemporary jazz groups of its time. It was probably the first really productive encounter at first hand between the *post-*Coleman and Coltrane conceptions of jazz and the folk music of the East. Joachim Berendt, who was on the tour, wrote 'On most occasions, the quintet played variations on themes taken from the folk or classical musics of the appropriate country. In Thailand the group transformed a ramwong – a native dance of the Thai – into a Coltranelike theme *à la My Favourite Things*, and I noticed two Thai girls in the front row moving their hands while listening to the music, as if they were dancing along with it'.

I would not be surprised if jazz records have reached the foothills of the Himalayas by now. Cab Calloway records were popular among Belgians in the Congo in the Forties. American record labels were being imported into South Africa in the Thirties. The music has been heard nearly everywhere. And some of the seeds have taken root. Almost every nationality boasts musicians who can express themselves through jazz. As they draw on the musical traditions of their own cultures fusing these elements with jazz elements and as the rules by which jazz is made become more flexible, so it becomes less and less an American idiom and more a bridge by which the gulf between musical traditions can be spanned.

In some respects it is surprising, in others quite natural, that South Africa should provide the best example of these developments occurring on a wide scale today. Jazz has been a force to be reckoned with there for twenty years and more. The number of first rate jazz musicians produced seems startling for a country halfway across the world from the source of American jazz. Dollar Brand stands out as one of the most important pianist-composers using the jazz idiom today. But European audiences are well aware of the fire, confidence and inventiveness of other expatriate South Africans; Mongezi Feza, Dudu Pukwana, Johnny Dyani, Louis Moholo, Harry Miller, Julian Bahula among them, and Chris MacGregor – whose 'Brotherhood of Breath' big band seems to sum up the distinctive, exuberant, highly emotional and swinging character of much South African jazz. These are not isolated individuals although they are some of the best jazz talents South Africa boasts. But, as Julian Bahula put it, 'I don't hear more jazz in London than there. In South Africa the cats are jazz cats. They dig jazz like mad.' Many fine instrumentalists who are hardly known outside their own country play at township gatherings and to audiences of twenty thousand or more at open-air festivals.

It is not possible here to go into the fascinating question of why jazz took root so strongly in this part of Africa while it had little influence in other parts of the continent. But it has been suggested that South African traditional music, which is quite different from West African or Congo-Angolan, has some remarkable similarities with jazz. One writer explains, 'it tends towards rhythmic complexity of singing voices over a regular beat; its polyrhythms come from the voices, which vary their accentuation relative to the basic rhythm. This is remarkably like jazz, especially the 1930s and 1940s music of Count Basie and others who riffed and soloed against a rock-solid four-four beat'.* Certainly big band jazz became popular in South Africa. Dollar Brand recalled in an interview, 'My first professional job was with a big band – there were big bands all over South Africa playing imported orchestrations like Erskine Hawkins and Tommy Dorsey'.

Significantly, South Africa seems to be a country where restrictive musical pigeonholes do not apply. A band like Batsumi, one of the best playing there, switches naturally and unselfconsciously from Coltraneish modal jazz to soul music to traditional music. Audiences seem to be equally open-minded. But this doesn't necessarily mean that the quality of the music must suffer. It may be that only where this open approach is present can there be the possibility of a real fusion which takes elements of different musics and links them into something new without bastardizing any of them. In the music of Dollar Brand it is difficult and ulti-mately pointless to try to isolate the elements which have been fused into a personal means of expression. Certain ingredients are obvious: Monk, Ellington, European classical influences, African rhythms. But beyond that there's

* John Storm Roberts, *Black Music of Two Worlds*, Allen Lane, London, 1973.

a danger of missing the point. In the melting pot of South Africa jazz has not simply had a few more colours mixed into its musical palette. It has been transmuted in a remarkable way into a means of expression for musicians of totally different experience and culture from that of the American creators of the jazz language. It is this phenomenon which is new and radically different from most of the 'fusions' which are part of jazz history. The obvious elements of rhythmic excitement and musical extroversion in some folk-based South African jazz exactly parallel the qualities which latin-jazz brought into the 1940s and 1950s jazz mainstream. But there the similarity ends because, with few exceptions, latin-jazz was the creation of musicians lacking a thorough understanding of one or other of the 'latin' or 'jazz' ingredients. Hence it tended to be either jazz or latin· music with a mere colouring of the other. In contrast, the Puerto Rican–Cuban 'Salsa' music which has evolved in New York in recent years seems to offer more possibilities for a real fusion with jazz on equal terms.

Like South Africa, Turkey is a country which has long been open to foreign musical influence and yet has powerful musical traditions of its own. When Dave Brubeck toured the country in 1958 he found in the intricacy of the folk themes and the fascinating complexity of the rhythms elements which could be adapted to a jazz context. The 9/8 rhythm common in Turkish music appeared in Brubeck's *Blue Rondo à la Turk* and, when copies of the record reached Turkey, the music attracted a young Cypriot pianist named Arman Ratip and helped to turn his attention to American jazz. Since then Ratip himself has produced two LPs which attempt to combine elements of jazz, Turkish folk music and European classical influences. In Sweden in 1971, Turkish jazz trumpeter Maffy Falay, a veteran of the Kenny Clarke-Francy Boland Band and a musician whom Gillespie had 'discovered' on that memorable 1956 tour, put together a group called Sevda, made up of Turkish and Swedish musicians, to play a mixture of Turkish music and jazz. During its existence Sevda produced three fascinating LPs and was, by all accounts, the biggest news on the Swedish jazz scene in quite a while.

Musically the fusion of Turkish folk music and jazz is perfectly feasible. Turkish music is improvised and modal. It makes use of powerful hypnotic themes and its most obvious characteristic is the complexity of its rhythms. 'It's natural to us,' Arman Ratip explained, '9/8, 7/8, 11/4 . . . these rhythms to us are like 2/4 or 4/4 because we have been listening to them since we were that small, you know.' The result is that Turkish folk musicians seem to achieve what jazz musicians have long been seeking to do. To swing effortlessly and create music of tremendous momentum in the most complex time signatures. At this stage it is hard to know whether Sevda's type of experiment will be carried into the mainstream of jazz and produce any major influence on contemporary jazz developments. But it is an example of the way the simplification of jazz harmony has allowed the music to link with a folk source that offers immense rhythmic vitality. And, as jazz musicians wander the world more widely than ever, ideas are carried further afield. So, for example, in 1972, Sevda's magnificent Turkish drummer Okay Temiz joined forces in Stockholm with two South Africans, Mongezi Feza and Johnny Dyani, to record 'Music for Xaba' (Sonet), a fine LP of jazz and traditional music.

These examples from Turkey and South Africa show genuine fusions of jazz and folk music of a kind which only seems to have become possible on a wide scale comparatively recently because of the changes occurring in jazz itself and because of the worldwide spread of its influence. At a far less significant level the use of folk elements as mere colouring for jazz without affecting its form and content has been widespread since the beginnings of the music. But there is also a third category which falls short of genuine fusion but is also much more than mere colouring.

It is typified by much of the music of Lars Gullin in Sweden and Zbigniew Namyslowski in Poland, by the jazz arrangements of Czechoslovak music by Karel Velebny and Jaromir Hnilicka, by some of the mid-Sixties work of the Zagreb Jazz Quartet in Yugoslavia and by a great deal of immensely beautiful music on record from Django Reinhardt to the present day. For musicians such as those mentioned folk music is a part of their heritage naturally expressed in their own jazz music. Their musical idiom is unmistakably jazz but the feeling of the music, its richness and emotional depth is often drawn from folk sources. It is no accident that much of the best music in this category has come from Europe – still rich in folk music which can often be adapted with little difficulty to jazz form.

Over the years baritonist and composer Lars Gullin has instilled into the best of his music a tranquillity and melancholy that is quite foreign to much American jazz. Although he was originally influenced by Americans such as Stan Getz, Lee Konitz and Gerry Mulligan, there is no doubt that his music today is unique and totally personal. The relation of Gullin's composing to folk music is a real one but hard to pin down; he rarely uses folk material as such and his music is far too complex and sophisticated for folk elements to play a significant part in the final product. But Gullin's love of Swedish folk music is genuine. His study of it has helped him to find himself in his music and, at its best, Gullin's composing hints at the timelessness of folk music which jazz rarely achieves.

By comparison, the Polish altoist Zbigniew Namyslowski has developed through the last two decades to become one of the finest *post*-Coleman and Coltrane alto players. Namyslowski's artistic path took him from traditional jazz to bebop to contemporary jazz in two decades of searching. He explored free jazz before it became fashionable and rejected it because of its denial of rhythm. 'I don't feel jazz when it lacks driving power. Free jazz was necessary – one had to go to extremes in order to ply back to the middle. But once rhythm is lost free stops being jazz.' Significantly it was in the folk music of Eastern Europe that Namyslowski found the rhythmic inspiration he was seeking. Roman Kowal wrote, 'Rhythmically, Namyslowski's jazz is marked by frequent oppositions between duple and triple times and their various combinations: 5/4, 7/8, 11/8. They go to make up that specific climate of many of his works and reflect his interest in the folklore of various peoples.' Like Gullin, Namyslowski draws strength in his music from folk roots but, again like Gullin, the musical language is still undoubtedly jazz. The folk element is more than just colouring but it is something latent underlying the music. 'Jazz means Jazz,' says Namyslowski. 'I believe that improvisations should be based on American musicians' patterns, on one of the several existing schools. Polishness should be manifested in themes which admit some home climate, a specific scale, a particular motif, melodic or harmonic phrase.'

Gullin and Namyslowski are two examples of musicians most of whose work is well within the jazz tradition but for whom folk sources have added something important to their music. It may well be that one path which jazz will follow in the future is towards a greater use of musical sources close to the people and their culture and towards the kind of open-minded meetings of musical traditions which the South African and Turkish examples illustrate. Labels may disappear but those for whom the jazz tradition is important and real need have no fears; swinging improvised music has a long future ahead of it. In whatever country it finds itself it can only grow stronger as it draws on long-lived musical traditions that seem appropriate. The sincerity of musicians and audience alike is perhaps a good enough guide in shaping the music of the future.*

* Linda (Bernhardt), Julian (Bahula), Arman (Ratip) – Thanks for answering my many questions about the music of your respective countries.

The musicians

THIS section lists current and recent musical activity of nearly 250 musicians presently active on the British jazz scene, together with recent records and details of their careers. Arranged in headings as follows:

B Date of birth. **A & T/Agent** Address and telephone for bookings and agent's address and telephone. **Curr** Musical activity *as at late September 1975*, bands and musicians worked with at that time. Where a group is not identified by the name of its leader, the leader or organizer is named in brackets after the group name. Under the entry for the leader of a group having a reasonably stable personnel, key members of the group are listed in brackets after the group name. **Prev** Bands worked with or led since the beginning of the musician's career. Not necessarily comprehensive but representative of the individual's musical experience: other career details are included where appropriate. **Tours, Conc, Fest** Recent tours, major concerts and festival appearances. Various other entries are based on questionnaire replies as follows: **Fav rec** The musician's best performance on record in his own view. **Mem/Imp event** Key events or experiences in musical career, not necessarily recent. **Pref** Preferences among other musicians' work, or favourite records or compositions by other musicians. Under the heading **Rec** most entries have a listing of recent records. For most musicians this extends back about five years and is a representative guide but not necessarily a comprehensive list. For major artists the listing extends back about ten years and is reasonably comprehensive. The listing is normally in reverse chronological order – i.e. most recent records are listed first. Where a musician's appearances on record have been mainly or extensively under other musicians' leadership cross referencing to the leader's entry in this section of the book has been used. The record listings give record titles, name of label and (in brackets) date of recording (not date of issue unless otherwise stated).

Abbreviations: **acc** accompanied; **alto** alto sax; **alto-f** alto flute; **app** appearance(s); **arr** arranger, arranged; **bari** baritone sax; **bs** bass; **clar** clarinet; **comp** composer, composed, composition; **comm** commissioned; **el** electric; **esp** especially; **f** flute; **flug-h** flugel-horn; **g** guitar; **ICA** Institute of Contemporary Arts London; **improv** improvised, improvisation; **JB** jazz band; **JF** Jazz Festival; **MD** musical director; **org** organ; **p** piano; **perc** percussion; **perf** performance; **QEH** Queen Elizabeth Hall London; **RFH** Royal Festival Hall London; **sop** soprano sax; **tbn** trombone; **tenor** tenor sax; **tpt** trumpet; **vib** vibraphone; **w** with

Neil Ardley

NEIL ARDLEY *comp, MD*

B 26.5.37 **A** 13a Priory Avenue, Bedford Park,
London W4. **T** 01–994 6513 & 062983 2753.
Curr Own orch & foreign radio orchestras.
Prev Leader New Jazz Orch '63–'68. **Fest**
Camden JF '74– special commission
'Biformal from Bali'. **Conc** Shakespeare
Anniv Southwark Cath '74 & '75, QEH
Oct '75. **Fav rec** 'A Symphony of Amaranths'
Regal Zonophone (1971). **Rec** 'Will Power'
(w Gibbs, Tracey etc) Argo (1974), 'Greek
Variations' (w Rendell, Carr) Columbia
(1969), 'Déjeuner Sur L'Herbe' (NJO) Verve
(1968), 'Western Reunion' (NJO) Decca
(1965). Ardley's writing often shows the
influence of Gil Evans but in recent years it
has steadily become more ambitious and
personal, d'splaying an individual and
impressive approach to extended composition.

VIC ASH *tenor, clar, f*

B 9.3.30 **A** 104 Morshead Road, London
W9 1LG. **T** 01–286 8926. **Curr** Freelance
session work & guest app at jazz clubs.
Prev Kenny Baker '51–'53, Vic Lewis '53–'55,
Dankworth, own quar, quin, etc. **Tours**
Europe w Frank Sinatra–Liza Minelli &
Jack Jones. **Fav rec** Own Jazz Five album
Tempo (*c*1961). **Mem events** Playing opposite
groups like Miles Davis, Dizzy Gillespie,
Dave Brubeck, & working w Sinatra. **Pref**
Thad Jones–Mel Lewis Orch, Getz, Goodman.

Bill Ashton

BILL ASHTON *sop, alto, tenor, bari, clar,
comp, arr, copyist, MD*

B 6.12.36 **A** 1 Victor Road, Harrow, Middx.
T 01–863 2717. **Curr** Musical Director Nat
Youth Jazz Orch since '64. **Prev** Oxford Univ
Big Band (leader), own octet, Red Bludd's
Bluesicians (Blues group inc Jon Lord),
schoolmaster until '73. **Tours, fest, conc**
(w NYJO) France '67 & '74, Poland '73,
Camden Fest '72, Greenwich Fest '75 & many
others. World Youth Fests: Sofia Bulgaria '68,
E Berlin '73. Wavendon '71 '72 '73 & '75.
UK tour May '75. TV appearances. **Mem
events** BBC TV 'In Concert' prog Jan '75,
Armstrong Mem Conc RFH July '75. **Rec**
'NYJO Live at LWT' RCA (1975), 'NYJO'
Charisma (*c*1973), 'National Youth Jazz
Orchestra' Philips (1971).

Ron Aspery

RON ASPERY *alto, sop, C melody sax, bari, f, p, el-p*
B 9.6.46 **A** 16 Dunraven Street, London W1 & 39 Cypress Road, Redcar, Cleveland.
T 01–499 0671 & Redcar 77615. **Curr** Back Door since *c*'72. **Fest** Montreux JF. **Tours** Numerous inc USA & Europe. **Fav rec** 'Back Door' (w Colin Hodgkinson, Tony Hicks) Warner Bros (1972). **Mem events** Recording w Carl Palmer & Mike Gibbs. **Pref** Gibbs, Ronnie Scott, Ellington, Elgar, Faure, Samuel Barber. **Rec** 'Another Fine Mess' (Back Door) Warner Bros (1974), '8th Street Nites' (Back Door) Warner Bros (1973).

ROY BABBINGTON *el-bs*
A 3a Lawrence Road, South Ealing, London W5. **T** 01–567 6840. **Curr** Soft Machine (inc Jenkins, Marshall, Mike Ratledge). **Prev** Alexis Korner, Mike D'Abo, Mike Gibbs, Nucleus (Carr), Ovary Lodge (Keith Tippett), Solid Gold Cadillac (Westbrook). **Rec** 'Bundles' (Soft Machine) Harvest (1974), 'Soft Machine 7' CBS (1973), & w Gibbs, Elton Dean, Carr, Tippett. **Other** Tutor Lambeth Jazz Summer School July '75. A strong, reliable bassist, Babbington's work has been largely in the rock and rock-jazz fields.

(SEBOTHANE) JULIAN BAHULA *African drums & perc*
B 13.3.38 **A** 4 Milner Road, Morden, Surrey.
T 01–648 1821. **Curr** Own band Malombo (w Feza, Ranku, Mothle) and Jabula–Spear (co-led w Pukwana). **Prev** Own band Malombo (in South Africa) 1st prize Castle Lager JF Johannesburg '64, own band Jabula, Jo'burg Hawk. **Tour, Conc** Swaziland, Basutoland, Mozambique, S. Africa before coming to Britain, Reading '73, Scandinavia '73. **Mem event** Coming to London from SA in '73. **Pref** 'Midnight Walk' (Elvin Jones), 'Tintinyana' (Dollar Brand). **Rec** 'Jabula' Virgin (*c*1973).

DEREK BAILEY *g*
A 33 Thornhill Road, London N1.
T 01–607 0367. **Curr** Solo concerts since *c*'71. **Prev** Commercial work Leeds '59–'60 & Manchester '63, trio w Tony Oxley & Gavin Bryars '63, came to London mid '60s, SME (Stevens) in '60s, Tony Oxley, London J

Comp Orch (Guy), Iskra 1903 (w Rutherford, Guy); Peter Brötzmann, Han Bennink, Alexander von Schlippenbach on Continent. **Tour, Conc** Wigmore Hall (w Anthony Braxton) June '74, Contemporary Music Network Tour Feb '75 (w Parker, Lytton), solo conc ICA May '75, frequently works on Continent. **Rec** 'Lot 74 – Solo Improvisations' Incus (1974), 'Duo' (w Anthony Braxton) Emanem (1974), 'The Crust' (Steve Lacy) Emanem (1973), 'Improvisation for Cello & Guitar' (w David Holland) ECM (1971), 'Solo Guitar' Incus (1971), 'Iskra 1903' Incus (1970-2), 'Music Improvisation Co' ECM (1970), 'Topography of the Lungs' Incus (1970), and w SME, Tony Oxley, London J Comp Orch, Wheeler. Tutor Barry J Summer School '73, formed Incus Records w Evan Parker etc *c*'70. A unique and completely original guitarist, Bailey has developed an entirely personal technique of free playing, relying on the exploration of sound structures and textures.

Keith Bailey

KEITH BAILEY *drums, perc, p*
B 14.9.48 **A** Flat 3, 148 Hornsey Lane, Highgate, London N6. **T** 01–272 0452 & 01–340 6285. **Curr** Own band Prana, Joy (Jim Dvorak), Naima (big band & trio) (Chris Francis), Arman Ratip. **Prev** Brotherhood of Breath (MacGregor), Chris MacGregor Quin, Dudu Pukwana, Isipingo (Harry Miller), Mike Osborne Quin, Keith Tippett Trio, Centipede (Tippett), Graham Bond, Brian Auger, Marc Charig Trio. **Rec** 'Spy from Istanbul' (Ratip) Regal Zonophone (1973), 'Blueprint' (Tippett) RCA (1972). **Pref** Bach, some Handel, Alan Hovhaness, Coltrane, Byzantine music and music of the great Himalayan range and Orient.

KENNY BAKER *tpt*
B 1.3.21 **A** 16 Avenue Rise, Bushey, Herts. **T** 01–950 1264 **Curr** plays w various groups, session work. **Prev** Numerous bands inc Lew Stone '39, Maurice Winnick, Jack Hylton, Ambrose, Sid Millward, Ted Heath Orch '46–'49 (lead tpt & arranger), also studio, film & TV work, own band Kenny Baker's Dozen. *Conc* 35 years celeb 100 Club '74. **Rec** 'Baker's Jam' 77 (1974), 'George Chisholm' Rediffusion Gold Star (1973), 'Along the

Chisholm Trail' (Chisholm) 77 (1971), 'London Date' (Benny Goodman) Philips (1969), and w Hayes, Tracey.

KENNY BALDOCK *bs*
A 4 Sandown House, Belsize Road, London NW6. **T** 01–624 1351. **Curr** Colin Purbrook Trio, Sext, Ronnie Scott Quar since Aug '75, own sext, Herman Wilson Chamber Group, Freddy Randall, Brian Lemon Trio, Dave Shepherd Quin. **Prev** Numerous groups inc Dankworth, Centipede (Tippett), Ovary Lodge (Tippett), Gene Cottrell Quin. **Rec** 'Live at Montreux' (Randall–Shepherd) Black Lion (1973).

KENNY (KENNETH DANIEL) BALL *tpt*
B 22.5.30 **A** Colin Hogg, London Management, Regent House, 235–241 Regent Street, London W1. **T** 01–734 8851. **Curr** Own Jazzmen. **Prev** Sid Phillips, Eric Delaney, Charlie Galbraith. **Tours** East Germany, Australia. **Fest** Breda JF (Holland) May '75. **Fav rec** 'Kenny Ball in Berlin' Fontana (1968). **Mem event** Playing in conc w Louis Armstrong, London. **Pref** Bunny Berigan, Bix Beiderbecke. **Rec** 'Let's All Sing A Happy Song' Pye (1973), 'Have A Drink On Me' Pye (1972), 'My Very Good Friend Fats Waller' Pye (1971–2), 'Fleet Street Lightning' Fontana (1969).

Chris Barber

CHRIS (DONALD CHRISTOPHER) BARBER *tbn, tpt*
B 17.4.30 **Agent** Colin Hogg, London Management, Regent House, 235–241 Regent Street, London W1. **T** 01–734 8851. **Curr** Own band. **Prev** First band '49, organized band w Colyer '53 taking it over '54, own band since '54. **Tours** Germany, Holland, Denmark, Switzerland, France, Sweden. **Fest** Hamburg, Dortmund (W. Germany), Reading, Newcastle JF '74. **Conc** Royal Fest Hall (Ellington Memorial) June '75, London Palladium, Fairfield Hall Croydon etc. **Fav rec** " 'Get Rollin' " Black Lion Double Album (1968–70). **Mem event** President Kennedy's Washington JF '62. **Pref** Armstrong early recordings. **Rec** 'In East Berlin' Black Lion (1968), 'Ragtime' Marble Arch (1970), 'Chris Barber Jubilee Album' (3 Vols–6 LPs) Black Lion (1949–1974). Barber's band is one of the best known and most widely travelled of

British jazz groups. Its style has evolved from strict traditionalism to one that takes in a variety of influences from rhythm & blues & rock to mainstream and modern jazz.

JOHNNY BARNES *alto, clar, bari, f*
A 16 Worton Road, Isleworth, Middx.
T 01–560 7593. **Curr** Alex Welsh Band. **Prev** Alan Elsdon, own quin w Bruce Turner. **Rec** 'John Barnes – Roy Williams Jazz Band' Rediffusion Gold Star (*c*1975), 'It's George' (Melly) Warner Bros (1974), and w Welsh.

JOHNNY (JOHN SIDNEY) BASTABLE
tenor banjo, g, mandolin
B 22.11.29 **A** 15 Cedar Road, Teddington, Middx TW11 9AN. **T** 01–977 5136. **Curr** Riverside Five Plus One. **Prev** Ken Colyer '55–'71, own Chosen Six '71–'74. **Tours** Germany '73, Belgium '74. **Fav rec** 'Johnny Bastable's Chosen Six Second Album' Joy (1972). **Mem event** Playing w George Lewis New Orleans Band on '59 tour. **Pref** All jazz, esp New Orleans style. **Rec** 'Exactly Like . . . Johnny Bastable's Chosen Six' Joy (1971) and w Colyer.

Gordon Beck

GORDON BECK *p, el-p*
A 21 North Drive, Hounslow, Middx. **T** 01–570 4183. **Curr** Own trio, Major Surgery (Don Weller) own group Gyroscope (reformed autumn '75). **Prev** Tony Kinsey, Tubby Hayes Quin, house pianist Ronnie Scott's Club in late 60s, The Band (R Scott) '68, Phil Woods' European Rhythm Machine '69–'72, own group Gyroscope '73–'74 (inc Sulzmann, Ricotti, Levin, Matthewson). **Tours, Conc** Travelled widely in Europe w Woods in early '70s. Montreux JF '72, Brussels, Germany, Switzerland (w Gyroscope) '73. BBC TV 'Open Door' w Gyroscope '74, Camden JF '74 (Piano Conclave). **Other** Tutor Barry Summer School '75. **Rec** Gyroscope 'One, Two, Three, Go' Jaguar (cassette) (*c*1974), 'Live at Montreux '72' (Woods) Cardin/Verve (1972), 'All In The Morning' (Beck–Matthewson–Humair Trio) Dire (Italy) (1972) reissued 1975 on Jaguar (cassette), 'At the Frankfurt Jazz Festival' (Woods) Embryo (1970), 'Experiments with Pops' Major Minor (1969), 'Gyroscope' Morgan (1968), 'Gordon Beck+2 plays Half A Jazz Sixpence' Major Minor (1968),

'Gordon Beck + 2 plays Dr Doolittle' Major
Minor (1968), and w Hayes, Ian Carr, Scott.
A pianist of prodigious technique, influenced by
Bill Evans but enjoying a well deserved
international reputation as an inventive and
adventurous soloist.

Harry Beckett

HARRY BECKETT *tpt, flug-h*
A 65 Cowper Road, London N16 8PB.
T 01–254 9113. **Curr** Own band S & R
Powerhouse Section (w Weller, Miller, Webb
etc). Own band Joy Unlimited, Ray Russell
Quin since early '70s, Graham Collier since
'60s, Brotherhood of Breath (MacGregor).
Prev Came to Britain from Barbados '54,
Herbie Goins & The Nightimers, Mike
Westbrook, Stan Tracey Big Band, John
Surman Octet, Keef Hartley Band, Gibbs,
Jack Bruce, Alan Cohen. **Tours** Germany w
John Warren Band, Europe w Collier '74.
Fest Holland w Brotherhood of Breath.
Other App in film 'All Night Long' w Mingus.
Tutor NYJO Easter J Course '74 & other
jazz educ activities. **Rec** 'Joy Unlimited',
Cadillac (1974), 'Themes for Fega' RCA
(1972), 'Warm Smiles' RCA (1971), & w
Collier, Russell, Mike Osborne, Westbrook,
Brotherhood of Breath, New J Orch (Ardley),
Keef Hartley, Ian Carr, Bob Downes, London
J Comp Orch (Guy). **Mem event** Featured
soloist w Swedish Jazz Orch. **Pref** 'Porgy &
Bess' & 'Sketches of Spain' (Davis), 'Where
Fortune Smiles' (Surman), 'Down Another
Road' (Collier). Much in demand in a wide
variety of contemporary jazz contexts,
Beckett's clear-toned and lyrical playing has
won him well deserved acclaim.

STEVE BERESFORD *p, toy p, toy
instruments, el–bs, bongos*
B 6.3.50. **A** 11 Wandsworth Bridge Road,
London SW6. **T** 01–931 5273. **Curr** Sorry, Four
Pullovers (w Nigel Coombes, Roger Smith,
Terry Day), solo perf, other free improv music
situations. **Prev** Derek Bailey Band, Bread &
Cheese. **Conc** Wigmore Hall London '75.
Rec 'Teatime' (w Coombes, Dave Solomons,
Gary Todd) Incus (to be released). **Pref** Derek
Bailey, Coombes, Solomons, Smith, Day,
Ginger Epstein, Stuart Jones, Eric Coates,
Prof Longhair.

BOB BERTLES *reeds*
B 6.3.39 **A** c/o Ian Carr. **Curr** Nucleus (Carr)
since '74. **Prev** Own groups in Australia (inc
MacRae, Mike Nock, Bryce Rohde), Max
Merritt & the Meteors '67–'74 in UK. **Pref**
Parker, Dolphy, Jackie McLean, Stewart
Spear, Bernie McGann.

RICHARD BESWICK *oboe, cor anglais*
A 3 Tavistock Avenue, Perivale, Middx.
T 01–997 8954. **Curr** Chamberpot (w
Wachsmann, Mayo etc) since '72, various free
improv music groups playing at Unity
Theatre, Little Theatre Club, Soho Poly,
London. BBC Radio 3 'Music In Our Time'
(w Chamberpot).

ACKER BILK *clar*
B 28.1.29 **Agent** Pamela Sutton, Acker's
International Jazz Agency, 6 Carlisle Street,
London W1V 5RG. **T** 01–437 7061. **Curr** Own
Paramount Jazz Band. **Prev** Came to London
w Ken Colyer Band '54. Formed own band in
Bristol and first brought it to London '57.
Tours, Conc Germany, Australia, Kuala
Lumpur, France. **Rec** 'Acker Bilk & the
Paramount Jazz Band' Pye (1972), 'Expo 70'
EMI Regal Starline (1970), numerous LPs for
EMI, since '71 records with Pye, 'We Love
You Madly' (Stan Tracey) Columbia (1968).
Mem event Duke Ellington recording *Stranger
On The Shore*, Reprise (1964). **Fav rec**
'Stranger On The Shore' Columbia (1961).
Pref Jazz clarinettists esp Edmond Hall,
George Lewis, Barney Bigard.

IAN BIRD *sop, alto, tenor*
A 40 Brackondale Road, Abbey Wood,
London SE2 9HS. **T** 01–855 4861. **Curr** Own
quin. **Prev** Ian Bird–John Curtis Quin from
'69. **Tours** Germany, Switzerland etc w
Bird–Curtis Quin. Residency at Greenwich
Theatre Club London for some years. **Fest**
Bird–Curtis Quin winners at Dunkirk JF '69.

CHRIS BISCOE *alto*
A 31 Windsor Road, London N3. **T**
01–349 1339. **Curr** Worlds In Collision
(Trevor Taylor). Own band Broken Biscuits
since '74 (w Pearce etc), Equus (Marshall) since
'75. **Prev** Nat Youth J Orch (Ashton). **Rec**
'NYJO' (Nat Youth J Orch) Charisma (c1973).

Gary Boyle

GARY BOYLE *g*
B 1941 **A** Rose Cottage, 52 Aspen Lane,
Earby, Colne, Lancs. **T** Colne 822799. **Curr**
Own rock-jazz band Isotope since '72. **Prev**
Came to England from India '49. Pro
musician since '62, Mike Westbrook, Caparius,
Eddie Harris, Stomo Yamash'ta, Keith
Tippett, Soft Machine, Kinkade (Alan
Jackson), Axiom (w Ron Herman etc), Cirrus
(Herman), Dankworth, Julie Driscoll–Brian
Auger. **Rec** 'Illusion' (Isotope) Gull (1974),
'Metropolis' (Westbrook) Cadillac (1971),
'Mike Westbrook Live' Cadillac (1972). UK
tour w Isotope Oct '74. Tutor Lambeth J
Summer School '73. A fine rock–jazz guitarist,
particularly effective in the context of the small
group he has led for some time.

MICK BRANNAN *alto*
B 29.3.44 **A** 145 Gloucester Avenue, London
NW1 8LA. **T** 01–722 3483. **Curr** Amazing
Band (w Marcio Mattos, Terry Day etc) since
'69, various Musicians Co-op & free music
groups. **Prev** AMM (Gare–Prevost), Mal
Dean, Rab Small, Lynn Dobson, People Band
(w George Khan, Day etc), rock & j groups in
France. **Fest** Little Theatre Club Free Music.
Conc Roundhouse (Eddie Prevost's Ritual
Theatre Music Orch). **Mem event** Discussing
music w late Mal Dean. **Pref** Parker, Monk,
Rollins, Coltrane, Coleman, Dolphy, Art
Ensemble of Chicago, Cecil Taylor, Max
Roach, Han Bennink, Evan Parker, Louis
Jordan, Charles Ives.

ALAN BRANSCOMBE *p, vib, alto, perc*
A 11 Bolton Gardens, London SW5. **T**
01–373 1464. **Curr** Ian Hamer Sext, session
work. **Prev** Bobby Lamb–Ray Premru Orch,
Stan Tracey Orch, Dankworth, Harry South
Big Band. **Conc** Stan Tracey Celeb Queen Eliz
Hall Nov '73. **Rec** 'George Chisholm'
Rediffusion Gold Star (1973), 'Humming Bird'
(Paul Gonsalves) Deram (*c*1968), and w
Tracey, Dankworth, Tubby Hayes, Ardley,
Wheeler.

IAN BRIGHTON *g*
A 44 Fairmead Avenue, Daws Heath, Benfleet,
Essex. **T** Southend 558307. **Curr** Organizer of
Alternative Music Orch since '74, various free

improv music groups. **Conc** at LSE w AMO & Touch of the Sun, May June '75. **Rec** 'SME + =SMO' (Stevens) A (1975).

LAWRIE (LAWRENCE) BROWN *tpt, flug-h*
B 31.5.35 **A** 14 Brixton Water Lane, London SW2. **T** 01-674 5292. **Curr** John Williams, John Walters, Matthew Hutchinson, Sound of Seventeen, Kinks pop group, own band Tundra. **Prev** New J Orch (Ardley), Alan Cohen, Mike Carr, Ken McCarthy, Tony Smith. **Tours** USA recently & UK w Kinks. **Pref** Clifford Brown, Rollins, Roach, Davis, Coltrane, Booker Little, Hubbard, Don Byas, Kenny Dorham etc.

Beryl Bryden

BERYL BRYDEN *singer, washboard*
A 52 Clifton Gardens, London W9 1AU. **T** 01-286 6879. **Curr** App w many European traditional bands. **Prev** Maxim Saury (Paris) '53, George Webb, Freddy Randall, Cy Laurie, Mike Daniels, Charlie Galbraith, Barber, Welsh, Sunshine, Fatty George (Germany), own group Beryl's Backroom Boys. **Tours** Far East '65, Africa '65, New York '70, Australia '71–'72. **Fest** Antibes, Luneray, Dendermonde, Zurich, Vienna, Breda, Biel–Bienne & in Britain, Czechoslovakia, Poland, etc. **Conc** In Holland May '75 w Bud Freeman, Jimmy McPartland. **Fav rec** 'Greatest Hits' CBS (Holland) (1967). **Mem events, etc** Singing for Princess Margaret Savoy Hotel London, knowing Armstrong & visiting him several times at home, visiting New Orleans. **Pref** Dixieland-Chicago style, Armstrong, Billie Holiday, Bessie Smith, Condon.

JOHN BURCH *p*
B 6.1.32 **A** 55 Millstrood Road, Whitstable, Kent. **T** 02-272 4898. **Curr** Own trio, octet, quin (inc Lowther, Themen, Rubin). **Prev** Jazzmakers (Ross–Ganley) '60, Don Rendell Quin '61, Tommy Whittle Quar. **Fest** Yugoslavia '74 (w Ron Russell–Al Gay Quin). **Tutor** Barry Summer School '75, NYJO Easter Jazz Course '74. **Fav rec** 'Roarin'' ' (Rendell) Jazzland (1961). **Mem events** Tour w Freddie Hubbard & at Scott's accompanying Roland Kirk '67. **Pref** Cedar Walton, Cliff Jordan, Parker, Powell, Peterson, Coltrane, Coleman, Jarrett, Hancock, Ellington.

CHARLES BURCHELL *tenor, f*
A 139 Wood End Gardens, Greenford,
Middx. **T** 01–422 9701. **Curr** Peter Ind Sext,
Quar. **Rec** 'Peter Ind Sextet' Wave (1975), 'No
kidding' (Ind) Wave (1974), 'Jazz at the 1969
Richmond Festival' (w Ind, Derek Phillips,
Bernie Cash) Wave (1969), and other Wave
releases. Burchell has never received much
publicity but his Warne Marsh influenced
tenor style is quietly impressive with its
consistent invention & intricate melodic lines.

LENNIE BUSH *bs*
B 6.6.27 **A** The Smithy, Rowley Hill Road,
Flamstead, Herts. **T** Markgate 479. **Curr**
Eight to One (Ronnie Ross), session work.
Prev Victor Feldman, Ronnie Scott, Tony
Crombie, Dizzy Reece, Jack Parnell, Jazz
Today Unit, Stephane Grappelli, Stan Tracey
Orch. **Rec** 'Stephane Grappelli & Friends'
(Grappelli) Philips (1970), 'Phil on Drums'
(Phil Seamen) 77 Records (1971), 'George
Chisholm' Rediffusion Gold Star (1973),
'Homage â Django Reinhardt' (Grappelli)
Festival Double album (1972), 'With Love from
Jazz' (Tracey) Columbia (1968), 'Hair at its
Hairiest' (Sandy Brown) Fontana (1969).

IAN CARR *tpt, flug-h, p, el-p, comp, author*
B 21.4.33 **A** 34 Englands Lane, London NW3.
T 01–722 1998. **Curr** Own band Nucleus since
'69. **Prev** EmCee 5 (w Gary Cox, M Carr,
Spike Heatley, Ronnie Stephenson) '60–'62,
Rendell–Carr Quin '63–'69, New J Orch
(Ardley), Michael Garrick Sext, Harold
McNair 5, Joe Harriott, Centipede (Tippett),
Animals Big Band. **Tours** Germany Jan–Feb
'75, Italy April '75, Germany May '75. **Fest**
European fest appearances, Newport JF '70.
Conc Shakespeare Birthday Celeb Southwark
Cath '74, perf 'Labyrinth' Camden JF Oct '74.
Fav rec 'Labyrinth' (1973), 'Belladonna' (1972),
'Snakehips etc' (1975), all on Vertigo; 'Dusk
Fire' (Rendell–Carr) Columbia (1966), 'Let's
Take 5' (EmCee 5) Columbia EP (1961).
Pref Davis, Armstrong, Gil Evans, Gibbs,
Keith Jarrett, Jelly Roll Morton, Fats Waller,
Ellington, Chester 'Howlin' Wolf' Burnett.
Other rec 'Will Power' (w Gibbs, Ardley,
Tracey) Argo (1974), 'Roots' (1973), 'Elastic
Rock' (1970), both on Vertigo; and w Rendell,
Garrick, Ardley, Guy Warren of Ghana,

Ian Carr

Amancio D'Silva, Joe Harriott. 'Springboard' (w Stevens, Watts, Clyne) Polydor (1966). **Book** *Music Outside* Latimer New Dimensions (1973). Carr is one of the comparatively few British jazz musicians to have whole-heartedly adopted the rock-jazz format and stayed with it unswervingly. His band has attained considerable popularity and success both in Britain and abroad.

Mike Carr

MIKE (MICHAEL ANTHONY) CARR *p, org, vib*
B 7.12.37 **A** 39 Clitterhouse Crescent, London NW2. **T** 01–458 1020. **Curr** Own trio (inc Dick Morrissey). **Prev** EmCee 5 (w I Carr, Gary Cox, Spike Heatley, Ronnie Stevenson) to '61, own trio in Africa, Nolan Ranger Orch (Africa), Herbie Goins & the Night-timers '66, own trio w John MacLaughlin, own trio w Terry Smith '67, Quintetto Academico Mais Dois (Portugal) '68, Earl Jordan (Mozambique) '69, Jimmy Witherspoon, Sahib Shihab Trio, Don Byas Trio, Johnny Griffin Trio, own trio w Harold McNair, Ronnie Scott '70–'75. **Tours** Australia & USA w Scott '74, Germany, Holland, Belgium, Luxembourg, Switzerland, France, Italy. **Mem event** Debut w Scott Trio at Carnegie Hall '74. **Pref** Tatum, Waller, Peterson, B Evans, Jarrett, Hank Mobley, Silver, Joe Pass etc. **Rec** Own trio 'P&O Blues' ad–Rhythm (1973).

MIKE CASIMIR *tbn*
B 14.9.36 **A** 21 Clarendon Road, London W11 4JB. **T** 01–727 1225/8643. **Curr** Paragon Brass Band (leader) since '59, New Iberia Stompers (leader) since '59. **Conc etc** NIS have acc Albert Nicholas, Kid Thomas Valentine, Alton Purnell, Louis Nelson, Paul Barnes, Emanuel Paul, Alvin Alcorn, Charlie Hamilton. **Fest** Jazz Band Ball Paris '70 & '71, Gentbrugge (Belgium) '73, New Orleans J & Heritage '73 & '75, Nice '74 & '75, Breda (Holland) '73, '74, '75. **Tours** Holland, Belgium, Germany, Italy, France etc. **Rec** 'Casimir's Paragon Brass Band Live' Paragon (1970), 'One Night With The New Iberia Stompers' 77 (1970), 'Kid Thomas & Louis Nelson with The New Iberia Stompers', Paragon (1973).

GEOFF CASTLE *keyboards*
B 8.6.49 **A** 36a Newington Green, London
N16. **T** 01–254 7752. **Curr** Nucleus (Carr) since
Jan '74, George Khan. **Prev** Studied
improvisation w Tubby Hayes, NYJO
(Ashton), Graham Collier '71–'74, Paz '73.
Pref Coltrane, Monk, Stanley Clark. **Rec** w
Collier, Nucleus.

DAVE CHAMBERS *tenor, clar, f, p*
B 26.8.43 **A** 87 Hornsey Lane, London N6.
T 01–340 6020. **Curr** Mike Westbrook,
Annette Peacock. **Prev** Alan Cohen, Adrian
Paton, Ken Gibson. **Pref** Keith Jarrett, Ali
Akbar Khan, Sandy Brown, Jimmy Yancey,
Bessie Smith, Armstrong, Bob Dylan.

Marc Charig

MARC CHARIG *flug-h, cornet*
A 40a Norland Square, London W11. **T**
01–229 7905. **Curr** Elton Dean's Ninesense
since '75 & Just Us since *c*'70, Brotherhood of
Breath (MacGregor). **Prev** Bluesology, Soft
Machine '69, Keith Tippett, Arman Ratip,
Centipede (Tippett), Georgie Fame '74,
Alternative Music Orch '74. **Rec** 'Elton Dean'
(Dean) CBS (1971), 'Septober Energy'
(Centipede) RCA (1971), 'The Spy from
Istanbul' (Ratip) Regal Zonophone (1973), &
w Brotherhood of Breath, Tippett, London J
Comp Orch (Guy).

JOHN JAMES CHILTON *tpt, flug-h, author*
B 16.7.32 **A** 18 Gordon Mansions, Torrington
Place, London WC1. **T** 01–580 2318. **Curr**
Own band Feetwarmers & working regularly
w George Melly since Jan '74. **Prev** Bruce
Turner Jump Band, Mike Daniels Big Band,
Alex Welsh Band, co-led band w Wally
Fawkes, also own Swing Kings. **Tour** w
George Melly USA '74. **Fest** Welsh JF
(Cardiff) May '75, Bracknell JF July '75.
Books *Who's Who Of Jazz – Storyville to
Swing Street* Bloomsbury Bookshop (1970) &
Chilton USA, *Louis* (w Max Jones) Studio
Vista (1971), *Billie's Blues* Quartet (1975).
Mem event acc Buck Clayton, Ben Webster,
Bill Coleman, Roy Eldridge, Matty Matlock.
Rec w Melly.

GEORGE CHISHOLM *tbn, euphonium, bari*
B 29.3.15 **A** 5 Oakwood View, Southgate,
London N14 6QJ. **T** 01–886 4999. **Curr** Own

George Chisholm

group Gentlemen of Jazz, freelance, solo &
guest appearances. **Prev** Teddy Joyce '36,
Benny Carter (Holland) '37, Ambrose '38,
Kenny Baker, Jack Parnell '59, BBC Show
Band '52 etc. Freelance work w many bands.
Tours, Fest Numerous inc Toronto Canada
(TV), Welsh JF (Cardiff) May '75, Bracknell
JF July '75, concerts as soloist w several brass
bands inc Grimethorpe Colliery. **Mem event**
Perf w Coleman Hawkins (rec w Hawkins '37),
Benny Carter, Fats Waller, Louis Armstrong.
Rec 'George Chisholm' Rediffusion Gold Star
(1973), 'Along the Chisholm Trail' 77 Records
(1971), 'An Evening With His Friends' (Alex
Welsh) 2 Vols Black Lion (1971), 'Hair at its
Hairiest' (Sandy Brown) Fontana (1969). Long
recognized as a world-class trombonist,
Chisholm at his best is one of the finest jazz
musicians of any style that Britain has
produced.

GEORGE CHISHOLM *tpt flug-h*
B 19.1.47 **A** Elm Avenue, Eastcote, Ruislip,
Middx. **T** 01–868 2695. **Curr** Impulse (Brian
Miller), Tony Milliner Sext, Alan Stuart Octet
John Williams Band. **Prev** Maynard Ferguson
Dankworth, Stan Tracey, Alan Cohen Band,
Tony Faulkner, Gibbs, European Broadcasting
Union Big Band. **Fav rec** 'Black, Brown &
Beige' (Cohen) Argo (1972) – lead tpt. **Mem
event** Oslo '73 w EBU Big Band. **Pref** Wheeler
Nat Adderley, Freddie Hubbard, Lee Morgan
Art Farmer, Faulkner.

(RONALD) KEITH CHRISTIE *tbn*
B 6.1.31 **A** 63a Westmoreland Terrace, London
SW1. **T** 01–834 9340. **Curr** Session work, Ian
Hamer Sext, Brian Cooper Orch, Gene
Cottrell Band. **Prev** Humphrey Lyttelton
'49–'51, own groups w brother Ian '51–'53,
Dankworth '53–'55, Tommy Whittle '55–'56,
freelance club work London '56–'57, Ted
Heath Orch '57–'59, Bobby Lamb–Ray
Premru Orch, various groups. **Rec** 'Phil on
Drums' (Seamen) 77 (1971), '21 Years On'
(Lyttelton) Polydor Double Album (1969),
'The World of Big Band Blues' (Heath)
Decca (rec 1959, reissued 1973), and w George
Chisholm, Tubby Hayes, Tracey,
Lamb–Premru.

KENNY CLARE *drums*
B 8.6.29 **A** The Hollies, Boxhill Road,
Tadworth, Surrey. **T** Betchworth 3644. **Curr**
Freelance. **Prev** Oscar Rabin '49–'54, Jack
Parnell '54–'55, Dankworth '55–'60, Ted
Heath '62–'65, Clarke–Boland Big Band
'67–'72, Peter Herbolzheimer '73–'74, Bobby
Lamb – Ray Premru Orch. **Fest** Hanover Dec
'74. **Tour** 3 years in USA etc w Tony Bennett
(working w Basie, Herman, Ellington). **Mem
event** 'Can't Buy Me Love' rec date w Ella
Fitzgerald, working w Ellington '59,
Clarke–Boland, Buddy Rich–Louie Bellson,
Lamb–Premru. **Rec** w Clarke–Boland,
Lamb–Premru, Dankworth, 'Afternoon In
Paris' (Stephane Grappelli), MPS (1971).
'Live At Ronnie Scott's' (Herbolzheimer)
MPS (1974).

DAVE (DAVID JOHN) CLIFF *g*
B 25.6.44 **A** 212 Old Brompton Road, London
SW5. **T** 01–373 3508. **Curr** Peter Ind Quar &
Sext, Cliff Manderson Band. **Prev** Studied at
Leeds Coll of Music w Ind. **Rec** 'Peter Ind
Sextet' Wave (1975), 'No Kidding' (Ind) Wave
(1974).

JEFF CLYNE *bs*, *el-bs*
B 24.1.37 **A** 10 Temple Gardens, London
NW11. **T** 01–455 2893. **Curr** Gilgamesh (w
Phil Lee etc). **Prev** Jazz Couriers (Scott–Hayes),
Tubby Hayes Quar, Gordon Beck Trio,
Dudley Moore Trio, Roy Budd Trio, Ronnie
Scott, SME (Stevens), Amalgam (Watts),
Stan Tracey, Centipede (Tippett), Nucleus
(Carr), Isotope (Boyle), Tony Oxley Sext,
London J Comp Orch (Guy), Bob Downes'
Open Music, Alan Skidmore. **Pref** Davis, Bill
Evans, Coleman, Scott La Faro, Stanley
Clarke, Stevie Wonder, Joni Mitchell, Chick
Corea, John MacLaughlin. **Rec** Numerous w
above musicians.

TONY (ANTHONY GEORGE) COE *clar*,
bass clar, *tenor*, *occasionally alto*
B 29.11.34 **Agent** Gabrielle Jones, 22 Glenton
Road, London SE13. **T** 01–278 6783 &
01–313 3476. **Curr** Coe Wheeler & Co (w
Kenny Wheeler), own quar, John Picard, own
Zeitgeist big band. **Prev** Humphrey Lyttelton
(late '50s), Al Fairweather. Nat Gonella,
Clarke–Boland Band, Matrix (Alan Hacker),

Neil Ardley, Ian Carr, own quin, Mike Carr Duo. **Fest** Proms '74, '75, Cologne, Belgium, Harrogate '75, Newcastle JF '75 (w Mike Carr).

Tour Contemp Music Network w own composition for orch 'Zeitgeist' Mar '75. **Conc** Shakespeare Celebration Southwark Cathedral '74. **Fav rec** 'Phil Seamen Story' Decibel (1972), *Lay By* from 'We Love You Madly' (Tracey) Columbia (1969), 'Faces' (Clarke–Boland). **Mem event** 'Zeitgeist' (first large scale work). **Pref** Armstrong, Webster, Gonsalves, Hodges, Bechet, Debussy, Schoenberg, Berg, Webern. **Rec** 'Will Power' (Gibbs etc) Argo (1974), 'George Chisholm' Rediffusion Gold Star (1973), 'Tony Coe w Brian Lemon Trio' 77 Records (1971), 'Our Kind of Music' (Lemon) 77 Records (1970), 'Duke Ellington Classics' (Lyttelton) Black Lion (1969), 'Black Marigolds' (Garrick) Argo (1966), and w Clarke–Boland, Ian Carr. Coe's tenor style is related to that of Paul Gonsalves but is personal and distinctive, timelessly transcending jazz categories.

Alan Cohen

ALAN COHEN *bari, clar, arr, comp, leader* **B** 25.11.34 **A** 6 Observatory Road, London SW14 7QD. **T** 01–876 1974. **Curr** Own bands, New Paul Whiteman Orch (Sudhalter). **Tour** Guest comp-cond w Danish Radio Big Band. **Pref** Wilhelm Mengelberg w Concertgebouw Orch & New York Philharmonic, Ellington, Gil Evans, Gerry Mulligan Concert JB, Serge Chaloff. **Rec** Orch 'Black, Brown & Beige' Argo (1972).

MAX COLLIE *tbn* **B** 21.2.39 **A** 26 Wendover Road, Bromley, Kent. **T** 01–460 1139. **Curr** Own Rhythm Aces. **Prev** Melbourne New Orleans JB, London City Stompers. **Tours, Fest** USA, Belgium, Holland, France, W Germany, Denmark, Sweden. **Fav rec** 'Battle of Trafalgar' Reality Double Album (1973), 'Recorded Live in the USA at the Big Horn Underground Atlanta, Georgia' GHB (1974). **Mem event** Rhythm Aces' first US tour '73 & seeing Louis Armstrong's All Stars in Melbourne, Australia. **Pref** Traditional, Dixieland & New Orleans Jazz. **Rec** 'In Concert' Reality (1971), and others on WAM & Happy Bird.

GRAHAM COLLIER *bs, comp, author*
B 21.2.37 **A** 51 Nevern Square, London SW5.
T 01–373 8634. **Curr** Graham Collier Music
(w Beckett, Wadsworth, Speight, Dean,
Webb). **Prev** Studied at Berklee School of
Music, Boston, Mass early '60s (1st Brit
graduate), returned to Britain '64, own band
since then. Film & TV scores & music for stage
play. **Fest** Montreux '71, Newcastle '74,
Middelheim Aug '75. Continental tour '74.
Swedish Radio comp commission '75. **Fav rec**
'Darius' Mosaic (1974). **Mem event** Two prizes
at Montreux JF '71. 1st jazz composer to
receive Arts Council grant '67 (for his comp
'Workpoints'). **Pref** Ellington, Mingus, Carla
Bley. **Books** *Inside Jazz* Quartet (1973),
Jazz Camb UP (1975). **Rec** 'Midnight Blue'
Mosaic (1974), 'Portraits' Saydisc (1972),
'Mosaics' Fontana (1970), 'Songs for my
Father' Fontana (1970), 'Down Another
Road' Fontana (1969), 'Deep Dark Blue
Centre' Deram (1967), and jazz educ records.
A noted figure in British contemp jazz, not
only as a composer and band leader but also
as a discoverer and promoter of jazz talent.
Also active in jazz educ.

KEN COLYER *tpt, vocal, g*
B 18.4.28 **A** 99 The Drive, Hounslow
TW3 1PW. **T** 01–560 8237. **Curr** Own
occasional band, various groups. **Prev** Crane
River JB '49 (leader), Christie Brothers'
Stompers '51, own group since Spring '53.
Rec 'I Want To Be Happy' Happy Bird (1975),
'Watch that Dirty Tone of Yours – There are
Ladies Present' Joy (1970), 'At the Thames
Hotel' Joy (1970), 'Ragtime Revisited' Joy
(*c*1970), 'Spirituals' (2 vols) Joy, 'Concert'
WAM, 'One For My Baby' Joy, 'K.C. and the
White Eagle New Orleans Band' WAM, 'The
Early Days' Storyville (1953 tracks reissued
1972). Colyer has never wavered in his
devotion to the principles of classic New
Orleans jazz. His various bands have remained
over the years a kind of mecca for British
jazz purists.

LES (LESLIE RICHARD) CONDON *tpt,*
flug-h
B 23.2.30 **A** 88 Belsize Lane, London NW3.
T 01–794 5978. **Curr** Ronnie Ross' 8 to 1,
Session work. **Prev** Tubby Hayes, Vic Lewis

Orch '53, Tony Crombie Orch '54–'56, Tony Kinsey '54–'59, Woody Herman Anglo-Amer Orch '59, New Departures Quin (Tracey) in early '60s, various groups. **Rec** w Hayes, Tracey, 'Jazz Tete-a-Tete' (Hayes) 77 (1966).

STEVE COOKE *el-bs, bs*
B 4.8.48 **A** 46 Holmbush Road, Putney, London SW15. **T** 01-788 8989. **Curr** Jubiaba (Barbara Thompson), Mike Westbrook, Kinkade (Alan Jackson), George Khan. **Prev** CMU, Seventh Wave, Gilgamesh (w Phil Lee etc), Tony Faulkner, Don Rendell, Michael Garrick, Paraphernalia (Thompson), Lol Coxhill, John Picard, E (Peter Lemer). **Tour** UK w Seventh Wave '74. **Pref** Tony Williams, Christian Vander, Coltrane, Larry Graham, Stanley Clarke, Rusty Allen.

Brian Cooper

BRIAN COOPER *drums, comp, arr, teacher, MD*
B 24.11.36 **A** 5 Ennerdale House, Woodberry Downs. London N4 2RP. **T** 01-802 5465. **Curr** Own Jazz Orch, own sept, quin, sext. **Prev** Nat Youth J Orch, Peter Titmus Orch, Ken Harrup Octet & Band '60, own trios, duos, many student bands. **Conc** w Orch, Mermaid Theatre Apr '75. **Pref** Kenton, Don Ellis, Gillespie, Rich, Ellington, Herman, Bill Holman, 'Miles Ahead' (Davis).

LINDSAY LANG COOPER *bs, el-bs, cello, tuba; also home made or adapted instruments*
B 18.1.40 **A** 1 St Ann's Park Road, London SW18 2RW. **T** 01-870 0943. **Curr** Peter Jacobson Trio, SME (Stevens), Ken Colyer, Ken McCarthy Quin, John Stevens' Dance Orch, Talisker (Hyder). **Prev** Amalgam (Watts), Strawbs, Stan Tracey Trio, Open Circle (Tracey). **Conc** Soloist in John Williams' 'Four Pieces for J Soloist & Orch' '74. **Mem event** Visits to New York and New Orleans, playing w Tracey, Stevens & Watts. **Pref** Gaelic mus, Ornette Coleman, Lee Konitz, Warne Marsh, Peter Ind, Derek Bailey, Webern, New Orleans Rock, Bunk Johnson, Bebop, anything holy, anything for dancing. **Rec** 'Dreaming Of Glenisla' (Talisker) Caroline (1975).

LOL COXHILL *sop; also alto, tenor, bari, 'minimal electronics', voice*

A 24 Coventon Road, Aylesbury, Bucks. **T** Aylesbury 81354 & 01–486 4031. **Curr** Brotherhood of Breath (MacGregor), solo perfs, Coxhill–Steve Miller Duo, John Stevens' Dance Orch, Welfare State (music theatre). **Prev** Whole World, Coxhill–David Bedford Duo, Mike Westbrook Brass Band and Cabaret, Paz, Hugh Hopper, Kevin Ayers, SME, Gas, Delivery, Chessmen, Otis Spann, Lowell Fulsom, Ed Speight–Coxhill Duo. **Tour** Holland (solo). **Fest** Berlin Free Music, Groningen, Rotterdam Science Fiction. **Fav rec** *Bath '72* on 'Miller/Coxhill/Coxhill/ Miller'. **Mem event** Recording w children for 'Ear of Beholder' album & w children of Aarhus Free School, Denmark. **Pref** Varèse, Pee Wee Russell, Evan Parker, Fred Frith, Delius, Jelly Roll Morton, Lee Konitz. **Rec** 'The Story So Far . . . Oh, Really?' Caroline (1974), 'Coxhill/Miller/Miller/Coxhill' Caroline (1972), 'Toverbal Sweet' Mushroom (1971), 'Ear Of The Beholder' Dandelion. A unique figure on the contemp jazz scene, Coxhill's typical solo performances mix quirky unpredictable humour with attractive free improvised soliloquies on soprano.

TONY (ANTHONY JOHN) CROMBIE
drums, comp, arr

B 27.8.25 **A** 18 Belvedere Court, Willesden Lane, London NW2. **T** 01–459 3393. **Curr** Freelance composing and arranging. **Prev** Own band '54, '59, Ronnie Scott Trio, Mike Carr Duo, Alan Haven, Pendulum (M Carr), Stephane Grappelli. **Tours** w Lena Horne, Carmen McRae, Annie Ross. Comp and arr of many film and TV scores.

Gordon Cruikshank

GORDON CRUIKSHANK *sop, tenor, f, clar, comp*

A 51 Spey Terrace, Edinburgh. **T** 031–553 2534. **Curr** Head (Glasgow based group inc MacColl, Kyle, John Davies) since '73, Windjammer (Robb) since '74, own quar in Edinburgh. **Fest** Dunkirk JF '75. Radio & Scottish TV broadcasts. **Rec** 'Red Dwarf' (Head) Canon (*c*1975).

JOHN TRELAWNEY CURTIS *fender-violin, tpt, flug-h*

B 23.8.40 **A** Woodcot, Cleanthus Road, London SE18 3DH. **T** 01–856 4985. **Curr**

Squeal Band (leader), See Saw Band (leader).
Prev South Bank JB (leader), Johnny Curtis
Jazz Group, Bird–Curtis Quin (w Ian Bird).
Tours Switzerland & Germany '73 & 3
previous tours. **Fest** Dunkirk JF, Zurich JF,
Ludlow Arts (2 years), Greenwich, East Coast
JF. **Mem event** Becoming pro musician in '74.
Pref Virtuoso musicians irrespective of
instrument or style, individuals rather than
copyists.

PETER CUSACK *g*
A 17 Crossway, London N16. **T** 01–254 2156.
Curr A Touch Of The Sun (free improvised
music duo w Simon Mayo). **Rec** 'Milk Teeth'
(A Touch of the Sun) Bead (1975).

JOHN DANKWORTH *alto, clar, comp*
B 20.9.27 **Agent** Laurie Mansfield, International
Artistes, Irving House, Irving Street, London
WC2. **T** 01–930 3046/5608. **Curr** Own orch,
comp for films, TV etc, occasional club app.
Prev Own septet March '50–'53, own big band
from '53. Numerous film & TV scores, also
classical compositions inc piano concerto '72.
Tours w Cleo Laine in Europe, Australia,
New Zealand, USA etc, first US visit w own
orch Newport JF '59. **Fest** Welsh JF (Cardiff)
May '75. For some years Dankworth has been
running the annual Wavendon Allmusic
Plan – a teaching–performing centre for
musicians – at Wavendon in Bucks w annual
Easter J Course. Also jazz workshop at Royal
Academy of Music. **Rec** 'Movies 'n Me' RCA
Victor (1974), 'Full Circle' Philips (1972),
'Million Dollar Collection' Fontana (1967),
'Zodiac Variations' Fontana (1964), 'What the
Dickens' Fontana (1963), 'The Big Band
Sound of JD' Roulette (tracks from 1959–61
reissued 1973). A founder figure in the British
modern jazz movement, Dankworth has led a
big band intermittently for more than two
decades.

John Davies

JOHN DAVIES *tpt, el-p, flug-h, keyboards,*
comp
A Muirhead Cottage, Riggend, Airdrie. **T**
Cumbernauld 22428. **Curr** Head (Glasgow
based group inc Cruikshank, MacColl, Kyle)
since '71, Windjammer (Robb) since '74, Dave
Saul Quin. **Fest** Dunkirk JF '71 & '72. BBC
Radio & Scottish TV broadcasts. **Tours** Arts

Centres, theatres, universities in Scotland and N England. **Rec** 'Red Dwarf' (Head) Canon (*c*1975), 'GTF' (Head) Head (*c*1972).

JOHN R T DAVIES *saxes, brass*
B 20.3.27 **A** 1 Walnut Tree Cottage, Burnham, Bucks. **T** Burnham 4811. **Curr** Crane River JB, New Paul Whiteman Orch (Sudhalter). **Prev** Mick Mulligan's Magnolia JB, Southern Stompers, Cy Laurie, Sandy Brown, Temperance Seven, Anglo-American Alliance (w Sudhalter etc). **Conc** w NPWO '74 & '75. **Fav rec** 'My Melancholy Baby' (Anglo-Amer Alliance) Ristic. **Mem event** First rehearsal of NPWO. **Pref** Jazz and early swing era (1917 – '40), Otto Hardwick. **Rec** 'Runnin' Wild' (NPWO) Argo (1975) 'Sweet and Hot' (Anglo-Amer Alliance) Regal (1968).

Elton Dean

ELTON DEAN *alto, saxello, el-p*
A 6 Walford Road, London N16. **T** 01–249 3342. **Curr** Own bands Just Us and Ninesense (inc Charig, Evans, Feza, Skidmore, Tippett, Miller, Moholo), Brotherhood of Breath (MacGregor), Loek Dikker's Band in Holland. **Prev** Various trad bands semi-pro, own soul band Soul Pushers, Long John Baldry's Bluesology (w Charig etc), Keith Tippett, Soft Machine '69–'72, Centipede (Tippett), Supersister (Dutch rock band), Georgie Fame '74. **Rec** 'Elton Dean' CBS (1971), 'Septober Energy' (Centipede) RCA (1971); '3', '4' & '5' (Soft Machine) CBS; 'Dedicated To You But You Weren't Listening' (Tippett) Vertigo (1970), 'You Are Here: I Am There' (Tippett) Polydor (1969).

ROGER DEAN *p, vib, bs*
B 6.9.48 **A** 18 Maidstone Road, London N11 2TP. **Curr** Own band Lysis, Graham Collier Music since '74. **Prev** Bassist w BBC Symphony Orch, English Sinfonia. **Tour** Europe (w Collier) Oct '74. **Fest** Middelheim (w Collier) Aug '75. **Fav rec** Solo on *Midnight Blue* from 'Midnight Blue' (Collier) Mosaic (1974). **Pref** Elliott Carter, Schoenberg, Ives, Varese, Ravel, Coltrane, Dolphy, Cecil Taylor.

JIMMIE DEUCHAR *tpt, flug-h, arr, comp*
B 26.6.30 **A** 16 Stracathro Terrace, Barnhill, Dundee. **T** Dundee 730730. **Curr** Arranger

Paul Kuhn SFB Berlin, & for BBC. **Prev** Dankworth, Geraldo, Jack Parnell, BBC Show Band, Ronnie Scott, Tubby Hayes, Kenny Clarke–Francy Boland Orch, Kurt Edelhagen Orch, own groups mostly for recording. **Fav rec** w Scott, Hayes, Crombie, Bush, Christie, Vic Feldman, Phil Seamen, Derek Humble etc in late '50s. **Mem event** App w Clarke–Boland. **Pref** (arrangers) Oliver Nelson, Boland, Quincy Jones, Thad Jones, Gil Evans, Ellington. **Rec** w Clarke–Boland, Edelhagen.

MARTIN DITCHAM *drums, perc*
B 22.3.51 **A** Flat 1, 47 The Drive, Ilford, Essex. **T** 01–554 6673. **Curr** Freelance, Embryo (Frank Roberts). **Prev** Nucleus (Carr), Henry Cow, Roger Barnes Trio, Tommy Bridges. **Tours** etc w Nucleus. **Pref** Elvin Jones, Tony Williams, Jack DeJohnette, Billy Cobham, Eric Gravatt.

Bob Downes

JIM DOUGLAS *g, banjo*
B 13.5.42 **A** 94 Butely Road, Luton, Beds. **T** Luton 592695. **Curr** Alex Welsh. **Prev** Clyde Valley Stompers. **Tours, Fest** W Germany, E Germany, Breda JF (Holland). **Mem event** Newport JF '67. **Pref** Joe Pass. **Rec** w Welsh, Freddy Randall.

BOB DOWNES *silver & bamboo f, tenor, alto, sop, western & oriental perc, voice, prepared tapes, Japanese gongs, cello, p, comp*
B 22.7.37 **A** 47 Lanark Road, London W9. **T** 01–286 6221. **Curr** Bob Downes' Open Music since '69 inc Solo, Trio (w Guy, Dennis Smith) & Triad (w Guy, Wendy Benka). **Tours** South America '73, Europe (w London Contemp Dance Theatre). **Conc** Wigmore Hall, Sadlers Wells, Roundhouse – comp for LCDT. **Mem event** Playing in S America '73. **Fav own comp** 'The Progression' (40 mins). **Rec** 'Hell's Angels' (1974), 'Episodes at 4 a.m.' (c1973), 'Diversions' (c1972) all on Openian; 'Deep Down Heavy' MFP (1970), 'Electric City' Vertigo (1970), 'Dream Journey' Philips (1969) and w London J Comp Orch (Guy), Ray Russell. Downes' 'open music' covers a wide range from rock & vocal blues to Colemanish contemporary jazz, spacey sound poems & lyrical flights on his various flutes. He has composed many scores for modern dance companies inc Ballet Rambert and for TV & Radio.

MARTIN DREW *drums, perc*
B 11.2.44 **A** 38 College Road, Wembley, Middx
HA9 8RJ. **T** 01–908 0558. **Curr** Ronnie Scott
Quar, Jubiaba (Thompson), Colin Purbrook
Trio, Bebop Preservation Society (Le Sage),
rock, pop, radio & TV work. **Prev** Tubby
Hayes, Joe Harriott, Tommy Whittle, Don
Rendell 5, Norma Winstone, Frank Rosolino,
Phil Woods, Tony Lee, Harry South, Annie
Ross. Pro musician since '73. **Mem events**
Working at Ronnie Scott's w visiting American
artists esp Oscar Peterson.

Amancio D'Silva

AMANCIO D'SILVA *g*
A 13 Gurton Road, Coggeshall, Essex. **T**
Coggeshall 61060. **Prev** Jazz Quar of the
Maharini of Jaipur, Joe Harriott, own band
Cosmic Eye, Ragalectric (Clem Alford). **Rec**
'Dream Sequence' (Cosmic Eye) Regal
Zonophone (c1972), 'The African Sounds'
(Guy Warren of Ghana) Regal Zonophone
(c1972), 'Reflections' (w Orch) Columbia
(1970), 'Integration' Columbia (1969), 'Hum
Dono' (w Harriott) Columbia (1969),
'Afro-Jazz' (Guy Warren) Columbia (1969).

JACK DUFF *tenor, sop, alto, clar, p*
B 13.8.40 **A** 2 Montrose Villas, Millbrook,
St Lawrence, Jersey, C.I. **T** 0534 31189. **Curr**
Own quin in Jersey. **Prev** Own band since '66.
Tours Resident band 'Sun Princess', Los
Angeles '73 & '74, resident band 'Canberra'
world cruise '75. **Fav rec** *The Old Curacao Shop*
from 'If The Cap Fits' (own quar w Bobby
Breen) York (1972). **Mem event** Conc w Philly
Joe Jones '72 & Johnny Griffin '73. **Pref** Sandy
Brown, Coleman Hawkins, Ellington. **Rec**
'The Enchanted Isle' (quin inc Wheeler)
Avenue (1971).

Jack Duff

JIM DVORAK *tpt*
A 148 Hornsey Lane, London N6. **T**
01–272 0452. **Curr** Own quin Joy (inc Francis,
Mothle, Bailey, Roberts) since Nov '73. A
stable personnel and regular work has helped
to make Joy one of London's tightest and
most stimulating small bands.

ALAN ELSDON *tpt, flug-h, pocket cornet*
B 15.10.34 **A** 29 Dorchester Road, Northolt,
Middx UB5 4PA. **T** 01–422 1055. **Curr** Own
traditional JB. **Prev** Cy Laurie. Graham

Stewart 7, Terry Lightfoot. **Fest** Dresden JF
'74, Hamburg '74. **Tour** E Germany Mar '75.
Fav rec 'Alan Elsdon & His Jazz Band'
Rediffusion Gold Star (1973). **Mem event**
Touring w Kid Ory, Red Allen, Howling Wolf,
Vic Dickenson, Edmond Hall, Albert Nicholas,
Wingy Manone. **Pref** Henry 'Red' Allen,
Armstrong, Ben Webster, Jack Teagarden.

Nick Evans

NICK EVANS *tbn*
A 6 Walford Road. London N16. **T**
01–249 3342. **Curr** Isipingo (Harry Miller),
Just Us & Ninesense (Elton Dean),
Brotherhood of Breath (MacGregor). **Prev**
Came to London from Wales '69, Graham
Collier, Keith Tippett Group, Centipede
(Tippett). **Rec** w MacGregor, Ray Russell,
Tippett, Collier, 'Septober Energy' (Centipede)
RCA (1971).

DIGBY FAIRWEATHER *tpt*
B 25.4.46 **A** Stannetts, Paglesham, Essex.
T Southend 612621 ext 39. **Curr** Ron Russell
Band, Lennie Hastings Band, Gene Allen
Jazzmen. **Prev** George Webb, Eric Silk, Hugh
Rainey – Eggy Ley, Colin Symons JB, own
Half Dozen. **Fest** Prague JF '74 (w Ron Russell
Orch inc Gay, Ingham, Pete Strange), Dresden
Dixieland '73 (w Symons). **Fav rec** *I'm
confessin'* on 'Les Page Dixieland Band'
Nicrosound (1973), 'John Barnes – Roy
Williams Jazz Band' Rediffusion (*c*1975).
Mem events Joining Russell; meeting, learning
from & occasionally depping for Alex Welsh.
Pref Colin Smith, Don Goldie, Bobby Hackett,
Wild Bill Davison, Billy Butterfield, Freddie
Randall, Ruby Braff, Charlie Teagarden,
Harry James, Johnny Windhurst, Beckett,
Wheeler, etc.

TONY FAULKNER *drums, arr, comp*
B 27.7.38 **A** 29 Hanover Square, Leeds
LS3 1AW. **T** Leeds 445786 & 01–680 2786.
Curr Own orch in Leeds since '75, teaching at
Leeds Coll of Music. **Prev** Own Jazz Orch
London '70–'72, Brian Miller, John Williams,
Lionel Grigson. **Fav rec** Compositions rec on
'Humming Bird' (Paul Gonsalves) Deram
(1968). **Pref** Arr/comp: Ellington, Gil Evans,
Gary McFarland, Thad Jones, Delius.
Drummers: Roach, E Jones, M Lewis, Haynes,
Cobham. **Rec** 'Mark Twain' (Frank Evans) 77
(1969).

LENNIE FELIX

B 16.8.20 **A** 233 Lauderdale Mansions, Lauderdale Road, London W9. **T** 01–286 4903. **Curr** Own trio. **Prev** Freddy Randall '50, Harry Gold '53, Far East tour '54, worked on Continent '55, '56 & '59. Solo & trio work, radio broadcasts. **Fest** Newcastle JF '74 & '75. **Conc** Wigmore Hall Dec '74.

Mongezi Feza

MONGEZI FEZA *tpt, f*

B South Africa 1945. *Died Dec 14th 1975 in London.* Brotherhood of Breath (MacGregor), Isipingo (H Miller), Arman Ratip, Elton Dean, Jabula – Spear (Bahula, Pukwana), Malombo Music (Bahula). **Prev** Pro musician from '60. Joined Chris MacGregor's Blue Notes '62, to Europe & Britain from SA w MacGregor '65, MacGregor Sext, Music for Xaba (w Okay Temiz, Johnny Dyani) in Sweden '72, Assagai (Pukwana), Spear (Pukwana), Centipede (Tippett). **Fest** Heidelberg JF June '75 & many app on Continent. Tutor Lambeth Jazz Summer School July '75. In Sweden '72–'73. **Pref** Don Cherry. **Rec** 'Music for Xaba', Sonet (1972) & w Pukwana, MacGregor, Bahula, Robert Wyatt. Feza's death, which occurred as this book was going to press has robbed the British contemp jazz scene of a vital, powerful trumpeter whose playing combined adventurousness and good humour with fine jazz feeling.

Chris Francis

RAY FOXLEY *p*

B 28.12.28 **A** 59a Old Birmingham Road, Bromsgrove, Worcs B60 1DD. **T** Bromsgrove 73941. **Curr** Own quin, Saratoga JB, Paragon JB. **Prev** Own Levee Ramblers '48–'50, Ken Colyer, Chris Barber, Mick Mulligan, Mike Daniels, Bobby Mickleburgh, Second City Jazzmen. **Conc** George Melly Band Show at Birmingham Rep Theatre March '75 (solo ragtime piano). **Mem event** Sitting in w Roland Kirk – B'ham '72. **Pref** Morton, Horace Silver, Monk, Mingus.

CHRIS FRANCIS *alto*

A 10a Putney High Street, London SW15. **T** 01–788 2551. **Curr** Joy (Jim Dvorak), own trio (w Mothle, Bailey), own orch Naima. **Prev** Own band Naima since '69 w various personnels, Amazing Band.

131

Lou Gare

MARTIN FRANKLIN *vib, p*
B 26.9.37 **A** 59 Valley Walk, Croxley Green,
Rickmansworth, Herts. **T** Watford 32890.
Curr Jimmy Skidmore, Tony Lee, own quar.
Prev Phil Seamen. **Mem event** Bobby Breen's
Benefit 100 Club w King, Brian Smith, Dudley
Moore, Clare & Matthewson '72. **Pref**
'Mellow Moods' (Oscar Peterson), Don
Rendell, Harry Beckett, Stan Robinson, comp
of Brian Miller, 'Cherry' (Milt Jackson,
Stanley Turrentine).

LOU (LESLIE ARTHUR) GARE *tenor*
A 17 Fairfax Road, Teddington, Middx.
Agent Music Now, 26 Avondale Park Gardens,
London W11 4PR. **T** 01-727 1133. **Curr** AMM
(w Eddie Prévost) since '65, Eddie Prévost
Band, AMM With Strings (Gare-Prévost+
Mattos, Meggido). **Prev** Early Mike Westbrook
Band. AMM has worked principally as a duo
since '72; earlier versions included Keith Rowe,
Cornelius Cardew. **Fav rec** 'AMM at the
Roundhouse' Incus EP (1972). **Tours** in USA,
Canada, Europe & Britain w AMM. **Rec**
'AMM Music' Electra (1966), 'Live Electronic
Music' (MEV/AMM) Mainstream (1968), 'To
Hear & Back Again' Emanem (1975). Gare's
partnership w Prévost in AMM has been the
basis of a unique & self-contained area of
activity within free improvised music for a
decade.

Michael Garrick

MICHAEL GARRICK *p, el-p, harpsichord,
pipe organ, comp*
B 30.5.33 **A** 12 Castle Street, Berkhamsted,
Herts. **T** Berkhamsted 4989. **Agent** Terry
Slasberg Associates, 33 Holland Street,
Kensington, London W8. **T** 01-937 6868.
Curr Own sext (inc Lowther, Themen,
Winstone, Green, Tomkins) since '69 & own
trio. **Prev** Don Rendell–Ian Carr Quin
'65–'69, New J Orch (Ardley) during '60s,
composer since '58. **Conc** 'Hobbit Suite'
(comm by Merseyside Arts Assoc) London
premiere QE Hall Nov '74, 'Jazz Praises' –
Glasgow Cathedral. **Fav rec** *Mirage* on
'Change Is' (Rendell–Carr) Columbia (1969).
Pref Herbie Hancock, John Taylor, Kenny
Wheeler, Chick Corea. **Rec** Own albums on
Argo inc 'Troppo' (1974), 'Home Stretch
Blues' (1972), 'Cold Mountain' (1972), 'Mr
Smith's Apocalypse' (1971), 'The Heart Is A

Lotus' (1970), 'Poetry & Jazz in Concert 250' (1969), 'Black Marigolds' (1966), 'Promises' (1965), 'October Woman' (1964), and w Rendell–Carr, Guy Warren of Ghana.

Al Gay

AL GAY *tenor*
A 26 Sanderson Road, Westoning, Beds.
T Westoning 3293. **Curr** Freelance, Freddy Randall, London J Big Band (Greig). **Prev** Ron Russell Orch, many mainstream orientated groups, Bob Wallis Storyville Jazzmen. **Fest** Prague JF '74 (w Russell). **Conc** w Alex Welsh Band at Welsh's 21st Anniv conc QE Hall May '75. **Rec** 'Dixieland Now & Then' (Dixieland A/S) Line (1974), 'Alex Welsh Dixieland Party' Columbia (1969).

DAVE GELLY *tenor, clar, bs-clar*
A 8 Kingswood Drive, London SE19 1UR.
T 01–670 0570. **Curr** Alan Cohen, Neil Ardley, own quin w Jeff Scott. **Prev** New J Orch (Ardley), own groups inc quin w Art Themen '66 and quar w Frank Ricotti '68–'69, Tony Faulkner. Tutor NYJO Easter J course '74, Lambeth J Summer School July '75. **Pref** Lester Young, Billie Holiday, Ellington, bebop, Coltrane. **Rec** w Ardley, Alan Cohen, Arthur 'Big Boy' Crudup, Johnny 'Guitar' Burns, McGuiness–Flint.

Michael Gibbs

MICHAEL GIBBS *tbn, arr, comp, leader*
B 25.9.37 **A** 91 Riversdale Road, Highbury, London N5. **Agent** Laurie Mansfield, International Artists Representation. **Curr** Own orch, John Warren Orch. **Prev** In Rhodesia to '59, studied at Berklee School of Music, Boston, USA '59–'63, Herb Pomeroy, settled in UK '65, Dankworth, Graham Collier, Tutor at Berklee '74–'75. **Conc** Rainbow London March '74, Shakespeare Celeb Southwark Cath Apr '74. **Fest** Berlin JF Nov '75. **Tour** UK March '74. **Mem event** Formation of own orch. **Fav rec** 'The Only Chrome-Waterfall Orchestra' Bronze (1975). **Pref** Gil Evans, Charles Ives. **Rec** 'Will Power' (w Ardley, Carr, Tracey) Argo Double Album (1974), 'In the Public Interest' (w Gary Burton) Polydor (1973), 'Just Ahead' Polydor (1972), 'Tanglewood '63' Deram (1970), 'Michael Gibbs' Deram (1969). Gibbs is one of the foremost arrangers & composers to have emerged in contemp jazz in Britain. Along w

Westbrook he was one of the first British composers for large jazz ensemble to make use of rock elements in a jazz content in a natural and effective manner. He has also written music for films & TV and for a ballet.

Brian Godding

BRIAN GODDING *g*
B 19.8.45 **A** 293 Finchley Road, London NW3 6DT. **T** 01–435 1172. **Curr** Mike Westbrook Orch, George Khan's Zagunga. **Prev** Blossom Toes, B.B. Blunder, Centipede (Tippett), Westbrook, Magma, Dick Morrissey etc. **Fest, Tours** (w Westbrook) UK tour & Camden JF '74, Bracknell JF '75. **Fav rec** 'Citadel/Room 315' (Westbrook) RCA Victor (1975), 'Septober Energy' (Centipede) RCA (1971). **Mem events** Working w Centipede (beginning of involvement w jazz), meeting & working w Westbrook. **Pref** Chick Corea (esp 'Hymn of The Seventh Galaxy'), early Weather Report and the associated musicians, 'Extrapolation' (MacLaughlin–Surman) Marmalade (1969) 'very important to me some years ago as it opened the door to jazz'.

GERRY GOLD *tpt*, *flug-h*
B 26.12.49 **A** 4 Queens Mansions, West End Lane, London NW6. **T** 01–794 9637. **Curr** Eddie Prevost Band. **Prev** London Jazz Comp Orch (Guy). **Mem event** Every perf w Prevost Band. **Pref** Sonny Terry.

Harry Gold

HARRY GOLD *alto, tenor, bass sax, clar, comp, arr*
B 26.2.07 **A** 3 Dartmouth Chambers, 8 Theobalds Road, London WC1X 8PN. **T** 01–405 3045 or 01–836 6699 ext 219. **Curr** Own Pieces of Eight, New Paul Whiteman Orch (Sudhalter), Commodore (Sudhalter), TV and recording sessions. **Prev** Oscar Rabin, Geraldo, Roy Fox, Bert Ambrose, Bert Firman's London Casino Band, Mantovani, Royal Philharmonic Orch, André Kostalanetz, Liverpool Philharmonic Orch. **Rec** 'Runnin' Wild' (New Paul Whiteman Orch) Argo (1975). **Conc** w NPWO '74 & '75. **Pref** Bach, Debussy, Schoenberg, Armstrong, Bix Beiderbecke, Bud Freeman, Don Byas, Rumanian folk music.

DAVE GREEN *bs*
B 5.3.42 **A** 86 Pine Gardens, Eastcote, Ruislip,

Dave Green

Middx HA4 9TJ. **T** 01–868 9891. **Curr** Stan Tracey, Humphrey Lyttelton, Michael Garrick since mid '60s, Quarternity (inc Lowther, Phil Lee) since '74. **Prev** Don Rendell–Ian Carr Quin '63–'69. **Tour** Germany w Lyttelton May '75. **Fest** Newcastle JF (Tracey w strings) June '75. **Fav rec** 'Integration' (Amancio D'Silva) Columbia (1969). **Mem event** Playing at Ronnie Scott's w Coleman Hawkins, Ben Webster & Sonny Rollins. **Pref** Jimmy Blanton w Ellington '40–'41, Parker, Coltrane. **Rec** Numerous w Garrick, Rendell–Carr, Tracey, Lyttelton.

STAN GREIG *p*
B 12.8.30 **A** 43 Tiverton Road, Potters Bar, Herts. **T** Potters Bar 56875. **Curr** Own trio, own Swing Band, London Jazz Big Band (leader). **Prev** Sandy Brown, Ken Colyer, Humphrey Lyttelton, Acker Bilk. **Tour** Danish Schools, Mar–Feb '75. **Fav rec** Own trio 'Boogie Woogie' Rediffusion (*c*1972). **Mem event** London J Big Band premiere perf at 100 Club. **Rec** 'Dixieland Now & Then' (Dixieland A/S) Line (1974).

MALCOLM GRIFFITHS *tbn*
A 2 Crescent Mansions, Elgin Crescent, London W11. **T** 01–727 1528. **Curr** Mike Westbrook Orch, John Warren Orch, Brian Cooper Orch, Mike Gibbs Orch. **Prev** Westbrook Concert Band in '60s, John Surman Octet '68–'69, Alan Skidmore Quin, 'Morning Glory' (w Surman, Taylor, Lawrence, Marshall, Terje Rypdal) '73, Solid Gold Cadillac (Westbrook), own quar (Skidmore, Jackson, Brian Odges), Brotherhood of Breath (MacGregor). **Tours** Germany (w Warren) Jan '75, UK (w Westbrook) Sept–Oct '74. **Fest** Camden JF '74 & Bracknell JF '75 (both w Westbrook & featured on Westbrook's extended comp 'Love, Dream & Variations'). **Rec** 'Citadel/Room 315' (Westbrook) RCA Victor (1975), 'Morning Glory' Island (1973), 'Black, Brown And Beige' (Alan Cohen) Argo (1972), 'TCB' (Skidmore) Philips (1970), and w Westbrook, Surman, Brotherhood of Breath, Dankworth, Gibbs. One of the best contemporary trombonists, Griffiths has been an associate of Mike Westbrook for a decade.

BARRY GUY *bs, comp*
B 22.4.47. **A** 6 Hassendean Road, Blackheath,

Barry Guy

London SE3 8TS. **Agent** Clarion Concert Agency Ltd, 64 Whitehall Park, London N19 3TN. **Curr** Howard Riley Trio, Tony Oxley, solo perf, duo w Jane Manning (soprano), Monteverdi Orch, Bob Downes' Open Music, Orch of St John's Smith Square, Richard Hickox Orch, London Bach Orch, Academy of St Martin in the Field, Spectrum, 20th Century Ensemble, London Sinfonietta, Musicians of London, Raglan Chamber Orch, own London Jazz Composers Orch. **Prev** Iskra 1903 (w Rutherford, Bailey), Evan Parker Group, MacGregor, Westbrook, BBC Symphony Orch, New Philharmonia Orch, Sonor, Dave Holdsworth Group. **Tour** Germany inc Donaueschingen Fest & Berlin JF '72. **Fest** English Bach '72, Guildford '73, Kingston '74 (w LJCO); as soloist La Rochelle '73, Brussels '75. Tutor Barry Summer School '75. **Pref** Gil Evans, Jelly Roll Morton, Armstrong, John Lewis, Dolphy, Mingus, Cecil Taylor, Varèse, Stravinsky, Monteverdi, Bach, Coltrane, Bartok, Richard Strauss, etc. **Rec** 'Ode' (LJCO) Incus (1972), 'Iskra 1903' Incus (1970–2) & w Howard Riley, Bob Downes, Tony Oxley, Amalgam (Watts). An exceptional virtuoso, Guy is equally at home in free improvised music, symphony orchs and conventional jazz.

Ian Hamer

IAN HAMER *tpt*, *flug-h*, *electric-tpt* **B** 11.9.32 **A** 35 Cambridge Crescent, Teddington, Middx. **Curr** Freelance, session work, Jubiaba (Barbara Thompson), own sext, Mike Gibbs. **Prev** Kenny Wheeler, Tubby Hayes, Woody Herman, Thad Jones–Mel Lewis Orch, Ted Heath, Jack Parnell. **Pref** Freddie Hubbard, Wheeler, Gillespie, Lowther, Davis, Booker Little, Clifford Brown, Jimmie Deuchar. **Rec** w Kenny Wheeler, Hayes.

EDDIE (EDWARD THOMAS) HARVEY *tbn*, *p*, *comp*, *arr*, *author* **B** 15.11.25 **A** 414 Ware Road, Hertford. **T** Hertford 2674. Various groups. Also teaching. **Prev** Founder member George Webb's Dixielanders '43–'46, RAF '46–'49, Freddy Randall '49–'50, Vic Lewis '50, Johnny Dankworth Seven '50–'53 & Dankworth Orch to '55, London jazz clubs '55–'57, Bert Courtley–Jack Seymour Orch '56, Don Rendell '57–'59, Humphrey Lyttelton. Arrangements for Lyttelton, Kenny Baker,

Oscar Rabin. Tutor Lambeth J Summer School '74 & '75 (comp, arr, harmony) & organizing tour. **Rec** w Lyttleton. **Book** *Teach Yourself Jazz Piano* E.U.P.

LENNIE HASTINGS *drums*
B 5.1.27 **A** 6 Exeter Road, Hanworth, Middx. **T** 01–894 9625. **Curr** Brian Lemon Trio, Dave Shepherd Quin, own band. **Prev** Freddy Randall, Alex Welsh, Johnny Duncan. **Fav rec** 'Love For Sale' (Tony Coe Quar) Nixa EP (1961). **Mem event** Newport JF '68 (w Alex Welsh). **Pref** 'Jammin' at Condons' (Eddie Condon), 'Throb' (Gary Burton). **Rec** 'Dixieland Now & Then' (Dixieland A/S) Line (1974) & w Welsh, Brian Lemon, Randall.

RON IAN HERMAN *el-bs, bs, p*
B 18.6.49 **A** 91 Hammersmith Road, Kensington, London W14. **T** 01–603 4310. **Prev** SME (Stevens), Amalgam (Watts), Bobby Bradford Quar, own group Beef Band (w Nigel Morris, Frank Roberts), Cirrus (w Boyle, Hurt, Morris, Roberts). **Fest** Black Arts Commonwealth Institute. **Fav rec** 'Birds of a Feather' (SME) Byg (1971). **Mem event** Joining SME, working w Bradford. **Pref** Bill Evans Trio '58–'61, Coleman, Coltrane, Albert Ayler. **Rec** 'Amalgam play Blackwell & Higgins' A (1972–3), 'Bobby Bradford plus SME' Freedom (1971).

TONY HICKS *drums*
A 66 Park Walk, Chelsea, London SW10. **T** 01–352 0365. **Curr** Pacific Eardrum (Dave MacRae). **Prev** Back Door (w Aspery, Hodgkinson). **Rec** 'Back Door' Warner Bros (1972).

PATRICK HIGGS *tpt, flug-h*
B 22.4.38 **A** 33 Ranelagh Gardens Mans, London SW6. **T** 01–736 5733. **Curr** Blue Diamonds w Jo–Ann Kelly. **Prev** Mike Westbrook, Chris MacGregor, John Walters, Gill Lyons, Ken Gibson, Alan Cohen. **Pref** Freddie Hubbard, Clifford Brown, Davis, Don Cherry, Wheeler, Gillespie, Coltrane.

PAUL HIRSH *g, bs, el-bs*
B 3.9.48 **A** 16 Colebrooke Avenue, London W13. **T** 01–997 1839. **Curr** John Walters. **Prev** Dudu Pukwana Sext, Action Music (Noel McGhie), Andrew Evans Trio,

Ken Gibson Big Band. **Mem event** Lambeth &
Barry Summer Schools '74. **Pref** Coltrane,
Rollins, Shepp, Davis, Hancock, Shorter,
Beck, Matthewson, Sulzmann.

JON HISEMAN *drums*
B 21.6.44. **Curr** Own band Colosseum
(re-formed July '75). **Prev** Group Sounds Five
(Lowther), Mike Taylor Quar & Trio, Don
Rendell 5, New J Orch (Ardley), Ian Bird
Sext, Graham Bond Organization, John
Mayall's Blues Breakers, Georgie Fame, Alan
Haven Duo, own band Colosseum '68–'71,
own band Tempest, Jubiaba (Thompson),
Barbara Thompson Quin, Neil Ardley Orch,
Howard Riley Trio. **Tours, Fest** World tours &
numerous major fests since '65. **Fav rec** 'Songs
for a Tailor' (Jack Bruce) Polydor (1969),
'Colosseum Live' Bronze (1971). **Imp event**
Deciding, after 3 weeks persuasion by Graham
Bond, to turn pro and replace Ginger Baker in
GBO in '66. **Mem event** The time w Mike
Taylor. **Other** Direction & record production.
Pref Mike Taylor, Coltrane, Bob Dylan,
Stevie Wonder, compositions of Barbara
Thompson. **Rec** 'Daughter of Time' Vertigo
(1970), 'Collectors Colosseum' Bronze
(1968–71), 'Those who are about To Die'
Philips (1968–69), 'Valentyne Suite' Vertigo
(1969), 'Grass is Greener' Dunhill (1969),
'Discussions' (Riley) Opportunity (1967).

DAVE HOLDSWORTH *tpt*
A 164 Broadfield Road, Catford, London SE6.
T 01–673 1873. **Curr** Tony Oxley Sext. **Prev**
Westbrook, own septet in early '70s. **Rec** w
Westbrook, London J Comp Orch (Guy).

PETE HURT *alto, tenor, clar, f*
B 5.1.50 **A** 169 Sheen Road, Richmond,
Surrey. **T** 01–940 5573. **Curr** Own 11 or 13 piece
band, Gill's band (Lyons). **Prev** Collier,
Narcissus (Phil Broadhurst), Cirrus (Herman).
Tours Italy, Germany, and England w
American singer Bobby Rydell. **Mem event**
Barry Summer School. **Pref** Gibbs, Wheeler,
Gil Evans, Stravinsky, Wayne Shorter,
Rollins, Coltrane, Warleigh, Davis. **Rec**
'Portraits' (Collier) Saydisc (1972).

KEN HYDER *drums*
B 29.6.46 **A** 71 Temperley Road, Balham,
London SW12. **T** 01–673 1873. **Curr** Own band

Talisker, duo w John Rangecroft. **Prev** Mal
Dean's Amazing Band, own band Put It All In
(w Stabbins, Mattos, Tippett), Jo'burg Hawk,
duo w Larry Stabbins. **Mem event** Playing at
Mal Dean's benefit conc ICA '74. **Pref**
Coltrane, Ayler, Rollins, Elvin Jones, Black
Watch Pipe Band, Pipe Major John Burgess,
David Webster. **Rec** 'Dreaming Of Glenisla'
(Talisker) Caroline (1975).

Peter Ind

PETER VINCENT IND *bs*

B 20.7.28 **A** 11 Swakeleys Drive, Ickenham,
Middx. **T** Uxbridge 38755. The Brynny,
Skyborry Green, Knighton, Powys. **T**
Knighton 732. **Curr** Own sext (inc Burchell,
Cliff, Gray Allard, Bernie Cash, Derek
Phillips), solo recitals, Alan Cohen Orch.
Prev Took up bs in '47, Freddie Barrat,
Tommy Sampson; working on transatlantic
liners '49; studied w Lennie Tristano in NYC;
emigrated to USA '51; app w Tristano;
joined Lee Konitz Feb '54; opened own rec
studio '57; teaching & playing in NYC,
worked w Buddy Rich, Coleman Hawkins,
Roy Eldridge, Warne Marsh, Ronnie Ball,
Sal Mosca; returned to UK '66. Teaching,
painting, work w various groups. Own record
label Wave. **Mem event** Arrival in New York as
as immigrant, 29.4.51. **Rec** (All on Wave)
'Peter Ind Sextet' (1975), 'Contra-bach' (duo w
Bernie Cash – bs) (1975), 'Your Friendly
Neighbourhood Rhythm Section' (duo w Tox
Drohar – drums) (*c*1974), quar 'No Kidding'
(w Burchell, Cliff etc) (1974), 'Jazz At The 1969
Richmond Festival' (w Burchell, Philips, Cash)
(1969), solo 'Time for Improvisation' (1969),
solo 'Improvisation' (1968), & earlier albums
on Wave & other labels w Tristano, Konitz,
Marsh, Mosca, Sheila Jordan, Ball etc. A
superb bassist who works in a variety of
contexts, Ind has remained closely associated w
Lennie Tristano's conceptions as reflected in
the music of his current sextet.

KEITH INGHAM *p*

A 9 Redcliffe Square, London SW10. **T**
01–373 8205. **Curr** Duo w Susannah McCorkle,
Ron Russell Band (inc Fairweather). **Prev**
Dick Williams, Wally Fawkes' Troglodytes,
Alan Littejohn, app w Bruce Turner Jump
Band, Sandy Brown; app w Wild Bill Davison,
Billy Butterfield, Bobby Hackett, Bud

Alan Jackson

Freeman, and (in USA) w Ben Webster, Zoot Sims; Commodore (Sudhalter). **Rec** 'Superbud' (w Freeman) 77 (1975).

ALAN JACKSON *drums*
A 6 Foxberry Court, Foxberry Road, London SE4. **T** 01–692 7988. **Curr** Own band Kinkade (inc Lowther, Themen), Mike Westbrook Orch, John Warren Orch, Alan Cohen Band. **Prev** Solid Gold Cadillac (Westbrook), Westbrook Sext & Concert Band, Howard Riley Trio, John Surman. **Tours** Germany w Warren '75. Tutor NYJO Easter Course '74. **Rec** w Westbrook, Riley, Warren, Surman, Tippett. Best known as a powerful & exciting big band drummer, Jackson has been a close associate of Westbrook for over a decade.

BARBARA JAY *singer*
B 15.8.37 **A** The Cottage, 13 Heathfield Road, Bushey, Watford WD2 2LH. **Curr** George Chisholm, Francisco Cavez, Tommy Whittle. **Prev** Ronnie Scott, Tito Burns, Ken Mackintosh, Sandy Brown, Joe Saye, Benny Goodman. **Tours** Europe w Goodman inc concerts at RFH & Albert Hall. **Mem event** Taking part in one of Ted Heath's swing concerts at London Palladium. **Pref** 'Listening to my husband, Tommy Whittle, playing in a jazz club.'

KARL JENKINS *comp, oboe, bari, sop, el-p, p*
A 3 Melina Court, Gipsy Lane, London SW15. **T** 01–878 1740. **Curr** Soft Machine (since June '72) (inc Mike Ratledge, Babbington, Marshall). **Prev** Graham Collier '68–'69, Nucleus (Carr) '69–'72. **Conc** Shakespeare Birthday Celeb Southwark Cath Apr '75. **Rec** 'Bundles' (Soft Machine) Harvest (1974), 'Soft Machine 7' CBS (1973), 'Soft Machine 6' CBS (1972) & w London J Comp Orch (Guy), Nucleus, Collier.

GEORGE (NISAR AHMED) KHAN *tenor, f, bari, sop, drums*
A 274 Liverpool Road, London N1.
T 01–607 2141. **Curr** Own band (Zagunga) (w Godding, Castle, Cooke, John Mitchell). **Prev** Westbrook Orch, Solid Gold Cadillac (Westbrook), own band Stagecoach (w Charlie Hart – bs, Terry Day – drums), Amazing Band. **Conc** Mixed Media work 'Zagunga' ICA

March '74. **Rec** 'Mike Westbrook Live'
Cadillac (1972), 'Solid Gold Cadillac' RCA
(1972) & other Westbrook albums, 'Local
Colour' (Peter Lemer) ESP (1966). Khan's
playing is explosive and colourful. He is at his
best combining his wild free tenor style with the
heavy swing of a rock beat on several of
Westbrook's albums.

PETER KING *alto*
A 15 Oakhill Place, London SW15. **T**
01–874 8646. **Curr** Bebop Preservation Soc
(Le Sage), Colin Purbrook, Stan Tracey, own
quar. **Prev** Tony Kinsey Quin, Splinters
(Tracey, Stevens etc), Dave Hancock Band.
Rec 'Free 'n One' (Tracey) Columbia (1970),
'Trailways Express' (Philly Joe Jones) Polydor
(1968), & w Bebop Preservation Soc.

TONY KINSEY *drums, comp, arr, p*
B 11.10.27 **A** 5 The Pennards, French Street,
Sunbury-on-Thames, Middx. **T** 01–768 3160.
Curr Session work, Colin Purbrook, own
group. **Prev** Studied in NYC while working on
transatlantic liners, Dankworth 7, own groups
since '53, own trio (w Bill Le Sage/Ronnie
Ball/Dill Jones), own quar & quin (inc at
various times Joe Harriott, Ross, Rendell,
Condon, Bob Efford etc) since mid '50's.

Bill Kyle

BILL (WILLIAM T) KYLE *drums, perc*
A 17 Royal Terrace, Glasgow. **T** 041–332 3743.
Curr Own band Head (based in Glasgow)
since '71, Windjammer (Robb), Dave Saul
Quar. **Fest** Dunkirk JF (w Head) '71 & '72
(prizewinners). Dunkirk JF '75 (w Saul). BBC
Radio & Scottish TV broadcasts. **Rec** 'Red
Dwarf' (Head) Canon (*c*1975), 'GTF' (Head)
(*c*1972).

CLEO LAINE *singer, actress*
Agent Laurie Mansfield, International
Artistes, Irving House, Irving Street,
London WC2. **T** 01–930 3046/5608. **Curr** Solo
star usually acc by John Dankworth Orch or
small group. **Prev** w Dankworth Septet &
Orch from '51. **Tours, Conc** In recent years
toured widely in USA, Australia, Europe etc w
Dankworth; annual 'Spring Collection' Brit.
tours since '69; Carnegie Hall NYC conc Apr
'73; conc & TV work Los Angeles Jan '75 (own
TV show w Dankworth), NZ & Australia
tour '75. Starred in 'Showboat' Adelphi

Cleo Laine

London '71 and has appeared in various plays. Numerous TV app Britain, USA, Australia etc. Gold Records – Phonogram, RCA, EMI '75. **Rec** 'Live at Carnegie Hall' (acc. Dankworth Quin) RCA (1973), 'I Am A Song' RCA (1973), 'Feel The Warm' Columbia (1972), 'If We Lived On Top Of A Mountain' Fontana (1968), 'Shakespeare And All That Jazz' (rec. Fontana 1964 re-issued), 'Portrait' Philips. Cleo Laine is a superb singer who now deservedly receives world wide acclaim. Her work transcends categories of jazz and popular music but retains, at its best, all the expressive qualities of jazz singing developed to a high degree.

CHRIS LAWRENCE *bs, el.bs*
A 49 Whitehouse Way, Southgate, London N14. **T** 01–368 5749. **Curr** Mike Westbrook Orch, John Taylor Sext, Mike Pyne Sext, Edge of Time (Norma Winstone). **Prev** w many groups inc Vic Ash, Frank Ricotti, Morning Glory (w Surman, Griffiths, Taylor, Marshall, Terje Rypdal) '73. **Rec** w Ricotti, Winstone, Taylor, Alan Skidmore, Harry Beckett, London J Comp Orch 'Ode' (Guy) Incus (1972), 'Morning Glory' Island (1973).

Chris Lawrence

PHIL LEE *g*
B 8.4.43 **A** 60 Fairhazel Gardens, London NW6 3SL. **T** 01–328 7208. **Curr** Gilgamesh (w Clyne etc) since *c*'73, Quarternity (w Lowther, Green, Tomkins). **Prev** Bob Stuckey Quar, Graham Collier, Mike Gibbs. **Conc** Performances of Tony Coe's 'Zeitgeist'. Radio broadcasts w Gilgamesh. **Fav rec** 'Gilgamesh' Caroline (1975). **Other rec** w Collier.

Phil Lee

TONY LEE *p*
A 50 Willesden Lane, London NW6. **T** 01–328 4934. **Curr** Own trio, Tommy Whittle Quar. **Conc** Wigmore Hall (London J Piano Series) Mar '75. **Rec** 'Phil Seamen Now . . . Live!' Verve (1968).

PETER LEMER *p, comp, arr*
A 31a Dollis Avenue, London N3.
T 01–349 9430. **Curr** Baker–Gurvitz Army. **Prev** Own band E, Barbara Thompson, Don Rendell 5, George Khan's Zagunga. **Conc** Own extended comp. 'The Tao Imprint' perf in

conc at ICA Sept '74 w Pepi Lemer – voice, Jane Bobertson – cello, etc.
Rec 'Oliv' (SME) Marmalade (1969), 'Local Colour' ESP (1966).

BRIAN LEMON *p*
B 11.2.37 **A** 8 Bloomsbury Close, Western Gardens, Ealing, London W5. **T** 01–992 1826. **Curr** Own trio, octet, and Dixielanders, Alex Welsh since Sept '75. **Prev** Freddy Randall, Betty Smith, Danny Moss, Dave Shepherd, George Chisholm, Sandy Brown. **Fest** Montreux '72 (w Danny Moss Quar) '73 (w Freddy Randall). **Fav rec** Own trio 'Taking Off' Jade. **Mem event** Working w Ben Webster, Charlie Shavers, Barney Kessel, Stephane Grappelli, Bud Freeman. Own trio conc Wigmore Hall '74, Armstrong Mem Conc Royal Fest Hall '74 acc Buddy Tate & Bill Coleman. **Pref** Art Tatum. **Rec** 'Live At Montreux' (Randall/Shepherd) Black Lion (1973), 'Freddy Randall – Dave Shepherd All Stars' Black Lion (1973), 'Sandy Brown with the Brian Lemon Trio' 77 (1971), 'Phil on Drums' (Phil Seamen) 77 (1971), 'Our Kind of Music' 77 (1970), 'Hall Of Fame' (Adelaide Hall) Columbia (1969), 'Shepherd's Delight' (Shepherd) 77 (1969), and w Tony Coe.

Bill Le Sage

BILL LE SAGE *p*, *vib*, *perc*, *comp*, *arr*
B 20.1.27 **A** 21 Park Road, Hanwell, London W7. **T** 01–567 2394. **Curr** Own trio, Bebop Preservation Society (leader) (quin inc Shaw, King), since '71, Jubiaba (Thompson). **Prev** Took up p '43, worked transatlantic liners at end of '40s, studied w Lennie Tristano NYC, Dankworth '50–'54, took up vib early '50s, Tony Kinsey '54–'61, Ronnie Ross, LeSage–Ross Quar early '60s, own Directions in Jazz Unit during '60s. Also involved in jazz educ. **Mem event** Working w Dizzy Gillespie. **Pref** Ellington, Gillespie, John Handy, Heitor Villa-Lobos, Andres Segovia. **Rec** 'The Bebop Preservation Society' Dawn (*c*1971) 'Cleopatra's Needle' (Ross) Fontana (1968), Directions in Jazz Unit – two albums on Philips (1964 & 1965), Bill Le Sage Orch Philips (1964), 'Bill Le Sage – Ronnie Ross Quartet' World Record Club (1963). A fluent bebop soloist on both piano and vibes.

TONY LEVIN *drums*
A 133 Oxford Road, Moseley, Birmingham 13.

Tony Levin

Henry Lowther

T 021–449 2345. **Curr** John Taylor Sext, Stan
Sulzmann Quar, Edge of Time (Norma
Winstone). **Prev** Tubby Hayes Quar (w Pyne,
Matthewson) mid '60s, Les Condon Quar,
Nucleus (Carr), Gyroscope (Gordon Beck)
'73–'74. **Rec** 'Pause And Think Again' (John
Taylor) Turtle (1971), 'TCB' (Alan Skidmore)
Philips (1970), 'Mexican Green' (Hayes)
Fontana (1967), and w Ian Carr, Winstone,
Beck, etc.

TERRY LIGHTFOOT *clar, vocalist*
Agent c/o Reg Tracey. **T** 01–500 1298. **Curr**
Own traditional band since '50s, touring
widely.

HENRY LOWTHER *tpt, flug-h, violin, comp*
B 11.7.41 **A** 63 Rosebery Road, Muswell Hill,
London N10 2LE. **T** 01–883 5005. **Curr**
Quarternity (w Lee, Green, Tomkins) + Art
Themen, Edge of Time (Norma Winstone),
Michael Garrick Sext, Kinkade (Alan
Jackson), Jubiaba (Barbara Thompson),
John Warren, Dankworth, Brian Cooper Orch,
John Stevens' Dance Orch. **Prev** Gibbs,
Westbrook Orch, own band, Manfred Mann,
John Mayall, Keef Hartley, Group Sounds
Five (own group w Lynn Dobson, Jon
Hiseman etc), BBC Symphony Orch, Radio
Band, Tony Faulkner Orch etc. **Fest, Conc,
Tours** Germany (w John Warren), USSR (w
Kurt Edelhagen), Bracknell JF '75 (w Jubiaba
& Westbrook), devised 'The Worlds of Inner
Space' conc of music & readings (w Martin
Bax) ICA Apr '75, comp 'Vietnam Symphony'
premiered at same conc, Shakespeare celeb
conc Southwark Cath '75. **Fav rec** *Anima* on
own album 'Child Song' Deram (1970). **Mem
event** Formation of Quarternity June '74.
Pref 'From Indian Music to Tony Oxley,
King Oliver to Weather Report, Dunstable to
Stockhausen, Mozart to Average White Band.'
Rec 'Citadel/Room 315' (Westbrook) RCA
Victor (1975), and w Garrick, Gibbs,
Dankworth, Winstone. A fine soloist with a
clear, brilliant tone, Lowther often sounds at
his best in a big band setting but he is a
consistent player much in demand in a variety
of contexts.

JIM LUXTON *sop, tenor, clar*
B 18.5.47 **A** 2 Steeds Terrace, Benter, Oakhill,

Bath, Avon. **T** Stratton-on-the-Fosse 232123. **Curr** Own bands in Cardiff (Crescent and Eclipse). **Mem event** Barry Summer School, playing w Henry Lowther at Scott's. **Pref** Coltrane (middle period), Surman, Skidmore, Ardley, Warren.

GILL LYONS *el-bs*
A 26 Ringford Road, London SW18.
T 01–874 6786. **Curr** Own big band Gill's Band. **Prev** Keith Tippett group, Centipede (Tippett).

Humphrey Lyttelton

HUMPHREY LYTTELTON *tpt, leader, author, broadcaster*
B 23.5.21 **Agent** Susan DaCosta, 35 Chesil Court, Chelsea Manor Street, London SW3.
T 01–352 4538. **Curr** Own band (inc Kathy Stobart, Bruce Turner etc), solo app w various groups. **Prev** George Webb's Dixielanders, own band since '48, Freddy Grant – Lyttelton Paseo JB '52. **Tour** Brit tour w own band Feb–Mar '75. TV app etc. **Conc** Ellington Memorial RFH June '75, Armstrong Memorial RFH July '75. **Other** Own weekly BBC Radio jazz prog. **Rec** 'Take It From the Top' Black Lion (1975), 'In Swinger' Happy Bird (1974), 'South Bank Swing Session' Black Lion (1973), 'Doggin' Around' WAM (1972), 'Duke Ellington Classics' Black Lion (1969), '21 Years On' Polydor Double Album (1969), 'Best of Humph 1949–56' Parlophone (issued 1972), 'Kansas City Woman' (w Buddy Tate) Black Lion. **Books** *I Play As I Please* MacGibbon & Kee (1954), *Second Chorus* MacGibbon & Kee (1958), *Take It From the the Top* Robson (1975). Lyttelton's career has taken him from an uncompromising traditional style to a mainstream approach rooted in the music of the Ellington small groups. Broadcaster, writer and celebrity, he nevertheless manages to remain one of the best British trumpeters within his style.

Paul Lytton

PAUL LYTTON *drums, perc*
A Flat 12a, Arkwright Mansions, 206 Finchley Road, London NW3. **T** 01–794 5197. **Curr** Duo w Evan Parker since *c*'70, trio (w Wachsmann, Malfatti), Freedom for a Change (Kenny Wheeler), various free improv music situations. **Prev** Own group in late '60s, NYJO (Ashton). **Tours** Contemp Music Network Feb '75 Britain. **Rec** 'Collective

Calls (Urban) (Two Microphones)' Incus
(1972) (duo w Parker), 'Live At the Unity
Theatre' (w Parker) Incus (1975).

KEN McCARTHY *p, el-p*
B 6.7.39 **A** 44 Elmbank Way, London W7.
T 01–578 4208. **Curr** Own quin (w Pearce,
L Cooper etc). **Prev** Mike Westbrook Orchs,
Group Sounds Five (Lowther). **Mem event**
Japanese tour as pianist/MD w Dutch singer
Ann Burton to play jazz clubs there and record
an LP. **Pref** Coltrane, Herbie Hancock,
Chick Corea.

LACHLAN MacCOLL *g*
A 23 Royal Crescent, Edinburgh. **T** Waverley
4237. **Curr** Head (w Cruikshank, Kyle etc)
since '73. Various groups in Edinburgh area.
Rec 'Red Dwarf' (Head) Canon (c1975).

SUSANNAH McCORKLE *singer*
B 1.1.46 **A** 9 Redcliffe Square, London SW10.
T 01–373 8205. **Curr** w pianist Keith Ingham
solo, duo and trio. **Prev** In California until
'70, then to Paris, Rome and London, Bruce
Turner Band, Jazz Without Walls (Sudhalter),
Commodore (Sudhalter), also app w Chilton,
Christie. **Fest** Camden JF '74, Edinburgh J and
Poetry F '75. **Fav rec** 'Cole' EMI. **Mem event**
Working w Ben Webster Copenhagen '73.
Pref 'The hundreds of very beautiful,
perceptive and witty American songs of the
'20s, '30s and '40s, and blues of every era.'

Chris MacGregor

CHRIS MacGREGOR *p, comp, arr, leader*
B 24.12.36 **A** Resident in Aquitaine, France
since '74 but commutes to Britain for
occasional app of his big band. **Agent** Hazel
Miller, 28 Richardson Court, Studley Estate,
Stockwell, London SW4 6RZ. **T** 01–622 1087.
Curr Own big band Brotherhood of Breath
since '70. **Prev** Early years in Transkei,
South Africa, studied classical music, own
group (Blue Notes) which won National J
Fest, Orlando Stadium, Johannesburg '63.
Antibes JF '64. To Britain w Blue Notes (inc
Feza, Pukwana, Moholo) '65. Own sext.
Tours Europe '73, numerous app on
Continent. **Other** Wrote score for film
'Kongi's Harvest'. **Rec** 'Live at Willisau'
(Brotherhood of Breath) Ogun (1974),
'Brotherhood' (BoB) RCA Victor (1971),
'Brotherhood of Breath' RCA Neon (1971),

sext 'Very Urgent' Polydor (1968), 'Kwela' 77 (1967–8), 'Outback' (Osborne) Turtle (1970). MacGregor brought his South African Blue Notes to Britain in 1965 and stayed for some years to revitalise the local scene. His big band is one of the raggedest to be heard but, at its best, also one of the most exciting and exhilarating.

Dave MacRae

DAVE (DAVID SCOTT) MacRAE *keyboards* **B** 2.4.40 **T** 01–235 3077 & 01–202 5736. **Curr** Own band Pacific Eardrum (inc Joy Yates, Big Jim Sullivan, Bob Bertles, Brian Smith). **Prev** Came to Britain from New Zealand (via USA) '71, rock bands inc Frank Reed's Powerhouse, Matching Mole, Nucleus (Carr), Gibbs, Westbrook, Back Door (w Aspery etc) '74, studio work, Buddy Rich in USA. **Tours** Europe (w Back Door) '74. **Fest** Newcastle JF (w Pacific Eardrum) June '75. **Mem event** Forming and devel. Pacific Eardrum. **Rec** w Carr, Westbrook, Gibbs. MacRae's involvement has been largely w the rock end of the jazz spectrum but he is also an excellent big band pianist.

RADU MALFATTI *tbn* **Curr** Brotherhood of Breath (MacGregor), Balance (w Wachsmann, Perry etc), trio w Wachsmann & Lytton. Just Us (Dean). **Rec** 'Live at Willisau' (MacGregor) Ogun (1974), 'Balance' Incus (1973), 'Ramifications' (Irene Schweitzer) Ogun (1973).

DAVE MARKEE *bs* **A** 71 South Ridge Road, Croydon, Surrey. **T** 01–680 2786. **Curr** Brian Cooper J Orch, Alan Price. **Prev** Maynard Ferguson Orch, Tony Faulkner Orch. **Rec** 'MF Horn' (Ferguson) CBS (1973).

JOHN MARSHALL *drums* **A** 28 Clonmore Street, London SW18. **T** 01–874 4981. **Curr** Soft Machine since '71. **Prev** Studied w Allan Ganley & Philly Joe Jones, Alexis Korner, Graham Collier '60s, Nucleus (Carr) '69–'71, Gibbs, Jack Bruce, Centipede (Tippett), Garrick, Morning Glory (w Surman, Griffiths etc) '73. **Rec** 'Bundles' (Soft Machine) Harvest (c1974), 'Soft Machine 7' CBS (1973), 'Morning Glory' Island (1973), 'Soft Machine 6' CBS (1972), 'Soft Machine 5'

CBS, 'Septober Energy' (Centipede) RCA
(1971), and w Bruce, Gibbs, Westbrook,
Surman, Collier.

JULIAN MARSHALL *p, el-p, violin*
B 16.3.54 **A** 8 Aldebert Terrace, Stockwell,
London SW8. **T** 01–735 6624. **Curr** Own band
Equus (sext inc Pearce, Nieman, Ormerod).
Prev Nat Youth J Orch (Ashton), free music
combinations at Little Theatre Club, own
band Quincicasm '74. **Fav rec** *Time & Motion* &
Trent Park Song from 'Quincicasm' Saydisc
(1974). **Pref** K. Jarrett, Stravinsky, Bartok,
Prokofiev, Chick Corea, J. MacLaughlin,
Stevie Wonder, Joni Mitchell, Herbie Hancock,
Westbrook etc.

RON MATTHEWSON *bs*
A 80 Sinclair Road, London W14.
T 01–603 9368. **Curr** Stan Sulzmann Quar,
bs duo w Ron Rubin, Freedom for a Change
(Kenny Wheeler). **Prev** John Cox, Tubby
Hayes Quar, Les Condon Quar, Mike Pyne
Trio, The Band (R Scott) '68, Francy Boland,
Ray Russell Quar, Phil Woods European
Rhythm Machine in early '70s, Ronnie Ross
Sext, WMWM (w Windo, Robert Wyatt,
MacRae) '73, Gyroscope (Beck) '73–'74, Pat
Smythe. **Other** Tutor Barry J Summer School
'75. **Rec** 'All in the Morning' (Beck–
Matthewson–Humair Trio) Jaguar cassette
(1972), 'Live at Montreux' (Woods) Verve
(1972), 'The Source' (SME) Tangent (1970),
'Trailways Express' (Philly Joe Jones) Polydor
(1968), and w Hayes, Russell, Wheeler, Ian
Carr.

MARCIO MATTOS *bs, acoustic g*
B 20.3.46 **A** 53 Foxbourne Road, London
SW17. **T** 01–767 2756. **Curr** Amazing Band,
AMM with strings (Gare–Prevost), Alternative
Music Orch (Brighton), Eddie Prevost Band,
Quar w Wachsmann, Brighton etc, Quar w
Larry Stabbins etc, West Square Ensemble.
Prev SME (Stevens), Spear (Pukwana),
Jabula (Bahula), Julian Marshall, Balance
(Wachsmann etc), Talisker (Hyder), Put It All
In (Hyder), Lyra Ventura, Moon and Sand.
Tour Belgium w AMM. **Conc** New Music
Formation LSE w AMO & Wachsmann/
Brighton/Mattos/Smith quar, West Square
Ensemble at St John's Smith Sq. **Rec** w SME

'The Source' Tangent (1970) and 'SME+=
SMO' A (1975), and w Brighton 'Pisces 44'
due for release.

SIMON MAYO *clar*
A c/o JCS
Curr A Touch Of The Sun (w Peter Cusack),
Chamberpot (w Wachsmann, Richard
Beswick, Tony Wren) since '72, free improv
music combinations. **Perf** Unity Theatre,
Little Theatre Club, Soho Poly w Chamberpot.
'Music in our Time' BBC Radio. **Rec** 'Milk
Teeth' (A Touch Of The Sun) Bead (1975).

MARC MEGGIDO *bs*
B 25.5.54 **A** 12a Arkwright Mansions, 206
Finchley Road, London NW3. **T** 01–794 5197.
Curr Eddie Prevost Band, AMM with strings
(Gare–Prevost), Alternative Music Orch
(Brighton), Town Cryer (Colin Towns),
Talisker (Hyder), Richard Leigh All Stars.
Prev Many bands at Little Theatre Club
'72–'74, e.g. Otherways, Free Space, Entourage
(Stevens). **Tour** Sunderland–Billingham
Colleges w Prevost Band Feb '75. **Rec** w
Hyder.

George Melly

GEORGE MELLY *singer, kazoo, author*
B 17.8.26 **Agent** c/o Ronnie Scott Directions,
47 Frith Street, London W1. **T** 01–439 0747.
Curr Solo appearances acc by John Chilton's
Feetwarmers. **Prev** Mick Mulligan's J Band
'49–'61, TV & film critic for *The Observer*
during '60s, returned to jazz singing in early
'70s. **Tours, Conc, Fest** USA May–June '74,
Reading Fest '74, Ronnie Scott's Club 5 wks
Dec '74, Lyceum Apr '75, Newcastle JF June
'75, Bracknell JF July '75, Welsh JF May '75
etc. **Fav rec** 'It's George' Warner Bros (1974).
Mem event Reading Fest '74. **Pref** Bessie
Smith, Armstrong. **Books** *Owning Up*
(autobiog) Weidenfeld & Nicolson (1965),
Revolt into Style Allen Lane (1970). **Rec**
'Son of Nuts' Warner Bros (1973). 'Nuts'
Warner Bros (1972), 'Meet George Melly with
Mick Mulligan' Pye (1959 rec re-issued 1974),
'The Fifties' (w Mulligan) Decca (1950s rec
re-issued 1973).

BRIAN MILLER *p, el-p, comp, arr*
A 55 Goldsmith Road, Friern Barnet,
London N11 3JG. **T** 01–368 7071. **Curr** Own
band Impulse (w Wakeman, Chisholm,

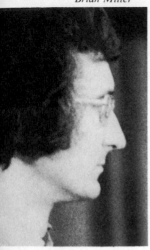

Ricotti etc), duo w Phil Lee, own trio, Jubiaba (Thompson), Harry Beckett's S & R Powerhouse Section, Joy Unlimited (Beckett). **Prev** Frank Ricotti, Tony Faulkner, Isotope (Boyle) '73–'74, Mike Osborne Quin, Westbrook. **Fest** Bracknell July '75 (w Westbrook). **Rec** 'Joy Unlimited' (Beckett) Cadillac (1974), and w Ray Russell.

HARRY MILLER *be, el-bs*
B 25.4.41 **Agent** Hazel Miller, 28 Richardson Court, Studley Estate, Stockwell, London SW4 6RZ. **T** 01–622 1087. **Curr** Own group Isipingo (inc Osborne, Feza, Evans, Moholo), Brotherhood of Breath (MacGregor), Mike Osborne Trio, Ovary Lodge (Tippett), Ninesense & Just Us (Dean), Quartette à Tête (co-led w Tippett, Malfatti, Lytton). **Prev** Vikings rock and roll band Johannesburg, Stan Tracey's Tentacles & Octet, Mike Westbrook Sext & Conc Band, John Surman Quar & Octet, John Warren Orch, Spear (Pukwana), Centipede (Tippett), Bob Downes Trio, Chris MacGregor Quin, Alan Skidmore Quin, Kenneth Terroade Group, Arman Ratip. **Tours, Fest** Numerous European Fest, works extensively on Continent, Heidelberg JF '75. Tutor Lambeth J Summer School July '75. **Rec** 'Children at Play' (solo bass) Ogun (1974) 'Border Crossing' (Mike Osborne Trio) Ogun (1974), 'Ramifications' (Irene Schweitzer) Ogun (1973), 'Once Upon a Time' (Skidmore) Decca (1969), 'Facets of the Universe' (Friendship Next Of Kin w Terroade, Feza, Osborne etc) Goody (1969) 'Jazz In Britain '68–'69' (w various musicians) Decca (1968–9), and w MacGregor, Warren, Westbrook, Surman, Downes.

TONY MILLINER *slide & valve tbn, bs-tpt*
B 28.12.29 **T** 01–493 6700 & 01–804 4167. **Curr** Own sext, own sept Mingus Music, Alan Stuart Octet, London J Big Band (Greig), Brian Lemon Octet. **Prev** Dave Carey, Al Fairweather–Sandy Brown All Stars late '50s & early '60s. **Fest** Camden JF '74 (w Sandy Brown). **Conc** Mingus Music ICA. **Fav rec** *Monsoon* from 'McJazz' (Fairweather–Brown) Columbia (1960). **Mem event** Joining Sandy Brown's band. **Pref** Mingus, Gil Evans, Parker, Jimmy Knepper, Jack Teagarden, Mike Gibbs, Carla Bley.

JOHN MITCHELL *drums, perc, vib*
A 35 Lynmouth Road, East Finchley,
London N2. **Curr** George Khan, Westbrook
Orch. **Rec** 'Citadel/Room 315' (Westbrook)
RCA Victor (1975).

LOUIS MOHOLO *drums*
A 148 Hornsey Lane, London N6.
T 01-263 2506. **Curr** Brotherhood of Breath
(MacGregor), Isipingo (H Miller), Mike
Osborne Trio, Elton Dean. **Prev** MacGregor
bands, Open Circle Quar (Tracey), Spear
(Pukwana). **Rec** w MacGregor, Osborne,
Pukwana. A fiery, powerful, extrovert drummer
equally effective in a trio setting w Osborne or
driving MacGregor's big band.

DICK MORRISSEY *tenor*
A 60 Wick Road, Teddington, Middx. **T**
01-977 5785. **Curr** Own quar, Mike Carr Trio
since Aug '75, various groups. **Prev** Own quar
(w Harry South, Phil Bates, Phil Seamen) in
'60s, Harry South Big Band, If (rock band) to
Nov '74. **Tours** USA, Germany etc w If. **Rec**
'Phil Seamen Story' Decibel (1972), 'Not Just
A Bunch Of Pretty Faces' (If) (1974), quar
'Storm Warning' Mercury (1965) etc, and w
Harry South.

DANNY MOSS *tenor*
A 129 Broomfield Avenue, Worthing, Sussex.
T Worthing 60370. **Curr** Own quar, session
work, Freddy Randall, appearances w many
mainstream bands, Dave Shepherd. **Prev**
Ted Heath, Dankworth. **Fest** Montreux '72
(w own quar) '73 (w Randall–Shepherd).
Welsh JF (Cardiff) May '75. **Conc** Alex Welsh
21st Anniv QEH May '75. **Rec** 'Live at
Montreux' (Randall–Shepherd) Black Lion
(1973). Good mid-period tenor.

ERNEST MOTHLE *bs, el-bs*
B 2.12.41 **A** 21 Westwood Road, London
SW13. **T** 01-876 4779. **Curr** Joy (Dvorak),
Jabula–Spear (Bahula–Pukwana), Embryo
(Roberts), Malombo Music (Bahula). **Prev**
Jabula (Bahula), HeShoo–BeShoo.

BRIAN NEWTON *tbn, comp, arr, leader*
B 2.4.38 **A** 29 Glaisdale Road, Birmingham
B28 8PY. **T** 021-777 2944. **Curr** Own Orch,
Johnny Lambe, Midland All Stars. **Prev**
Various groups and big bands. **Conc** w own
orch around the Midlands. **Pref** Post-war big
bands.

Ernest Mothle

KEITH NICHOLS *p, tbn, arr*
B 13.2.45 **A** 33 Rosemary Drive, Ilford, Essex.
Curr Own ragtime orch, tbn w New Paul
Whiteman Orch (Sudhalter), solo ragtime p.
Prev Mike Daniels '64–'66, Anglo-American
All Stars '66–'67, Levity Lancers (novelty
band) '67–'74. **Conc** Ragtime QEH Feb,
June '75, Fairfield Hall Apr '75, New Paul
Whiteman Orch Camden JF '74 & Fairfield
Hall '75. **Pref** James P Johnson, Fats Waller.
Rec 'Keith Nichols plays Scott Joplin and the
Classic Rag Masters' EMI One-Up (1973).

Maggie Nichols

MAGGIE NICHOLS *singer*
A 53 Chesham Buildings, Brown Hart
Gardens, London W1. **T** 01–499 4680. **Curr**
Arman Ratip, Alternative Music Orch
(Brighton), own band Okuren (inc Derek
Foster, Nicki Francis etc). **Prev** Centipede
(Tippett), SME (Stevens). Co-organizer &
tutor (w John Stevens) Rochelle School Music
Workshops. **Conc** Soloist w John Williams'
'Four Pieces For Jazz Soloists and Orchestra'
'74. W own quin on BBC TV 'Open Door'
prog May '74. **Rec** 'Oliv' (SME) Marmalade
(1969).

PAUL NIEMAN *tbn*
B 19.6.50 **A** 21 Well Walk, Hampstead,
London NW3 1BY. **T** 01–435 8834. **Curr** John
Warren, Equus (Julian Marshall), London J
Comp Orch (Guy). **Prev** Dankworth, Gibbs,
Brotherhood of Breath (MacGregor),
Westbrook Concert Band, Centipede
(Tippett), Soft Machine, Stan Tracey Big Band,
Ballet Rambert, Northern Sinfonietta. **Tours**
Germany twice w Warren, Music Theatre w
John Surman & Barre Phillips in Avignon.
Pref Mingus, Jimmy Knepper, Stockhausen,
Coltrane. **Rec** w London J Comp Orch.

PAUL NOSSITER *clar, sax, oboe*
B 1.8.30 **A** 40 Belsize Square, London NW3.
T 01–794 5973. **Curr** New Paul Whiteman
Orch (Sudhalter). **Prev** Teddy Wilson, Bobby
Hackett, Ruby Braff, Jimmy Rushing in USA;
Commodore (co-leader w Sudhalter). **Conc** w
New Paul Whiteman Orch Camden JF '74 &
Fairfield Hall '75, w Bobby Hackett &
Commodore Camden JF Sept '74. **Fav rec**
'Runnin' Wild' (New Paul Whiteman Orch)
Argo (1975). **Mem event** Coming to England
from USA. **Pref** Stravinsky, piano music of
Satie, Billie Holiday.

Mike Osborne

MIKE OSBORNE *alto*
A Flat 1, 44 Gleneagle Road, Streatham, London SW16. **T** 01–769 2834. **Curr** Own trio (w Miller, Moholo) since '69, SOS (w Skidmore, Surman) since '73 – 1st UK app 100 Club Apr '74, Isipingo (Miller), Brotherhood of Breath (MacGregor). **Prev** To London from Hereford early '60s, studied at Guildhall School of Music. Mike Westbrook during '60s, John Surman Octet '68–'69, duo w Stan Tracey in early '70s, Harry Beckett. Tutor Lambeth J Summer School '74 & '75. **Tours, Conc** Germany, Switzerland, Austria w own trio '74 & '75, six wks at Paris Opera House '74 w SOS, QEH conc w SOS & London Saxophone Quar Mar '75. **Rec** Trio 'Border Crossing' Ogun (1974), 'Outback' Turtle (1970), 'SOS' (w Skidmore, Surman) Ogun (1975), 'Original' (duo w Tracey) Cadillac (1972), 'TCB' (Skidmore) Philips (1970), 'The Sun Is Coming Up' (Rik Colbeck Quar) Fontana (1970), 'Facets of the Universe' (Friendship Next Of Kin w Feza, Miller, Kenneth Terroade) Goody (1969), 'Jazz In Britain '68–'69' (w various musicians) Decca (1968-9), and w Surman, Westbrook, Beckett, Warren, London J Comp Orch (Guy), Brotherhood of Breath. An important and original contemp jazz stylist, Osborne has worked through an early Konitz influence to a style which makes full use of harmonic freedom while remaining, at its best, melodic and swinging.

Tony Oxley

TONY OXLEY *drums, perc, comp*
A Burghley, Masham Way, Gerrards Cross, Bucks. **T** Gerrards Cross 82015. **Curr** Own sext The Angular Apron (inc Riley, Guy, D Holdsworth, Alan Davie etc), Howard Riley Trio, London J Comp Orch (Guy). **Prev** House drummer Ronnie Scott's Club during '60s, The Band (R Scott) '68, Gordon Beck, Alan Skidmore, Mike Pyne Trio, Compositions for London J Comp Orch. Founder member Musicians' Co-Op and Incus Records '71. Organizing tutor annual Barry J Summer School since '73. **Tour** Brit tour w sext Nov '74. **Conc** ICA Aug '75. **Rec** 'Solo, Sextet and Quartet' Incus (1975), 'Icnos' RCA (1972), 'Four Compositions For Sextet' CBS (1970), 'The Baptised Traveller' CBS (1969), 'Extrapolation' (John

MacLaughlin) Marmalade (1969), 'Once
Upon A Time' (Skidmore) Decca (1969), 'Jazz
In Britain '68–'69' (w various musicians)
Decca (1968–9), 'Gyroscope' (Beck) Morgan
(1968), and w Riley, London J Comp Orch,
Gibbs. Oxley is a superb percussionist who has
shown, in his conventional jazz drumming, a
mastery of phrasing and time which few
drummers can equal. With his own groups and
with Riley he has gradually evolved a style
which integrates percussion totally into the
textures and sound patterns of free collective
improvisation.

MIKE PAGE *alto, tenor, bari, bs-clar, f, alto-f*
B 9.5.47 **A** 5 Hawarden Road, Caterham,
Surrey CR3 5QT. **T** Caterham 48557. **Curr**
Westbrook, Dankworth, Alan Cohen, Gill's
Band (Lyons). **Prev** Nat Youth J Orch
(Ashton), Warren. **Tours** Cleo Laine's Spring
Collection w Dankworth '75, Dionne
Warwicke, Diana Ross, Three Degrees. **Fav
rec** Lead alto on 'Citadel/Room 315'
(Westbrook) RCA Victor (1975). **Mem event**
Ellington Memorial Service St Martin's in the
Fields London '74. **Pref** Most kinds of music
esp big bands.

DAVID PANTON *alto, p, oboe, also
home-made perc. viola. violin*
B 20.10.46 **A** 9 The Hawthorns, Woodbridge
Road, Birmingham B13 9DY. **Curr** One
Music Ensemble (solo perf) since '70. **Prev**
Forest, Ashbury–Panton Duo '72–'73,
Laboratory Theatre '72–'74, Entourage
(Stevens) '73, B'ham New Music Ensemble
'68–'69 (leader). **Fav rec** 'The Other Side'
(One Music Ensemble) (alto/perc) Nondo.
Pref Cecil Taylor, Evan Parker, Stravinsky,
Bartok, Varèse, Coleman, Parker, Dolphy,
Cage, early music to avant-garde, bird song to
pneumatic drills. **Rec** 'One Music' Nondo
(1971).

EVAN PARKER *tenor, sop*
B 5.4.44 **A** 87 Third Cross Road, Twickenham,
Middx. **T** 01–878 4095. **Curr** Duo w Paul
Lytton since *c*'70, Alexander von
Schlippenbach Quar since late '60s, Kenny
Wheeler, Tony Oxley. **Prev** SME (Stevens),
Music Improvisation Company (w Bailey,
Jamie Muir, Hugh Davies, Christine Jeffrey),

Evan Parker

Peter Kowald Quin, Globe Unity Orch
(Schlippenbach, Kowald), Tentacles (Tracey),
Brotherhood of Breath (MacGregor),
Alternative Music Orch. **Fest, tours, conc**
Free Music Workshop Berlin, Contemp
Music Network Tour Feb '75, Saxophone
Special conc (w Steve Lacy, Watts, Steve
Potts) Wigmore Hall Dec '74. **Imp event**
Estab Incus Records (w Bailey, Oxley) '71.
Rec 'Live At the Unity Theatre' (w Lytton)
Incus (1975), 'Live In Wuppertal' (Globe
Unity Orch) FMP (Incus import) (1973),
'Collective Calls (Urban) (Two Microphones)'
(w Lytton) Incus (1972), 'Music Improvisation
Company' ECM, (1970), 'Topography of the
Lungs' (w Bailey, Han Bennink) Incus (1970),
and w Oxley, SME, London J Comp Orch
(Guy), MacGregor. Parker's intricate style
frequently dispenses with both harmonic
reference and constant rhythm while retaining
an inventiveness and expressiveness that mark
him as a key figure in the European avant
garde.

DICK PEARCE *tpt, flug-h*
A 61 Avonmore Road, London W14.
T 01–603 4111. **Curr** Embryo (Frank Roberts),
Equus (Julian Marshall), Ken McCarthy Quin.
Prev Nat Youth J Orch (Ashton), Collier,
Quincicasm (Marshall), Narcissus (Phil
Broadhurst). **Conc** Soloist w John Williams
'Four Pieces For Jazz Soloists And Orchestra'
'74. **Rec** 'NYJO' (Nat Youth J Orch) Charisma
(c1973), 'Quincicasm' Saydisc (1974),
'Portraits' (Collier) Saydisc (1972), 'National
Youth Jazz Orchestra' Philips (1971).

DAVE PERROTTET *slide & valve tbn,*
comp, arr
B 17.2.40 **T** 01–743 8000 ext 2153/8. **Curr**
Gill's Band (Lyons), Tony Faulkner. **Prev**
Westbrook, MacGregor, Centipede (Tippett),
New Jazz Orch Reunion (Ardley), Pat Evans.
Pref Carla Bley, Jazz Composers' Orch, Gil
Evans, Roswell Rudd, Armstrong, Mingus.
Rec 'Septober Energy' (Centipede) RCA (1971).

FRANK ERNEST JOHN PERRY *perc,*
bamboo f, sheng
B 25.6.48 **A** 44 Weatherbury House, Wedmore
Street, London N19 4RB. **Curr** Ovary Lodge
(Tippett), own band Balance (w Wachsmann,

Malfatti, Brighton etc), solo recitals. **Prev** Own
trio, Derek Bailey & Evan Parker, Mistral,
Chris MacGregor Trio, Alternative Music
Orch (Brighton). **Tours** France & Germany.
Mem event Solo conc Wigmore Hall. **Pref**
Cesar Franck, Alan Hovhaness, Wagner,
Debussy, Ravel, Messaien; Tibetan, Japanese,
Javanese, Indian, Chinese, Balinese ethnic
music; Samuel Barber, Coltrane, Ayler, Cecil
Taylor, Moondog. **Rec** 'Balance' Incus (1973),
'Blueprint' (Tippett) RCA Victor (1972).

TIM PHAROAH *bs, el-bs*
B 11.5.44 **A** 26 Elm Park Mansions, Park
Walk, London SW10. **T** 01–352 5628. **Curr**
Nicky Francis Quin, John MacNicol Quin.
Prev Pete Martin Band (Edinburgh), John
MacNicol Band (Edin), Ken Rogers Sext.
Pref Burton, Corea, Davis, Rollins, Weather
Report, Gibbs, Beck, Rendell, Guy,
Matthewson, Derek Bailey.

JOHN PICARD *tbn*
B 17.5.34 **A** North Lodge, Essendon, Herts.
T Essendon 519 & Potters Bar 58191. **Agent**
Coda Promotions. **T** 01–607 4272. **Curr** Own
band, London J Big Band (Greig). **Prev**
Humphrey Lyttelton, Tony Coe Quin, own
bands, Bruce Turner Jump Band. **Pref**
Coltrane, Rollins, Mingus, Ellington, Monk,
Coe, Kenny Wheeler, Herbie Hancock,
Frank Rosolino, Freddie Hubbard, Elvin
Jones. **Rec** 'Phil On Drums' (Phil Seamen) 77
(1971), 'Our Kind Of Music' (Brian Lemon)
77 (1970), and w Lyttelton, Turner.

ROGER 'BUTCH' POTTER *el-bs, bs, g*
B 29.7.43 **A** 48 Brownlow Road, Bounds
Green, London N11. **Prev** Pete Brown's
Battered Ornaments, Arthur Brown,
Westbrook, Stagecoach (Khan). **Rec** 'Mike
Westbrook Live' Cadillac (1972).

RAY PREMRU *bs-tbn, bs-tpt, comp, conductor*
B 6.6.34 **A** 33 Springfield Gardens, London
NW9 0RY. **T** 01–205 0475. **Curr** Bobby
Lamb–Premru Orch. **Prev** Larry Crosley
Octet (USA), Kenny Baker Dozen, Dill Jones
Quin, Eddie Thompson Quin, Friedrich Gulda
Euro-jazz Orch. **Fest, conc** Camden JF '74,
Shaw Theatre, QEH (guests Gulda, Buddy
Rich, Louie Bellson). **Fav rec** 'Live At Ronnie

Scott's Club' (Lamb–Premru) BBC (1971).
Mem events Concerts w Lamb–Premru Orch
and Gulda Euro-jazz Orch (inc J J Johnson,
Art Farmer, Cannonball Adderley, Ron
Carter, Mel Lewis). **Pref** Bill Holman,
Wheeler, George Russell, Mulligan, Parker,
Gulda, Brookmeyer, Teagarden, Armstrong,
Getz, Alan Branscombe, Alan Clare, Ralph
Burns, Johnny Mandel etc. **Rec** 'Conversations
– A Drum Spectacular' (Lamb–Premru
featuring Rich, Bellson. Kenny Clare)
Parlophone (1971).

EDDIE PRÉVOST *drums*
B 22.6.42 **Agent** Victor Schonfield, 26 Avondale
Park Gardens, London W11 4PR.
T 01-727 1133. **Curr** AMM (duo w Lou Gare)
since '65, AMM With Strings (w Gare,
Mattos, Meggido), Eddie Prevost Band (inc
Gare, Gold, Meggido, Mattos, Geoff
Hawkins). **Prev** Various editions of AMM
since '65 (originally trio w Keith Rowe and
inc at various times Cornelius Cardew &
Mike Westbrook, working mainly as duo
since '72). **Fav rec** 'To Hear And Back Again'
Emanem (due for release). **Mem event**
Meeting Gare. **Rec** w AMM listed under
Gare's name. Prevost is an exceptionally
inventive and individual musician whose
long term partnership w Gare has produced
one of the most sympathetic duos in free
improvised music.

DUDU PUKWANA *alto, p*
B 18.7.38 **A** 52 Fordingley Road, London W9.
T 01-969 1175. **Agent** John Jack, 41
Sandringham Buildings, Charing Cross Road,
London WC2. **T** 01-836 6006. **Curr** Own band
Jabula–Spear (co-led w Bahula), Brotherhood
of Breath (MacGregor). **Prev** Chris
MacGregor's Blue Notes & Sext, came to
UK w MacGregor '65, Bob Stuckey Quar,
Centipede (Tippett), Isipingo (Miller), John
Martyn, own band Assagai (inc Feza, Gred
Coker, Bizo Mngqikana), own band Spear (inc
Feza, Moholo, Miller etc). **Conc** Lambeth
New Music Soc Brixton Town Hall '73. **Fest**
Berlin (w Brotherhood of Breath) '74,
Amsterdam (w Spear) '74, Heidelberg '75.
Tours Many app on Continent inc Willisau,
Bregenz, Innsbruck, Rheims, Rouen '75.
Fav rec 'Flute Music' (Spear) Caroline (1974),

Dudu Pukwana

'Brotherhood' (MacGregor) RCA Victor (1971). **Mam events** Berlin F '74 w MacGregor, Jabula–Spear at 100 Club Apr '75. **Pref** Coleman, Ellington, Ben Webster, Stevie Wonder, John & Beverley Martyn. **Rec** 'In The Townships' (Spear) Caroline (1973), 'Septober Energy' (Centipede) RCA (1971), and w MacGregor. An explosive extrovert alto stylist.

COLIN PURBROOK *p, bs, arr*
B 26.2.36 **A** Flat 55, Apsley House, Finchley Road, St John's Wood, London NW8.
T 01–722 8463. **Curr** Own trio, sext. **Prev** Sandy Brown–Dick Heckstall Smith (bs), Sandy Brown '57–'60, Ronnie Scott '60, Allan Ganley '61, own group co-led w Tony Coe '61–'63, acc Benny Goodman '64, Gene Cottrell. **Rec** w Tubby Hayes.

CHRIS PYNE *tbn*
T 01–986 8388. **Curr** Mike Pyne Sext, John Taylor Sext, Alan Cohen Band, John Stevens' Dance Orch, Ronnie Ross' 8 To 1. **Prev** The Band (R Scott), Dankworth, Gibbs, Coe Wheeler & Co, Bobby Lamb–Ray Premru Orch. **Rec** 'The Source' (SME) Tangent (1970), 'Trailways Express' (Philly Joe Jones) Polydor (1968), and w Tracey, Taylor, Gibbs, Wheeler, Dankworth, Scott.

MIKE PYNE *p, occasionally cornet & tpt*
A 5a Pixham Court, Lake Road, London SW19. **T** 01–946 8838. **Curr** Humphrey Lyttelton, own trio, own sext (inc Warleigh, Wheeler, C Pyne, Matthewson, Levin). **Prev** Own quar, played tenor w Alexis Korner in early '60s, Les Condon Quar, Tubby Hayes Quar in mid '60s; acc Hank Mobley, Roland Kirk, Philly Joe Jones in London in late '60s. **Rec** 'In Swinger' (Lyttelton) Happy Bird (1974), 'The Source' (SME) Tangent (1970), '21 Years On' (Lyttelton) Polydor (1969), 'Change-Is' (Rendell–Carr) Columbia (1969), 'Trailways Express' (Philly Joe Jones) Polydor (1968), 'Mexican Green' (Hayes) Fontana (1967), and w Gibbs.

TERRI QUAYE *conga, singer*
A 10 Balham Park Mansions, Balham Park Road, London SW12. **T** 01–675 1208. **Curr** Amalgam (Watts), John Stevens' Dance Orch.

Prev With her father Cab Kaye's group as a child, w Roland Kirk at Scott's '70, Osibisa, Assagai (w Pukwana etc), Chris MacGregor in Paris '71, Elvin Jones & Lee Morgan in USA '71. **Tours** Travelled widely on Continent, France, Germany, Poland, Switzerland, Mediterranean, Ghana '70, New York '71. Also jazz photographer since '71 w her photos included in John Jeremy's 'Jazz Is Our Religion' film.

FREDDY RANDALL *tpt, cornet*
B 6.5.21 **A** 5 Epping New Road, Buckhurst Hill, Essex. **T** 01–504 1183. **Agent** Miss H Carey, The Shieling, Epping New Road, Buckhurst Hill, Essex. **T** 01–504 6053. **Curr** Own All Stars since '72. **Prev** Took up tpt '37, Will DeBarr '38, own St Louis 4 '39, own Dixieland Band '43, Freddy Mirfield Garbage Men '44, guest soloist w Ted Heath, Stanley Black, Cyril Stapleton, Henry Hall, Harry Parry, Ambrose, Paul Fenoulhet. App w Pee Wee Russell, Wild Bill Davison, Bud Freeman, Teddy Wilson, Sidney Bechet, Bill Coleman, Dorseys, McPartlands, Rex Stewart. **Fest** Montreux '73 (w own band). **Mem events** Conc RFH and presentation afterwards to Princess Elizabeth June '51, US tour May '56. **Pref** Eddie Condon & Chicago style jazz. **Rec** 'Freddie Randall–Dave Shepherd All Stars Live At The Montreux Jazz Fest' Black Lion (1973), 'Black Lion At Montreux' (various groups) Black Lion (1973), 'Freddy Randall–Dave Shepherd All Stars' Black Lion (1972), 'Freddie Randall And His Famous Jazz Band' Rediffusion (1971).

LUCKY RANKU *g*
A 4 Milner Road, Morden, Surrey. **T** 01–648 1821. **Curr** Malombo Music (Bahula), Jabula–Spear (Bahula, Pukwana). **Prev** Malombo during '60s (in S Africa), came to UK from SA '73.

ARMAN RATIP *p, comp, arr*
B 7.10.42 **A** 35 Willoughby Road, London N8 0JG; Cengiz Sok, Yuva Apt, Kat 2 No 9, Lefkosa, Mersin 10, Turkey. **T** 01–340 7452. **Curr** Own trio, quar, quin (inc Feza, M Nichols, Bailey), solo perf. **Prev** Came to UK from Cyprus '60, studied European

Arman Ratip

classical music in Cyprus. **Fav rec** *Nightmare*
on 'The Spy From Istanbul' (own quar)
Regal Zonophone (1973). **Pref** Turkish music,
Dave Brubeck, Lalo Schifrin. **Rec** 'Introducing
The Arman Ratip Trio' Columbia (1970).

KEN RATTENBURY *tpt, p, comp*
B 10.9.20 **A** Way Down Yonder, 299
Birmingham Road, Walsall WS5 3QA. **Curr**
Own Jazzman, own Jazz Four. **Prev** Freelance,
many associations. Radio broadcasts of own
compositions inc Jazz Piano Concerto '51,
'Mirror To Bix' Suite, 'Seven Ages Of Man'
tone poem, 'Rime Of The Ancient Mariner'.
Fav rec Series of records of fairy stories w
jazz-tinged incidental music under own name
on EMI. **Mem events** Entertaining Bobby
Hackett at home and playing trumpet duets w
him into the small hours. **Pref** Armstrong,
Hackett, Ellington, Benjamin Britten,
Vaughan Williams, Beethoven, Mozart,
Dankworth.

Don Rendell

DON (DONALD PERCY) RENDELL *tenor,
sop, clar, f*
B 4.3.26 **A** 24 Weir Hall Gardens, London
N18 1BH. **T** 01–807 7831. **Curr** Own 5 (inc
Barbara Thompson), Dankworth, Herman
Wilson Orch, Dave Hancock Band, freelance
solo work. **Prev** Duncan Whyte, George
Evans, Oscar Rabin, Frank Weir, Dankworth 7
'50–'53, own group '54–'55, Ted Heath '55,
European tour w Stan Kenton '56, Woody
Herman '59, own quin inc Graham Bond
'61–'62, own quin w Ian Carr '64–'69, own
quin inc Stan Robinson '70–'71, Garrick.
Fest Antibes '68, Hamburg J Workshop '68
Jazz Expo '69 (Royal Fest Hall), Newcastle
'70 & '72, Belfast '71, Camden '73, Camden
JF '74, Newcastle JF '75. **Fav rec** 'Dusk Fire'
(Rendell–Carr) Columbia (1966), 'Space
Walk' (own 5) Columbia (1971). **Mem events**
Working w Billie Holiday '55, Kenton,
Herman, Bond, Carr, Robinson, Thompson.
Pref Herman, Davis, Coltrane, Young,
Parker, Garrick, Ardley, Lowther, Themen,
Lemer, Herman Wilson, B Thompson,
Robinson, Dave Green, Tomkins. Active in
music educ e.g. Barry Summer School '74 &
'75, Dankworth's Wavendon Easter Course,
Royal Academy of Music workshop. **Rec**
'Change-Is' (1969) 'Live' (1969) 'Phase III'

(1968) 'Shades of Blue' (1965) (Rendell–Carr,
all on Columbia), 'Live at the Avgarde
Gallery' Spotlite (1973), 'Greek Variations'
(Ardley) Columbia (1969), Integration'
(D'Silva) Columbia (1969), 'We Love You
Madly' (Tracey) Columbia (1969), 'Afro–Jazz'
(Guy Warren) Columbia (1968), 'Roarin' '
(quin feat Bond) Jazzland (1961), and w
Garrick, Dankworth. Rendell is one of the
most widely respected and consistent British
jazz musicians of his generation. Influenced
originally by Lester Young, in the '60s his
playing began to show the impact of Coltrane,
developing to a personal and highly expressive
style.

TONY RICHARDS *drums*
B 14.1.38 **A** 22 Balfour Crescent, Tettenhall
Road, Wolverhampton. **T** 0902–751901. **Curr**
Own trio, quar. **Conc** at various coll & univ.
Mem events Working w Johnny Griffin,
Sonny Stitt, Gerry Mulligan, Bobby Hackett,
Bud Freeman. **Pref** Elvin Jones, Tony
Williams, Roy Haynes, Jack DeJohnette,
Oxley, Coltrane, Parker, Rollins, Davis,
Tyner, Hancock, Joe Henderson.

Howard Riley

FRANK RICOTTI *vib, perc, alto, clar*
A 12 Sefton Avenue, London NW7.
T 01–959 1205. **Curr** Impulse (Brian Miller),
Ian Hamer Sext. **Prev** NYJO (Ashton), Collier,
Gibbs, New J Orch (Ardley), own quar (inc
Spedding, Lawrence), quar w Dave Gelly
'68–'69, Gyroscope (Beck) '73–'74. **Rec**
'Ricotti and Albuquerque' (w Michael
Albuquerque) Pegasus (1971), quar 'Our
Point Of View' CBS (1969), and w Ardley,
Beck, Tracey, Beckett, Gibbs, Winstone.

HOWARD RILEY *p, comp*
B 16.2.43 **A** 2 Bennett Park, Blackheath,
London SE3 9RB. **T** 01–852 0219. **Curr** Own
trio (w Guy, Oxley), Tony Oxley Sext, solo perf,
London J Comp Orch (Guy). **Prev** Bachelor
and Master's degree in music Bangor Univ '66,
Master of Music degree Indiana Univ '67,
Evan Parker Quar '65, Dave Baker (USA),
duo w John MacLaughlin, own trio since '67.
Conc Comp for chorus, orch, trio, scat singer,
coloratura soprano and electronics perf at
Proms '69. Comp for string quar, chamber
ensemble etc. **Fest** Donaueschingen New

Music, Berlin JF, Paris Bi-ennale, York. Tutor
in jazz/improv music Guildhall School of
Music since '70, tutor Barry J Summer School
'74 & '75. **Fav rec** 'Synopsis' (trio) Incus,
'Singleness' (solo) Chariavari due for release.
Pref Creative rather than imitative music in
any idiom. **Rec** trio 'Flight' Turtle (1971),
'The Day Will Come' CBS (1970), 'Angle'
CBS Realm (1968–9), 'Discussions'
Opportunity (1967), solo 'Solo Imprints'
Jaguar (cassette), and w Oxley, London J
Comp Orch. Riley has been at the forefront of
the jazz avant garde in Britain for some years.
His close knit trio comprises three of the most
talented musicians in free improvised music in
this country at present.

SAMMY RIMINGTON *clar, alto, sop, tenor,
f, g*
B 29.4.42 **A** 37 Stradella Road, Herne Hill,
London SE24. **T** 01–274 5766. **US Agent**
Crescent Jazz Productions. **Curr** Louisiana
Shakers (Duke Burrell) (USA) since '74, own
quar on Continent. **Prev** Ken Colyer, Henry
Red Allen, Zutty Singleton, Thomas
Jefferson, own band. **Tours** USA w Louisiana
Shakers, Europe w Barney Bigard Wingy
Manone & Legends of Jazz '75, Holland &
Belgium w own quar '75. Breda J Fest May
'75. **Fav rec** 'Louisiana Shakers On Tour'
Crescent Jazz Productions (USA) (1974).
Mem event 'A Night In New Orleans' conc w
Barney Bigard etc Los Angeles Sept '74. **Rec**
Quin 'New Orleans Music' California Condor
(US Import) (1973), 'Everybody's Talking
'Bout Sammy' 77 (1969).

Frank Roberts

GRAHAM ROBB *bs, el-bs, keyboards, comp,
arr*
B 7.8.50 **A** 33 Kersland Street, Glasgow.
T Kelvin 7829. **Curr** Own band Windjammer
since '74, BBC Scottish Symphony Orch (bs),
Head (w Kyle etc) (el-bs). Graduate RSAM
'71. **Fest** Dunkirk JF '71, '72 & '75. **Rec**
'Red Dwarf' (Head) Canon (*c*1975), 'GTF'
(Head) Head (*c*1972).

FRANK ROBERTS *p, el-p*
A 17 Castellain Road, London W9.
T 01–286 6208. **Curr** Own quin Embryo (w
Pearce, Mothle etc), Joy (Dvorak),
Jabula–Spear (Bahula, Pukwana), own trio.

Prev Cirrus (Herman), Band Tank (Frank Tankowski), Klaus Doldinger, Naima (Francis).

STAN ROBINSON *tenor, clar, f*
A 92 Trowbridge Road, Harold Hill, Essex. **T** Ingrebourne 4235. **Curr** Own quin. **Prev** Don Rendell 5, Ronnie Ross Sext. **Rec** 'Space Walk' (Rendell) (1971), 'Greek Variations' (Ardley) (1969), 'Change-Is' (Rendell–Carr) (1969) – all on Columbia.

JIMMY ROCHE *g*
B 24.8.47 **A** 26c Sharsted Street, London SE17. **T** 01–735 8990. **Curr** Major Surgery (Don Weller). **Prev** Colosseum (Jon Hiseman), Boris (w Jamie Muir etc) *c* '71, East of Eden (rock group). **Rec** 'St Vitus' Dance' (Major Surgery) Jaguar (Cassette).

NEIL ROGERS *drums*
B 30.5.45 **A** 16a Upper Park Road, London NW3. **T** 01–722 1833. **Curr** John Macnicol Quin, Broken Biscuits (Biscoe), Pete Saberton Sext, teaching. **Prev** John Williams Octet, Jeff Scott Quin, Alan Wakeman, Phil Broadhurst 10 piece, dance bands. **Tours** Spain w Bob Weedon Trio '73 & '74. **Mem events** Playing w Sulzmann, Beck, Matthewson. **Pref** Jack DeJohnette, Tony Williams, Bobby Hutcherson, Joe Henderson, Woody Shaw, Chick Corea, Ron Carter, Stanley Clarke, Pharoah Sanders, Elvin Jones.

ANNIE ROSS
singer, songwriter, actress
B 25.7.30 **Agent** Don Norman, 37 Devonshire Place, London W1. **T** 01–486 5643. **Curr** Theatre work as actress, occasional conc etc. **Prev** Lionel Hampton Orch in Europe '53, Jack Parnell '54, Tony Crombie '54, Lambert–Hendrix–Ross (w Dave Lambert, Jon Hendrix) '58–'62, many stage reviews & cabaret work in England, Europe & USA, own night club Annie's Room in London '60s, own one woman show Hampstead Theatre Club '71. **Conc** w Nat Youth J Orch at Wavendon May '75. Radio Manchester F May '74.
Rec 'You And Me Baby' Decca (*c*1970).
Annie Ross' comparative inactivity in jazz at present is a cause for regret. One of the finest jazz singers to have come out of Britain, she

couples sophistication and superb technique in standards and songs of her own composition.

RONNIE ROSS *bari, f, also tenor, alto, clar, piccolo, bs-clar, alto-f*
B 2.10.33 **A** 49a Oakhead Road, Balham, London SW12. **T** 01–673 2056. **Curr** Own band 8 To 1, Stan Tracey, Duncan Lamont, Tony Kinsey, Bob Leaper. **Prev** Kinsey, Ted Heath, Don Rendell, Newport International Band Newport JF '58, Woody Herman, Jazz Makers (co-led w Allan Ganley) formed '58 & US tour '59, MJQ Brit conc Nov '59, Maynard Ferguson, Friedrich Gulda, John Lewis, Tubby Hayes, Bill LeSage, own quar, quin, sext. **Fav rec** 'European Windows' (John Lewis Orch) RCA (rec Stuttgart 1958). **Pref** Parker, Coltrane, Wheeler, Mulligan, Clifford Brown. **Rec** 'Skid Marks' (Jimmy Skidmore) Silverline (1972), sext 'Cleopatra's Needle' Fontana (1968), 'Bill LeSage–Ronnie Ross Quartet' World Record Club (1963), and w Hayes, Tracey, LeSage. Originally strongly influenced by Gerry Mulligan, Ross has been widely recognized in Britain and abroad as an excellent and inventive baritone stylist.

Daryl Runswick

RON RUBIN *p, bs*
B 8.7.33 **A** 4 Willoughby Road, London NW3. **T** 01–435 5548. **Curr** John Picard Band, Lennie Best Quar, Johnny Burch Trio, own trio, duo w Ron Matthewson, solo p. **Prev** Sandy Brown–Al Fairweather All Stars, Bruce Turner Jump Band, Mike Taylor Trio, Lennie Felix Trio, Michael Garrick Sext, Barbara Thompson–Art Themen. Solo p residency in Spain for 3 years. **Fest** Bracknell July '75 (w Lennie Best). **Mem event** Tour w Billy Eckstine, Charlie Persip, Bobby Tucker. **Pref** Ellington, Bill Evans, Webster, Tatum, Hank Jones, Ray Bryant, Teddy Wilson, Cliff Jackson, Phineas Newborn Jr. **Rec** 'Mike Taylor Trio' Columbia (1966).

DARYL RUNSWICK *bs, el-bs*
A 61 Ellesmere Avenue, London NW7 3EX. **T** 01–959 5796. **Curr** Ray Russell, Brian Cooper Orch, session work. **Prev** Dankworth. **Tours** w Dankworth. **Rec** 'Joy Unlimited' (Harry Beckett) Cadillac (1974), 'Live At Carnegie Hall' (Cleo Laine) RCA (1973), 'Child Song' (Lowther) Deram (1970),

'Atlantic Bridge' (w Jim Phillip, Mike McNaught, Mike Travis) Dawn (1970), and w Russell, Dankworth.

ALAN RUSHTON *drums*
A c/o 37 Limes Gardens, Southfields, London SW18. **T** 01–874 0329. **Curr** Ray Russell Quin. Resident on BBC TV children's prog 'Play Away'. **Rec** w Russell.

RAY RUSSELL *g*
A 37 Limes Gardens, Southfields, London SW18. **T** 01–874 0329. **Curr** Own quin (w Beckett, Windo, Runswick, Rushton), Joy Unlimited (Beckett). **Prev** Graham Bond, own quar in late '60s, own groups since '60s. **Rec** 'Secret Asylum' Freedom (1973), 'Running Man' RCA Neon (1972), 'Live At The ICA' RCA Victor (1971), 'The Very Last Time' CBS (1971), 'Rock Workshop' CBS (1970), 'Rites And Rituals' CBS (1970), 'Dragon Hill' CBS (1969), 'Turn Circle' CBS (1968), and w Bob Downes, Beckett, Gibbs. An exciting and original guitarist who combines influences from jazz and rock in a style which uses the sound capabilities of the guitar to the full.

PAUL RUTHERFORD *tbn*

Paul Rutherford

A 60 Ashburnham Place, Greenwich, London SE10. **T** 01–691 1697. **Curr** Solo perf, John Stevens' Dance Orch, Alan Cohen, Westbrook. **Prev** SME (Stevens), Iskra 1903 (w Bailey, Guy), London J Comp Orch (Guy), Tony Oxley Sext, New J Orch (Ardley), Globe Unity Orch (Alexander von Schlippenbach, Peter Kowald), Peter Kowald Quin. **Other** Tutor Lambeth J Summer School July '75. **Rec** 'Live In Wuppertal' (Globe Unity Orch) FMP (Incus import) (1973), 'Peter Kowald Quintet' Free Music Production (1972), 'Iskra 1903' Incus double album (1970–2), 'Challenge' (SME) Eyemark (1966), and w Oxley, LJCO. A superb trombonist who can function effectively in a wide range of jazz contexts, Rutherford's lyrical approach to free music is typified in the work of Iskra 1903.

DAVE SAUL *p, el-p, comp*
A 33 Kersland Street, Glasgow. **T** Kelvin 7829. **Curr** Own band Equinox since '73. Various groups in Glasgow & Edinburgh. Scottish TV broadcasts w Oxley & Matthewson. **Rec** Solo track on 'Red Dwarf' (Head) Canon (*c*1975).

RONNIE SCOTT *tenor, sop*
B 28.1.27 **A** c/o Ronnie Scott's Club, 47 Frith
Street, London W1. **T** 01–439 0747. **Curr** Own
quar (inc Louis Stewart, Martin Drew, Kenny
Baldock) since '75. **Prev** Johnny Claes,
Ambrose, Tito Burns, Cab Kaye, Ted Heath,
Jack Parnell '52, own band '53–'55, Jazz
Couriers (co-led w Tubby Hayes) '57–'59,
Clarke-Boland Orch, own group The Band
(inc Surman, Warleigh, Pyne, Beck,
Matthewson, Clare, Oxley) '68, own trio
(w Mike Carr, Bobby Gien/Tony
Crombie) '72–'75. **Tours** Portugal France
Belgium Switzerland Germany w own trio
'73, Europe w Francy Boland Sext '73, USA &
Australia w own trio '74 (Carnegie Hall NYC
conc). Own jazz night club since '59. **Rec** trio
'Scott At Ronnie's' RCA (1973), 'Live At
Ronnie Scott's' (The Band) CBS Realm (1968),
and w Clarke–Boland Orch, Hayes. Scott is as
well known for the club he has been running
for a decade and a half as for his booting
swinging hard bop tenor. In recent years,
touring in Britain and abroad w his trio, he
has reaffirmed his status as a dependable and
often exciting player.

HANK SHAW (HENRY SHALOFSKY) *tpt*
B 23.6.26 **A** 111 Dargate Road, Yorkletts,
New Whitstable, Kent. **T** Whitstable 63381.
Curr Bebop Preservation Society (LeSage)
since '71, Colin Purbrook Sext, Dankworth.
Prev Teddy Foster, Oscar Rabin '42, Vic Lewis
'48, Maynard Ferguson & Oscar Peterson in
Montreal '49, Jack Parnell '52, Ronnie Scott
'54, Tony Crombie, Joe Harriott Quin
'59–'60. **Rec** w Stan Tracey, Dankworth. A
crackling fleet bop stylist.

DAVE SHEPHERD *clar*
B 7.2.29 **A** 41 Blackacre Road, Theydon Bois,
Essex. **T** Theydon Bois 2669. **Curr** Own quin,
sext. **Prev** Joe Daniels, various pick-up
touring units (eg Jazz Today Unit), Freddy
Randall. **Fest, conc** Montreux JF '73, app w
Teddy Wilson, Bud Freeman. **Fav rec** 'Running
Wild' (Wilson) Black Lion (1973). **Pref**
Goodman, Artie Shaw, Irving Fazola, Bob
Wilber, Tatum, Getz, Peterson, Condon. **Rec**
'Live At Montreux' (Randall–Shepherd)
Black Lion (1973), 'Freddy Randall–Dave

Shepherd All Stars' Black Lion (1972), quin 'Shepherd's Delight' 77 (1969), and w Teddy Wilson.

Alan Skidmore

ALAN SKIDMORE *tenor, sop, f, alto-f, drums*
B 21.4.42 **A** 9 Badminton Close, Boreham Wood, Herts. **T** 01–953 0533. **Curr** SOS (w Surman, Osborne) since '73 – first UK app Apr '74, John Warren Orch, Ninesense (Dean), own quar. **Prev** Eric Delaney, Dankworth, Ronnie Scott, Tubby Hayes, Graham Collier, Alexis Korner, Westbrook, Gibbs, Maynard Ferguson, Surman, Brotherhood of Breath (MacGregor), Keith Tippett, Irene Schweitzer, Volker Kriegel, Rolf Kuhn, Chick Corea, Ian Carr, Georgie Fame, Stan Tracey, own quin. Toured Germany w John Warren Orch summer '75. **Mem event** Montreux JF '69. **Rec** 'SOS' Ogun (1975), quin 'TCB' Philips (1970), quin 'Once Upon A Time' Decca (1969), 'Jazz In Britain '68–'69' (w various musicians) Decca (1968-9), and w Gibbs, Westbrook, MacGregor, Surman, Tracey, Harry Beckett, Norma Winstone etc. Skidmore's tenor style is marked by a big tone and a muscular multinoted approach. He is an exciting soloist who fits easily and effectively into many areas of contemporary jazz.

JIMMY SKIDMORE *tenor*
B 8.2.16 **A** 22 Heath Lodge, Danesbury Park Road, Welwyn, Herts. **T** Welwyn 5515. **Curr** Own band. **Prev** Harry Parry, George Shearing '42–'45, Ralph Sharon '50–'52, own band '52, Jack Parnell Orch, Vic Lewis Orch, George Chisholm, Eric Delaney Orch '54–'56, Humphrey Lyttelton '56–'61. **Rec** 'Skid Marks' (w Willie Garnett, Ronnie Ross, Branscombe etc) Silverline (c1972), 'Humphrey Lyttelton Plays Standards' Columbia (1960) reissued on Marble Arch.

BRIAN SMITH *tenor, sop, f, alto-f, clar*
B 3.1.39 **A** 7b Gunnersbury Avenue, Ealing Common, London W5. **T** 01–992 2411.
Agent Irene Smith, address above. **Curr** Pacific Eardrum (MacRae), own quar. **Prev** Nucleus (Carr), Maynard Ferguson, Gyroscope (Beck), Gibbs, Westbrook, Collier, Alan Price, Tubby Hayes. **Tours** USA w

Ferguson '74, Carnegie Hall NYC (Newport
Fest) July '74, Japan May '74; Newport JF
'70 w Nucleus. **Fav rec** *MacArthur Park* on
'MF Horn' (Ferguson) CBS (1973), *Whapatiti*
on 'Roots' (Nucleus) Vertigo (1973). **Pref** Ed
Hall, Clifford Brown–Max Roach, 'Kind of
Blue' (Davis), 'Live At The Village Vanguard'
(Coltrane), Frank Zappa, Herbie Hancock.
Rec w Carr, 'The Source' (SME) Tangent
(1970), 'Septober Energy' (Tippett) RCA
(1971).

COLIN (RANGER) SMITH *tpt, flug-h*
B 20.11.34 **A** 42 Hillfield Road, London
NW6 1PZ. **T** 01-435 2499. **Curr** John Picard,
Stan Greig. **Prev** Acker Bilk. **Fav rec** 'Dixieland
Now And Then' (Dixieland A/S) Line (1974).
Pref Armstrong, Buck Clayton, Henry Red
Allen, Clifford Brown, Eldridge, Hubbard,
Ellington.

PAT SMYTHE *keyboards*
A 54 Duncan Terrace, London N1. **T**
01-226 0910. **Curr** Coe Wheeler & Co, Ronnie
Ross' 8 To 1. **Prev** Dankworth, Dizzy Reece,
Joe Harriott Quin, Harriott–John Mayer
Double Quin, Holdsworth–Warleigh Quin.
Fest Chateauvallon '73 w own trio plus Alan
Holdsworth. **Mem events** Recording w Getz &
Paul Gonsalves, playing w Harriott, Ben
Webster, Coe, Wheeler, Holdsworth. **Pref**
Tatum, Jarrett, B Evans, Parker, Coltrane,
Dolphy, Rollins. **Rec** w Harriott inc 'Indo–Jazz
Fusions II' Columbia (1967), 'Movement'
Columbia (1963), 'Abstract' Columbia
(1961–2), 'Free Form' Jazzland (1960), 'Joe
Harriott Memorial' One-Up (1960–7).
Smythe's best work on record is on the early
'60s albums by Harriott's remarkable
pioneering free form quintet.

HARRY SOUTH *p, comp, arr, MD*
B 7.9.29 **A** 17 Palace Court, Palace Road,
London SW2 3ED. **Curr** Own big band since
'60. **Prev** Basil Kirchin (arr), Ronnie Scott Big
Band '55 (arr), Tony Crombie '56, Tubby
Hayes, Joe Harriott '58–'60, Ronnie Ross,
Dankworth, 4 yrs w Dick Morrissey. Comp for
films etc. **Fav rec** 'After Lights Out' (Tubby
Hayes Quin) Tempo (1956). **Mem event**
Playing w Count Basie for 2 wks while acting
as MD for Georgie Fame. **Rec** 'Presenting

The Harry South Big Band' Mercury (1966),
'Sound Venture' (w Georgie Fame) Columbia
(1965) and w Morrissey etc.

CHRIS SPEDDING *g*
A 7 Roundacre, Inner Park Road, Wimbledon,
London SW19. **T** 01–788 4959. **Curr** Session
work in rock and pop music & w various
groups, John Cale, Roy Harper. **Prev** Nat
Temple, Tommy Kinsman, Sid Phillips,
Frank Ricotti Quar, Gibbs, Pete Brown's
Battered Ornaments '67–'69 Westbrook,
Nucleus (Carr) '70–'71, Jack Bruce, Sharks
(rock group) '72–'74, extensive session work.
Tours w Cale '74, Harper '75, USA w Sharks
'74. **Rec** 'Harmony Row' (Bruce) Polydor
(1971), 'Deep Down Heavy' (Bob Downes)
Music for Pleasure (1970), 'Songs For A Tailor'
(Bruce) Polydor (1969), 'Greek Variations'
(Ardley) Columbia (1969), 'Our Point Of View'
(Ricotti) CBS (1969), numerous rock albums,
and w Nucleus, Gibbs, Westbrook, Dick
Heckstall-Smith.

ED SPEIGHT *g*
A c/o Langsett, Westfields, Whiteleaf, Nr
Aylesbury, Bucks. **T** Princes Risborough 5808.
Curr Graham Collier since '72, Paz (w
Warleigh, Dick Crouch etc). **Prev** Ken Gibson,
duo w Lol Coxhill. **Conc** Sweden w Collier '75
– featured soloist on Collier's extended comp
comm by Swedish Radio. **Rec** w Collier,
Coxhill.

Bryan Spring

BRYAN SPRING *drums*
A 101 St Dunstan's Road, Barons Court,
London W6. **T** 01–748 3581. **Curr** Stan Tracey
Trio & Quar, Own trio. **Prev** Studied w
Philly Joe Jones; Frank Ricotti, Passport
(Klaus Doldinger), Bebop Preservation
Society (LeSage), Nucleus (Carr), Centipede
(Tippett). Tutor Lambeth J Summer School
July '75. **Rec** w Tracey, Joe Harriott,
Doldinger, Tippett. An excellent drummer
with a superb technique.

LARRY STABBINS *tenor, sop, f*
B 9.9.49 **A** 10 St Andrews Road, London W14.
T 01–385 5771. **Curr** Air, Gill's Band (Lyons).
Prev Centipede (Tippett), Solid Gold Cadillac
(Westbrook), duo w Ken Hyder, Nick Collins,
Put It All In (Hyder). **Pref** Coltrane, Rollins,
Derek Bailey. **Rec** 'Septober Energy'
(Centipede) RCA (1971).

John Stevens

JOHN STEVENS *drums, perc, cornet*
A Flat 4, 14 Blackesley Avenue, London W5.
T 01–998 4320. **Curr** Spontaneous Music
Ensemble (leader) since '66 (currently a duo w
Trevor Watts), Amalgam (Watts) since '68,
own Dance Orch (inc Watts, Tippett, Quaye,
Wheeler etc) since July '74, own jazz-rock
group Away (w Watts, Steve Hayton, Peter
Cowling) since Aug '75, Splinters (w Watts,
Tracey etc formerly inc Tubby Hayes, Phil
Seamen) since '72. **Prev** Playing drums since
'58, RAF School of Music, left RAF '64, club
gigs London '64–'66, house drummer at
Scott's Club '66, w John Tchicai on
Continent, Open Circle Quar (Tracey), Free
Space, Spontaneous Music Orch, Bobby
Bradford Quar, numerous earlier versions of
SME (inc Bailey, Rutherford, Parker, Wheeler,
Guy etc). **Tours, conc** Berlin '71 (SME),
concerts w Steve Lacy UK '74. Organizer
Little Theatre Club since '66, tutor in many
teaching situations & workshops. **Rec** 'SME
+ =SMO' A (1975), 'Face To Face' (SME)
Emanem (1973), 'The Crust' (Steve Lacy)
Emanem (1973), 'Love's Dream' (Bradford)
Emanem (1973), 'Bobby Bradford & SME'
Freedom (1971), SME 'So What Do You
Thing?' Tangent (1971), 'Birds Of A Feather'
Byg (1971), 'SME For CND' A Records (1970')
'The Source' Tangent (1970), 'Oliv' Marmalade
(1969), 'Karyobin' Island (1968), 'Challenge'
Eyemark (1966); for Amalgam albums see
under Watts' name. A key figure in the
British avant garde for a decade; Stevens'
SME has gone through numerous permutations
but has always remained influential, original
and in the forefront of European free
improvised music.

Louis Stewart

LOUIS STEWART *g*
B 5.1.44 **A** 1 St Anthony's Crescent,
Walkinstown, Dublin 12, Eire. **T** Dublin
506052. **Agent** Ronan Wilmot. **T** Dublin
685967. **Curr** Ronnie Scott Quar, own trio,
quar. **Prev** Tubby Hayes Quar & Orch,
Richard 'Groove' Holmes, Harry South,
Gerry Mulligan, Clark Terry, toured Europe 3
times w Benny Goodman Orch. Scholarship
to Berklee School of Music, Boston '69.
Working in Eire since '69. **Fest** Montreux '68
& '69, Bracknell July '75. **Mem event** Working
w Hayes. **Pref** Parker, Getz, Chick Corea,
B Evans.

Kathy Stobart

KATHY (KATHLEEN) STOBART *tenor, bari*
B 1.4.25 **A** 26 Norbury Court Road, Norbury, London SW16. **T** 01–764 0587. **Curr** Humphrey Lyttelton, freelance work. **Prev** Vic Lewis in late '40s & early '50s, own groups. **Conc** season at Scott's Club '74. **Tutor** NYJO Easter Course '74. **Rec** w Lyttelton.

ALAN STUART *tenor*
B 31.8.31 **A** 605 Uxbridge Road, Hatch End, Middx. **T** 01–428 4591. **Curr** Maurice Earl, Ray Crane, own octet. **Prev** Various j club work over 20 years. **Mem events** Broadcasts w own octet. **Pref** B Miller, Lowther, Sulzmann, etc.

Richard Sudhalter

RICHARD SUDHALTER *cornet, author*
B 28.12.38 **A** 61 Riverview Gardens, London SW13. **T** 01–748 1989. **Curr** New Paul Whiteman Orch (leader) since '74, own sext Commodore. **Prev** Various bands in USA, W Germany, own band Jazz Without Walls, Anglo–American Alliance (w J R T Davies etc). **Conc, fest** Camden JF '74 w NPWO & backing Bobby Hackett w Commodore. Fairfield Hall & QEH w NPWO, New York J Repertory Co Bix Beiderbecke Conc Carnegie Hall NYC '75. **Rec** 'Runnin' Wild' (NPWO) Argo (1975), 'Sweet and Hot' (Anglo–Amer Alliance) Regal (1968). **Book** *Bix – Man And Legend* Quartet (1974) (co-author).

Stan Sulzmann

STAN SULZMANN *sop, alto, tenor, f alto-f, piccolo, clar*
B 30.11.48 **A** 17 Meadow Gardens, Staines, Middx. **T** Staines 56313. **Curr** Own quar, John Taylor Sext, Gibbs, Warren, Brian Cooper Orch, Alan Cohen. **Prev** Dankworth, Clarke–Boland Orch, Kenny Wheeler, Gyroscope (Beck), Nat Youth J Orch, Collier. **Pref** Wheeler, Davis, Ravel, Debussy, Delius, Stockhausen (*Hymnen* & *Stimmung*), Frank Zappa. **Rec** w Collier, Dankworth, Warren, Beck, Gibbs.

MONTY SUNSHINE *clar*
Agent c/o Reg Tracey. **T** 01–500 1298. **Curr** Own band, freelance work. **Prev** Ken Colyer, Chris Barber through '50s, recreated Crane River JB (w Colyer, J R T Davies etc). **Tours** W Germany etc '75, works frequently on

Continent. **Rec** 'Monty Sunshine' Happy Bird (1974).

John Surman

JOHN SURMAN *bari, sop, bs-clar, p, synthesizer, comp*
A Knowle House, Warren Street, Charing, Ashford, Kent. **T** Charing (Kent) 2746. **Curr** SOS (w Skidmore, Osborne) (first app Brussels Oct '73, first UK app Apr '74). **Prev** J Workshop Plymouth Arts Centre w Westbrook while still at school, to London in early '60s, Westbrook '58–'68, The Band (R Scott) '68, own quar, octet (inc Beckett, Griffiths, Osborne, Skidmore, Taylor, Jackson, Miller) '68–'69, The Trio (w Stu Martin, Barre Phillips) '69–'72, Morning Glory (w Griffiths, Taylor, Terje Rypdal, Lawrence, Marshall) '73. **Tours, fest** Travelled widely in Europe and beyond w The Trio, Japan '70, many foriegn fests, conc, tours; Italy '73 (SOS), 6 wks at Paris Opera House w SOS '74, comp & perf music for contemp ballet 'Sablier Prison'. Top soloist award Montreux JF '68 & numerous awards & poll successes since. Tutor Lambeth J Summer School '74 & '75. **Rec** 'SOS' Ogun (1975), 'Citadel/Room 315' (Westbrook) RCA Victor (1975), 'Morning Glory' Island (1973), solo 'Westering Home' Island (1972), 'Conflagration' Dawn (1971), 'Tales Of The Algonquin' (John Warren) Deram (1971), 'The Trio' Dawn (1970), 'Where Fortune Smiles' (w John MacLaughlin) Dawn (1970), 'Bass Is' (Peter Warren) Enja (1970), 'How Many Clouds Can You See?' Deram (1969), 'Extrapolation' (MacLaughlin) Marmalade (1969), 'John Surman' Deram (1968), and w Gibbs, Westbrook, Lyttelton, Beckett. Surman has received world wide acclaim as possibly the finest baritonist in contemporary jazz. A strong personality and a creative adventurous musician, his playing on Westbrook's magnificent 'Citadel/Room 315' is some of his best recorded work to date.

CHRIS SUTTON *g*
A 15 Dundonald Road, Glasgow. **T** Western 2027. **Curr** Windjammer (Robb) since '74, Bobby Deans Big Band, teaching. **Prev** Studied at Berklee School of Music USA. **Rec** w Windjammer on 'Red Dwarf' (Head) Canon (*c*1975).

John Taylor

JOHN TAYLOR *p, comp, arr*
A 234 Conisborough Crescent, London SE6.
T 01–698 5296. **Curr** Own sext (inc Wheeler,
C Pyne, Sulzmann, Lawrence, Levin), Edge Of
Time (Winstone), Stan Sulzmann Quar. **Prev**
John Surman Quar & Octet, Dankworth,
Morning Glory (w Surman etc), Alan Skidmore
Quin, Gibbs. **Tutor** Lambeth J Summer
School July '75. **Rec** Sext 'Fragment' Jaguar
(Cassette) (c1974), 'Morning Glory' Island
(1973), trio/septet 'Pause And Think Again'
Turtle (1971), and w Surman, Skidmore,
Warren, Winstone, Gibbs, Beckett.

Art Themen

ART THEMEN *tenor, sop*
A 47 Montpelier Grove, Kentish Town,
London NW5. **T** 01–485 7750. **Curr** Michael
Garrick Sext, Stan Tracey Quar, Kinkade
(Alan Jackson), Alan Cohen Band, Themen–
Don Weller Quin. **Prev** Quin w Dave Gelly
'66, Barbara Thompson, Jack Bruce, Graham
Bond, Alexis Korner. **Fest** Bracknell JF July
'75 w Tracey. **Conc** Stan Tracey–Spike
Milligan 'Small Dreams Of A Scorpion'
Fairfield Hall Sept '75. **Rec** w Garrick, Alan
Cohen, Jack Bruce. Themen is also a surgeon
and only plays jazz part-time. He is
nevertheless one of the most impressive tenor
and soprano stylists currently active in
Britain.

Barbara Thompson

BARBARA THOMPSON *tenor, f, sop, alto,
bari, clar, piccolo, alto-f*
A c/o JCS. **Agent** Robert Masters. **Curr** Own
band Jubiaba (inc Wadsworth, Lowther,
Miller, LeSage, Cooke, Drew), own quar
since autumn '75, Don Rendell 5, Ardley,
Dankworth, Major Surgery (Weller), Derek
Wadsworth Sext. **Prev** Studied at Royal Coll
Music 'clar, f, p), New J Orch (Ardley) '60s,
Gibbs, Keef Hartley Band, Humble Pie,
Keith Emerson, own quin Paraphernalia to
'75. **Tours** Germany & Belgium (& TV
recordings), UK. **Fest** Camden JF '74 (perf of
own extended comp 'The Awakening'),
Merton, Chelmsford, Newcastle, Bracknell
JF '75. **Mem event** Transition from classical
music to jazz via New J Orch. **Pref** Ardley,
Rendell, Gibbs, Hiseman, Coltrane, Roland
Kirk, Tom Scott LA Fxpress, Stevie Wonder's
songs. **Rec** w New J Orch, Hiseman.

EDDIE (EDGAR CHARLES) THOMPSON
p, org

B 31.5.25 **A** 48 Kingswood Road, Goodmayes, Ilford, Essex. **T** 01–590 3798. **Curr** Own trio, solo perf. **Prev** Tony Crombie, Ronnie Scott, Carlo Krahmer; played in Paris w Parker, Davis, Hot Lips Page, Kenny Clarke. Moved to USA '62, played w many star musicians & resident at Hickory House NYC '63–'67 mostly as solo p. Returned to UK '72. **Conc** Wigmore Hall, Fairfield Hall, Edinburgh, Stockport, Manchester, Leeds, Southampton, Leicester. Newcastle JF '75. Acc Billy Butterfield in UK June '75. **Fav rec** *Tea For Two* (trio) & *Spring Is Here* (solo) on 'Out Of Sight' MPS (1970). **Mem event** Carnegie Hall conc NYC. **Pref** Tatum, Peterson, Getz, Ellington, Webster, Gershwin, Ravel, Bach, Delius, Carmichael, Kern. **Rec** Solo 'By Myself' 77 (1970). A fine pianist with a timeless style.

PETER THOMS *tbn*

B 8.10.47 **A** 61 Avonmore Road, West Kensington, London W14. **T** 01–603 4111. **Curr** Landscape (Walters), Tundra (Lawrie Brown), Brian Johnston Big Band. **Prev** Crumbs, Mick Collins Big Band, Renaissance. **Mem event** Coming to London from Australia. **Pref** Weather Report, Bruce Fowler, Tom Scott, Julian Priester, Gibbs, MacLaughlin, Billy Cobham. **Rec** 'Thursday 12th' (Landscape) Jaguar (cassette) (1974–5).

KEITH TIPPETT *p*

Keith Tippett

B 1947 **A** 21 Apex Close, The Avenue, Beckenham, Kent. **T** 01–658 0156. **Curr** Own band Ovary Lodge since '73 (inc Miller, Perry), Just Us (Dean), Isipingo (Miller), Amalgam (Watts), John Stevens' Dance Orch, Ninesense (Dean), Centipede (reformed '75). **Prev** Moved to London from Bristol '67, own group, own 50 piece orch Centipede, TNT (duo w Tracey) '74. App w Amalgam in Jack Gelber's play 'The Connection' Hampstead Theatre Club Sept–Oct '74. **Rec** 'Blueprint' RCA Victor (1972), 'Septober Energy' (Centipede) RCA double album (1971), 'Dedicated To You But You Weren't Listening' Vertigo (1970), 'You Are Here I Am There' Polydor (1969), and w King Crimson, Harold McNair. Tippett's monster orch of the early '70s is remembered with mixed affection

Trevor Tomkins

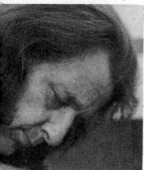

Stan Tracey

and amazement. Since then he has acted as catalyst to a great variety of contemporary jazz activity.

TREVOR TOMKINS *drums*
A 70 Rathfern Road, London SE6. **T** 01–690 1434. **Curr** Michael Garrick Trio, Sext since '60s, Quarternity (w Lowther, Lee, Green) since '74. **Prev** Took up drums at 18, mainstream bands, Roy Budd, transatlantic liners mid '60s, Don Rendell–Ian Carr Quin '64–'69, Rendell 5. Tutor Barry Summer School '75. **Rec** w Garrick, Rendell, Rendell–Carr, Amancio D'Silva, Guy Warren.

STAN TRACEY *p, previously also vib*
B 30.12.27 **A** 11 Mount Ephraim Road, Streatham, London SW16. **T** 01-769 4310. **Curr** Own trio (Green, Spring), quar (w Themen), octet. **Prev** Roy Fox, Eddie Thompson Quar '50, Laurie Morgan's Elevated Music, played on transatlantic liners '51, Kenny Baker, Ronnie Scott, Tony Crombie, Ted Heath Orch '57–'59, house pianist Ronnie Scott's Club '60–'68, own orch from '65, New Departures Quar (w Bobby Wellins), Open Circle Quar (w Watts, Stevens etc), duo w Mike Osborne, Amalgam (Watts), Tentacles (own big band) formed '72, TNT (duo w Tippett) '74. **Fest** Camden JF '74, Bracknell JF '75. **Conc** '30 Years In Jazz' celeb QEH Nov '73, 'Poems' Suite inspired by Spike Milligan's 'Small Dreams Of A Scorpion' premiere at Newcastle JF June '75 & London perf Fairfield Hall Sept '75, Shakespeare Birthday celeb Southwark Cath '74. **Other** Tutor Lambeth J Summer School July '75. **Rec** quar 'Captain Adventure' Steam (1975), 'Will Power' (w Gibbs, Ardley, Carr) Argo (1974), solo 'Alone At Wigmore Hall' Cadillac (1974), 'Original' (duo w Osborne) Cadillac (1972), trio 'Perspectives' Columbia (1972), quar 'Free'N' One' Columbia (1970), orch 'Seven Ages Of Man' (1970) 'We Love You Madly' (1969) 'Latin American Caper' (1969) 'Alice In Jazzland' (1966) – all on Columbia, quar 'With Love From Jazz' Columbia (1968) 'Under Milk Wood' Columbia (1965) reissued on Steam, 'Humming Bird' (Paul Gonsalves) Deram (*c*1968). Tracey has probably the most individual and instantly recognizable style of any British

jazz instrumentalist. Working through the influence of Ellington and Monk, he developed through the '60s to produce a recorded masterpiece in 'Under Milk Wood', explored free improvisation and, more recently, seems to be returning to more conventional music. Tracey's further explorations seem likely to add to his already significant contribution to jazz.

Bruce Turner

BRUCE TURNER *alto, clar*
B 5.7.22 **A** 1 Compton Lodge, Green Lanes, London N21. **T** 01–360 6734. **Curr** Humphrey Lyttelton since '70; app w John Chilton's Feetwarmers, Peter Ind Octet & Duo. **Prev** Billy Kay, Freddy Randall '48–'53, Kenny Baker's Dozen, Lyttelton '53–'57, Fawkes–Chilton Feetwarmers, own Jump Band '57–'64, Acker Bilk '66–'70. **Tours** Germany, Austria, Switzerland etc. 'In Concert' BBC TV '75. **Fav rec** 'In Swinger' (Lyttelton) Happy Bird (1974). **Mem event** Jump Band tour w Ben Webster '65. **Pref** Early Lee Konitz ('50–'55), Armstrong, Hodges, Mahler, Prokofiev. **Rec** 'Dixieland Now And Then' (Dixieland A/S) Line (1974), 'It's George' (Melly) Warner Bros (1974), 'South Bank Swing Session' (Lyttelton) Black Lion (1973), 'Doggin' Around' (Lyttelton) WAM (1972), 'An Evening With His Friends' (Alex Welsh) Black Lion (2 vols) (1971), 'Our Kind Of Music' (Brian Lemon) 77 (1970), 'Melody Maker Tribute To Louis Armstrong' Polydor (1970). A fine soloist whose style often reflects the strangely disparate influences of Hodges and Konitz.

PHILIPP WACHSMANN *violin w stereo amplification*
B 5.8.44 **A** 8 Alexandra House, St Mary's Terrace, London W2 1SF. **T** 01–262 8461. **Curr** Chamberpot (w Beswick, Mayo, Tony Wren) since '72, Alternative Music Orch (Brighton), Balance (w Malfatti, Perry etc), trio w Lytton & Malfatti, various free improv music groups. **Prev** Yggdrasil, Derek Bailey Band. **Tour** Sweden w Bailey & Evan Parker (trio) (& Radio recording). BBC 'Music In Our Time' broadcast '75 w Parker, Lytton, Bailey & Chamberpot. **Pref** Ethnic music & avant garde. Interest in improv & extension of conventional instrumental practices. **Rec**

'Balance' Incus (1973), Wachsmann–Lytton–
Malfatti Trio LP due for release on Rat Race.

DEREK WADSWORTH *tbn, arr, MD*
A 40 Brookwood Avenue, Barnes, London
SW13. **T** 01–876 1712. **Curr** Own sext, Jubiaba
(Thompson), Collier, session work & arranging
for various artists. **Prev** Jack Dorsey, Dusty
Springfield, Georgie Fame, own group (w
Lemer, Pyne etc), New J Orch (Ardley), John
Burch Octet, Diana Ross etc. Arrangements
for Alan Price, Georgie Fame, Humble Pie.
MD for musical 'Hair'. Rock session work,
film work. Directs MU jazz-rock workshops.
Rec w Ray Russell, New J Orch, Joh
Hiseman, Collier.

ALAN WAKEMAN *tenor, sop, Also alto, bari,
clar, bs-clar, f, p*
B 13.10.47 **A** 7 Wyndham Crescent, Hounslow,
Middx. **T** 01–572 1262. **Curr** Westbrook Orch,
Impulse (Brian Miller), own trio. **Prev** Nat
Youth J Orch (Ashton), Collier, London J
Comp Orch (Guy), Dankworth, Tony
Faulkner, Harry Beckett. **Tours** Most
recent Germany '74 w Beckett, Brit tour w
Westbrook '74. Soloist w John Williams'
'Four Pieces For Jazz Soloists &
Orchestra' '74. **Fav rec** 'Songs For My
Father' (Collier) Fontana (1970). **Imp event**
Montreux JF '71 w Collier. **Pref** Many Brit
musicians, Coltrane, King Curtis. **Rec**
'Citadel/Room 315' (Westbrook) RCA Victor
(1975), 'Mosaics' (Collier) Fontana (1971).

BOB WALLIS *tpt, singer*
A 15 Hatherleigh Gardens, Potters Bar,
Herts. **T** Potters Bar 56909. **Curr** Own
traditional band Storyville Jazzmen since '58.
Prev Formed own band in Bridlington,
Yorkshire '50 & led it until '57, Papa Bue's
Viking JB (Denmark) '56, Diz Disley JB '57,
Acker Bilk '58. **Tours** Germany,
Switzerland, Italy, Belgium, Denmark,
Sweden, Holland, Luxembourg etc. **Rec** 'Bob
Wallis' Storyville Jazzmen' WAM (c1974)
(same title) Storyville (1973).

JOHN WALTERS *f, sop, alto, comp*
A 7 Holder's Hill Drive, London NW4 1NC.
T 01–203 4335. **Agent** Rock Orchestrals,
32 Middleburg Street, Newbridge Road, Hull.

Ray Warleigh

T Hull 76842. **Curr** Own sext Landscape since
March '75 (w Thoms, Lee etc). **Prev** Landscape
(octet) '74–'75, John Walters Band '73–'74,
arrangements for Mick Collins, John Williams,
Gill Lyons. **Pref** Gil Evans, Ellington, Mingus,
Monk, 'Bitches Brew' (Davies), 'Fresh' (Sly
Stone), 'The Unanswered Question' (Charles
Ives). **Rec** 'Thursday 12th' (Landscape)
Jaguar (Cassette) (1974–5).

RAY WARLEIGH *alto, f*
A 80 Sinclair Road, London W14. **T**
01–603 8904. **Curr** Kenny Wheeler, Mike Pyne
Sext, John Stevens Dance Orch, Paz (w
Speight, Castle etc), session work. **Prev**
Warleigh–Alan Holdsworth Quin, Ronnie
Scott, Gibbs. **Rec** 'Metropolis' (Westbrook)
RCA (1971), 'The Source' (SME) Tangent
(1970), 'Duke Ellington Classics' (Lyttelton)
Black Lion (1969), 'Live At Ronnie Scott's'
(Scott) CBS Realm (1968), 'Ray Warleigh's
First Album' Philips (1968).

JOHN WARREN *bari, f, comp, arr, leader*
A 2 Crescent Mansions, Elgin Crescent,
London W11. **T** 01–727 1528. **Curr** Own orch
since '68, Westbrook Orch, Alan Cohen Band.
Tours Germany & Switzerland '73 & Germany
'75 w orch. **Rec** Orch 'Tales Of The
Algonquin' (feat Surman) Deram (1971), and w
Surman, Westbrook. An impressive
arranger/composer whose orch's appearances
are usually rewarding musical experiences.

TREVOR CHARLES WATTS *alto, sop*
B 26.2.39 A 10 Great North Road, Highgate,
London N6. **T** 01–348 7106. **Curr** Own group
Amalgam (inc Stevens, Tippett, Quaye, Peter
Cowling), SME (Stevens) since '66, John
Stevens' Dance Orch, Splinters (w Tracey,
Stevens etc) since '72, Open Circle since '73.
Prev RAF School of Music '59, left RAF '63,
New J Orch (Ardley) during '60s, many
prev versions of Amalgam (orig duo w Guy)
since '67, Pierre Favre '70, London J Comp
Orch (Guy), Bobby Bradford Quar '72–'73,
Tentacles (Tracey). **Tours, fest** Germany &
Switzerland '75. San Sebastian '74.
Amalgam took part as musicians & actors in a
revival of Jack Gelber's play 'The Connection'
Hampstead Theatre Club '74. **Rec** 'Love's
Dream' (Bradford) Emanem (1973), 'Amalgam

Trevor Watts

Play Blackwell And Higgins' A Records (1972–3), 'Prayer For Peace' (Amalgam) Transatlantic (1969), 'Springboard' Polydor (1966), and w London J Comp Orch (Guy). For SME albums see under John Stevens' name. Watts favours a powerful and confident post-Coleman style which finds its best expression w his Amalgam group. Nevertheless hé contributes effectively in the more fragmented musical territory of the SME in which he has collaborated w Stevens for a decade.

JOHN WEBB *drums*
B 28.5.44 **A** 6 Clydesdale House, Kale Road, Erith, Kent. **Y** 01–310 7630. **Curr** Collier, Beckett. **Prev** Bird–Curtis Quin, Tim Rose, David McWilliams, Blossom Dearie, Jon Hendrix, Marian Montgomery. **Fav rec** 'Flare Up' (Beckett) Philips (1970). **Mem event** Montreux JF '71 w Collier. **Pref** Davis, Mingus, Coltrane, Weather Report, Jarrett, Hancock. **Rec** w Collier, Beckett.

Don Weller

DON WELLER *tenor*
A 9 Upwood Road, Norbury, London SW16. **T** 01–764 2623. **Curr** Own band Major Surgery (inc Roche, Beck, Bruce Colcutt, Tony Marsh), quin w Art Themen, Stan Tracey Octet, Harry Beckett's S & R Powerhouse Section, freelance w various groups. **Prev** East Of Eden rock group. **Rec** 'St Vitus Dance' (Major Surgery) Jaguar (cassette) (c1975).

ALEX WELSH *tpt, cornet*
B 9.7.29 **A** 10 Pennant Mews, London W8. **T** 01–373 1428. **Agent** Contact Colin Hogg 01–437 3326 or June Elsdon 01–422 1055 or Reg Tracey 01–500 1298. **Curr** Own band since '54. **Conc** Annual Armstrong Mem Conc since '70 – Royal Fest Hall July '75, 21st Anniv conc Queen Eliz Hall May '75. **Fest** Breda JF May '75, Bracknell JF (w Wild Bill Davison) July '75. **Mem event** Playing at Newport JF '68. **Rec** 'Dixieland Party' Black Lion (1973), 'An Evening With His Friends' (2 vols) Black Lion (1971), 'If I Had A Talking Picture Of You' Black Lion (1971).

MIKE WESTBROOK *comp, leader p, baritone horn*
B 21.3.36 **A** 26 Susannah Street, London

Mike Westbrook

E14 6LS. **T** 01–515 2824. **Curr** Own orch (re-formed '74), own Brass Band (inc Phil Minton, Chambers, Rutherford, Kate Barnard) since '73. **Prev** Jazz workshop in Plymouth, to London in early '60s, own Band, own sext (Surman, Osborne, Griffiths, Jackson, Miller), own Concert Band, Cosmic Circus multi media group '70–'72, own rock-jazz band Solid Gold Cadillac '72–74'. **Tours, conc** Premiere of 'Citadel/Room 315' extended comp perf by Swedish Radio J Orch Stockholm March '74, Camden JF '74, Brit tour w orch Sept–Oct '74, Bracknell JF w orch July '75. **Fav rec** 'Citadel/Room 315' RCA Victor (1975). Compositions for films, TV, theatre. Music for Adrian Mitchell's play 'Man Friday'. National Theatre mixed media presentation 'Tyger'. **Rec** 'Mike Westbrook Live' Cadillac (1972), 'Solid Gold Cadillac' RCA (1972), 'Tyger' RCA Red Seal (1971), 'Metropolis' RCA Neon (1971), 'Love Songs' Deram (1970), 'Marching Song' (2 Vols) Deram (1969), 'Release' Deram (1968), 'Celebration' Deram (1967). One of the most important composers in contemporary jazz and a restless musical explorer, Westbrook fuses tradition and innovation naturally and unselfconsciously in the best of his work. 'Citadel/Room 315', which marks his return to extended jazz composition for a large orchestra is a new impressive pinnacle in his career.

Kenny Wheeler

KENNY WHEELER *tpt, flug-h*
A 141 Wallwood Road, Leytonstone, London E11. **T** 01–556 0639. **Curr** Own orch, own band Freedom For A Change (inc Parker, Warleigh, Lytton), Coe Wheeler & Co (w Tony Coe), Mike Pyne Sext, John Taylor Sext, John Stevens' Dance Orch, numerous other groups on occasional basis. **Prev** Ronnie Scott '68, Alan Skidmore Quin, SME (Stevens), Gibbs, Globe Unity Orch (Alexander von Schlippenbach, Peter Kowald), Dankworth. **Tour** Germany w John Warren Orch '75. Tutor Lambeth J Summer School July '75. **Rec** Orch 'Song For Someone' Incus (1973), 'Will Power' (Gibbs etc) Argo (1974), 'Live In Wuppertal' (Globe Unity Orch) FMP (1973) (Incus Import), orch 'Windmill Tilter' Fontana (1968), 'The Enchanted Isle' (Duff) Avenue (1971), 'Jazz In Britain '68–'69' (w various

musicians) Decca (1968–9), 'Trailways Express' (Philly Joe Jones) Polydor (1968), 'Humming Bird' (Paul Gonsalves) Deram (*c*1968), and numerous LPs w Oxley, SME. Skidmore, Gibbs, Westbrook, Hayes, Warren, Dankworth, Scott, Surman, Collier, Clarke–Boland Orch, Winstone etc. The clarity, lyricism and brilliance of Wheeler's playing mark him as one of the finest trumpeters in jazz, able to express himself musically with directness and poise in almost any context from free improvisation to more conventional settings.

Tommy Whittle

TOMMY WHITTLE *tenor, clar, bs-clar, f, alto, piccolo*
B 13.10.26 **A** The Cottage, 13 Heathfield Road, Bushey, Watford WD2 2LH. **T** Watford 43385. **Curr** Own quar, Jack Parnell Orch, Peter Knight Orch, Laurie Johnson Orch, Robert Farnon Orch. **Prev** Harry Hayes, Lew Stone, Johnny Claes, Cyril Stapleton, Ted Heath, Tony Kinsey, Geraldo, Frank Cordell, own sext, quin, quar. **Tours** USA & France '56 & '57. Holland recently. **Conc** Ted Heath Orch re-union shows. Ran own club at Hopbine North Wembley for some years until recently. **Fav rec** *Just One Of Those Things* from 'The Memory Lingers On' (Frank Cordell Orch). **Mem event** From an emotional viewpoint, playing to the crew of the 'Queen Mary' crossing Atlantic. **Rec** 'George Chisholm' Rediffusion Gold Star (1973), 'Along The Chisholm Trail' (Chisholm) 77 (1971), 'Phil On Drums' (Phil Seamen) 77 (1971). A consistently swinging mainstream modern tenor stylist originally influenced by Lester Young.

JOHN WILLIAMS *bari, sop, alto-f, bs-clar, bs-sax, contrabass-clar, comp*
B 8.2.41 **A** 22 Villiers Road, Southall, Middx UB1 3BP. **T** 01–574 0417. **Curr** Own big band. **Prev** Centipede (Tippett), Alan Cohen, John Warren, Herman Wilson, Tony Faulkner, Brian Cooper, Barry Guy, Mike Westbrook. **Mem event** Perf of own comp 'Four Pieces For Jazz Soloists And Orchestra' w West London Sinfonia Mar '74 (soloists inc Pearce, Nichols, Wakeman, L Cooper). **Pref** Ellington, Cecil Payne, Gil Evans, Coltrane, Hubert Laws.

ROY WILLIAMS *tbn*
A 2 Nightingale Close, Stopley, Luton, Beds.
T Luton 27208. **Curr** Alex Welsh. **Prev** Terry
Lightfoot. **Rec** 'John Barnes–Roy Williams
Jazz Band' Rediffusion Gold Star (c1975),
'Dixieland Now And Then' (Dixieland A/S)
Line (1974), 'It's George' (Melly) Warner Bros
(1974).

GARY WINDO *tenor*, *bs-clar*, *f*
A Flat 31, Brookfield, 5 Highgate West Hill,
London N6. T 01–348 4811. **Curr** Ray Russell
Quin, Brotherhood of Breath (MacGregor),
session work. **Prev** Centipede (Tippett),
Lemonspie III (w Tippett etc) '74, WMWM (w
Matthewson, Robert Wyatt, MacRae) '73.
Rec 'Secret Asylum' (Russell) Freedom (1973),
'Running Man' (Russell) RCA Neon (1972),
and w MacGregor, Centipede.

NORMA WINSTONE *singer*
A 234 Conisborough Crescent, London SE6.
T 01-698 5296. **Curr** Michael Garrick Sext
since summer '68, own group Edge Of Time
(inc Lowther, Taylor, Lawrence). **Prev** Gibbs,
Westbrook, Wheeler, Ian Carr, New J Orch
(Ardley). **Fest** Baden-Baden New J Meeting
'74, Stuttgart '75. **Conc** Shakespeare Celeb
Southwark Cath '74. Tony Coe's 'Zeitgeist'.
App w own group on BBC TV 'Open Door'
prog May '74. **Rec** 'Will Power' (Ardley–
Gibbs–Tracey–Carr) Argo (1974), 'Edge Of
Time' Argo (1971), 'Hum-Dono' (Harriott–
DaSilva) Columbia (1969), and w Carr,
Wheeler, Taylor, Westbrook. Winstone is
one of several singers who have adapted
contemporary instrumental improvisatory
styles to their own purposes. Her technique
and musicianship have made her much in
demand in many contemporary jazz contexts.

Norma Winstone

Jazz on record

Jazz record issuing labels currently available in Britain

British major companies:
DECCA

Ace of Clubs	Reissues from Decca and Brunswick archives
Argo	New recordings by British artists: Garrick, Winstone, Carr etc
BASF/MPS	Issues from German parent co of material by current American and European artists: George Shearing; O Peterson; Bill Evans; Willie 'the Lion' Smith; Clarke-Boland Orch
BUK	Big band swing
Eclipse	Reissue/budget items from main Decca lists
Deram	British modern jazz
Gull	Jazz/rock, principally Isotope (Boyle)
London	American material, currently from Commodore
York	British artists, Frank Evans, Jack Duff etc

EMI

Arista	New Jazz from 'Freedom' catalogue
B & C	American 'soul jazz' from Groove Merchant list
Coral/MCA	Reissues from US Decca, Brunswick '30s and '40s lists
Fantasy	From American parent company
Capitol	
HMV	
Liberty	
Sunset	
United Artists/Blue Note	
One-up	Material from Lansdowne catalogue
Virgin/Caroline/Watt	Current jazz-rock & New Jazz: Spear; Carla Bley Gilgamesh; Jazz Composers Orch etc

ANCHOR

Impulse	Coltrane, P Saunders, B Evans, Shepp, Hodges, Mingus etc

CBS
Douglas
Embassy

Midi
Ode
Realm
PHONOGRAM/POLYDOR
Chess
Checker
Contour
CTI/Kudu
Carnival
Fontana
Metro
MGM
Onyx
Pablo
Philips
Verve
Vertigo
PYE
DJM
Ember
Mainstream
Probe
Sonet
Vanguard
Vogue
RCA
Flying Dutchman
RCA
Prestige

British independent and musician-owned companies:

A RECORDS *Owned by Trevor Watts and John Stevens*
Issues to date:
A001 'Spontaneous Music Ensemble for CND . . .'
A002 'Amalgam play Blackwell & Higgins'
A003 SME+, equals SMO
A004 'Ripple' (Amalgam)
CADILLAC *Owned by Mike Westbrook and John Jack*
Issues to date:
SGC1001 'Live' Mike Westbrook Quin
SGC1002 'Original' (Osborne/Tracey)
SGC1003 'Alone' Stan Tracey at Wigmore Hall
SGC1004 'Joy Unlimited' (Harry Beckett)
CARROT
TWO: Father Al Lewis with Bill Brunskill JB
DECIBEL *Owned by Paul Howarth*
BSN103 Phil Seamen Story; memorial to a great drummer
EMANEM *Owned by Martin & Mandy Davison (Now based in US)*
301 Steve Lacy solo concert
302 'Love's Dream' Bobby Bradford Quar
303 'Face to Face' John Stevens & Trevor Watts
304 'The Crust' Steve Lacy, Steve Potts, John Stevens etc

601 'Duo' Anthony Braxton & Derek Bailey (double album reissued as two single LPs)

ESQUIRE/DELMARK *Owned by Carlo & Gretta Kramer*
  D1202 George Lewis NO JB
    207 Albert Nicholas Quar
    210 Clancy Hayes with the Salty Dogs
    211 Barney Bigard with Art Hodes
    212 Earl Hines solo
    402 Ira Sullivan Quin with Johnny Griffin
    404 Jimmy Forrest
    408 Roscoe Mitchell
    410 Joseph Jarman
    411 Sun Ra Arkestra
    413 Richard Abrams
    414 Sun Ra Arkestra
    415 Anthony Braxton
    416 Leon Sash Trio
    417 Joseph Jarman
    419 Maurice McIntyre
    422 Ira Sullivan
    423 Richard Abrams
    424 George Freeman
    425 Maurice McIntyre
    426 Sonny Stitt
    427 Jimmy Forrest
    600 series. All blues releases

FIRST HEARD
  1 Benny Goodman & his Musicians 1946–49
  2 Woody Herman 1944–46
  3 Tommy Dorsey band & Dorsey leading H James band
  4 Jimmy Dorsey bands 1944–47
  5 Buddy Rich 1946–47 band
  6 Artie Shaw 1949
  7 Gene Krupa Orch
  8 Boyd Raeburn Orch
  9 Harry James 1945–49
  10 Woody Herman Vol 2

FOUNTAIN
  FG/FV/FB/FJ prefixes. Classic American black and white jazz of the '20s including Ida Cox, Armstrong & Red Onion Jazz Babies, Freddie Keppard, Morton, Ladd's Black Aces, ODJB, Louisiana Five, Red Nichols, Spanier, Annette Hanshaw

JAGUAR CASSETTES *Organized by Gordon Beck and the artists on each tape*
  CS1 Howard Riley solo
  JS1 Beck, Matthewson, Humair trio
  JS2 Gyroscope (Beck, Sulzmann, Ricotti, Levin, Matthewson)
  JS3 John Taylor Sext
  JS4 Major Surgery (Weller)
  JS5 Landscape (John Walters)

HEP
  Limited editions of big bands such as Boyd Raeburn

JOY; division of President Records drawing mainly from the American VeeJay catalogue of jazz, blues and gospel, but also albums by Ken Colyer; John Bastable's Chosen Six; Malc Murphy's quar

MELODISC *Owned by Emil Shalit; oldest British-based independent*
Albums by Bunk Johnson 1942 band; Wild Bill Davison Commodore sessions, Max Kaminsky Commodores; Joe Harriott and blues by Leadbelly, Broonzy, Memphis Slim etc

MOSAIC *Owned by Graham Collier*
GCM 741 'Darius' Graham Collier Music
GCM 751 'Midnight Blue' Graham Collier Music

NOLA *Owned by Tom Stagg*
Albums of authentic New Orleans music by Bunk Johnson, Pete Bocage, Thomas Jefferson etc

OGUN *Owned by Harry & Hazel Miller and Keith Beale*
OG100 Chris MacGregor's Brotherhood of Breath
OG200 Harry Miller solo
OG300 Mike Osborne Trio
OG400 SOS – Surman, Osborne, Skidmore
OG500 'Ramifications' Irene Schweitzer

OPENIAN *Owned by Bob Downes and Wendy Benka*
BDOM 001 'Diversions' Bob Downes Open Music
002 'Episodes at 4AM' Bob Downes
003 'Hells Angels' Bob Downes large group

PARAGON *Owned by Mike Casimir*
PLE S103 Kid Thomas & Louis Nelson with New Iberia Stompers

REALITY *Owned by Max Collie*
R105 Max Collie Rhythm Aces live in Bremen
R106 Max Collie Rhythm Aces 'Battle of Trafalgar' double album and cassettes

RHAPSODY
RHA 6021 'The Jelly Roll Morton Rarities'

SAGA
6000 series. Extensive budget/medium priced catalogue of '40s bebop, big bands & swing: including Charlie Parker Dial material and b/casts, Ellington, Basie, Armstrong, Holiday, Bechet, Tatum, Condon etc

SAYDISC
SDL 244 'Portraits' Graham Collier Music
Other albums by Clyde Bernhart Allstars, Miss Rhapsody, etc

SCAM
JPG 1 'Dance of the infidels' Charlie Parker
2 'Cheers' Charlie Parker
3 'What's This' Parker Royal Roost Feb/March '49 b/casts

77 *Owned by Doug Dobell*
Extensive catalogue of New Orleans, mainstream, swing and piano solos by Ken Colyer, Humphrey Lyttelton, Buck Clayton, Kid Thomas, George Lewis, Barry Martyn, Albert Nicholas, Pete Brown, New Orleans Joymakers, Sandy Brown, Don Ewell, Nat Gonella, Dick Wellstood, Billy Butterfield, Bill Coleman, Dick Sudhalter, Fred Hunt, Lennie Felix etc; many blues and folk items

SPOTLITE *Owned by Tony Williams*

The definitive edition of Charlie Parker's Dial recordings, plus his first ever records with Jay McShann, various b/casts; new sessions by Joe Albany, Cecil Payne, Pepper Adams, Al Haig, etc: plus b/casts by Coleman Hawkins, Lester Young, and the Billy Eckstine band. New releases will feature Red Rodney with the Bebop Preservation Society (Le Sage), and a BPS album

WORLD JAZZ *Owned by Bark Hickox and Jerry Finingley*

WJLPS 1 'Century Plaza' World Greatest Jazz Band
2 'Hark the Herald Angels Swing' WGJB
3 WGJB in concert Massey Hall vol 1
4 WGJB vol 2 Carnegie Hall with B Hackett and Maxine Sullivan
5 'Soprano Summit' Bob Wilber & Kenny Davern
6 WGJB play Cole Porter

WAVE *Owned by Peter Ind*

The catalogue documents Ind's work with various members of the Lennie Tristano 'school' both in Britain and America from 1959 to today, and includes sessions with Warne Marsh, Sheila Jordan, Ronnie Ball, Chas Burchell; plus solo and duo albums designed to serve as rhythm sections for musicians to accompany at home

CANON

CNN5970 'Red Dwarf' Head (Bill Kyle)

STEAM *Owned by Stan & Jackie Tracey*

SJ101 'Under Milk Wood' Stan Tracey quartet
SJ102 'Captain Adventure' Stan Tracey quartet

INCUS *Owned by the Compatible Recording and Publishing company*

Incus 1 'Topography of the Lungs' Evan Parker, Derek Bailey, Han Bennink
8 Tony Oxley 'Solo, Quartet, And Sextet'
9 Derek Bailey and Han Bennink
11 'Balance' Ian Brighton, Radu Malfatti, Frank Perry, Phil Wachsmann, Colin Wood
10 'Song for someone' Kenny Wheeler Orch
12 Derek Bailey solo
13 Howard Riley Trio
14 Evan Parker/Paul Lytton
15 'Teatime' Steve Beresford, Nigel Coombes, Dave Solomons, John Russell, Gary Todd

BEAD 1

'Milk Teeth'/A touch of the sun (Simon Mayo & Peter Cusack)

NEW ORLEANS RARITIES/LA CROIX.

Both devoted to authentic NO music

COLLECTORS ITEMS/GANNET/BLUES OBSCURITIES

Reissues of vintage collectors material, including 6 vol set of Ida Cox; Savoy Bearcats etc

MONO

Recent recordings of veteran NO musicians

REDIFFUSION GOLD STAR

US material from Roulette, and current British mainstream/dixieland

Some Foreign Jazz Labels Currently Being Imported Into Britain

ALAMAC Reissues of American material from '30s, '40s & '50s

ARISTON Italian: reissues of Goodman, Hampton, Wilson, Armstrong, Hodges, Tatum etc

CARDIN French: reissues from Riverside classic jazz lists; recent material by Phil Woods etc

CENTRE OF THE WORLD French label owned by Frank Wright & his musicians

CJM Swedish: reissues of Morton Library of Congress recordings, C Williams, NORK, etc

BANDSTAND Swing Bands

BIG BAND ARCHIVES

BROADWAY Beiderbecke, Nicholls, Pollack etc

CRESCENT JAZZ New Orleans jazz today

DAWN CLUB American reissues of Bunk Johnson, Lu Watters, Kid Ory

DOGWOOD Canadian concert by Armstrong Allstars '51

DIXIE Barry Martyn, New Orleans musicians

ENJA New German recordings by D Brand, M Waldron, Elvin Jones, Bobby Jones etc

ECM German: K Jarrett, Jan Garbarek, R Towner, Terje Rypdal

FAIRMONT USA: Ellington, Armstrong, Watters

CHIAROSCURIO USA: Current recordings by Buck Clayton, Ruby Braff-George Barnes, B Tate

CONCORD Braff-Barnes, Zoot Sims

CICALA Italian reissues: M Davis nine piece band, Hampton, Glenn Miller, Lunceford

HAPPY BIRD German sessions by Colyer, Wallis, Sunshine, Collie etc

JAZZ SOCIETY Swedish: reissues of Don Byas, Basie, Ellington, Carter, Hawkins, etc

JAZZ ARCHIVES Ben Webster, Lester Young, Bunny Berigan, Lips Page, Basie etc

JAZZ SHOWCASE Broadcasts – Parker, Davis, Gillespie Big Band, Howard McGhee

MAX Ellington broadcasts '40s

MUSICMOUTH Armstrong Copenhagen broadcast '33

PDU Italian contemporary jazz

PHOENIX C Williams '44, Gillespie '45–'46, Hawkins '39, Charlie Ventura, Nat Cole

QUEENDISC Italian: L Young, Parker, Ellington, Gillespie, Armstrong, Carter, Condon, Noone

STEEPLECHASE Danish: current recordings by Dexter Gordon, P Woods, Duke Jordan, Joe Albany

SACKVILLE Canadian: Braxton, Brand, Wild Bill Davison, Willie 'The Lion' Smith

STRATA-EAST Charles Tolliver, Bill Hardman

SWAGGIE Australian bands & reissues of classic jazz

SUN French recordings by Oliver Lake

TAX Swedish: Young, Eldridge, Hodges, Freeman, Ellington, Kirby, Newton

TRIP Reissues of Clifford Brown, Hawkins, Vaughan etc from
  Mercury lists
WAM German sessions by Lyttelton, Collier, Wallis, Temperance 7
  etc

French, German, American, Italian, Scandinavian, Benelux etc
issues of major labels

Principal importers and trade distributors of these and the local
specialist labels:
  CRD. Lyon Way, Rockware Avenue, Greenford, Middx UB6 0BN.
    01–578 4311
  Cadillac Music. 1a Belmont Street, London NW1. 01–836 6006
    & 01-267 1542
  Flyright/Swift. 18 Endwell Road, Bexhill-on-Sea, East Sussex.
    Bexhill 220028
  Jazz Services Unlimited. 7 Kildare Road, Swinton, Manchester
    M27 3AB. 016–794 3525/4859
  Chris Wellard. 4 Chequers Parade, London SE9 1DD. 01–859 2748
  Vixen Records. 34 Station Road, West Croydon, Surrey

Jazz societies, clubs
and promoters

It has only been possible to include here a brief selection of some of the societies and promoters active on the jazz scene at present. There are hundreds of pubs throughout the country which regularly provide a venue for local bands but the following list is limited mainly to societies, clubs and promoters which present jazz on several evenings a week or which arrange a diverse programme using guest musicians. The listing of clubs outside the London area is based on returns to questionnaires.

Further details of jazz clubs and concerts may be obtained from the local press, MELODY MAKER, *and for the London area,* JAZZ IN LONDON *(published by the Jazz Centre Society) and* TIME OUT. *Every care has been taken to ensure accuracy in the information printed but, although some clubs such as the Peanuts Club have a thirteen year history and the Opposite Lock Club has presented jazz since 1966, many others are much less permanent establishments and details of venues, days, etc. may change from time to time.*

JAZZ CENTRE SOCIETY, c/o ICA, 12 Carlton House Terrace, London SW1. **T** 01–930 4261. **Admin** Charles Alexander. **Asst Admin** Peter Budge.

The JCS was formed in 1968 and is a registered charity. It is non-profit making and is run by an elected committee of 15 with a full-time staff of 4. The current membership exceeds 1500 and the membership fee is £3 pa (£2 for students and MU members). Other sources of finance include the Arts Council of Great Britain, Arts Association regional, the Musicians' Union and the Performing Right Society.

The JCS organizes weekly events at the Phoenix, Cavendish Square, W1 on Wednesdays and the Seven Dials Social Club, Shelton Street, WC2 on Thursdays. Concerts are frequently presented at other venues including the ICA. There are also occasional seasons of jazz and blues films at the ICA, Nash House, The Mall, SW1. The JCS has taken part in arranging festivals including the Camden Jazz Festival (Autumn '74) and Bracknell Jazz Festival (July '75).

Present activities include acting as an advisory body to other jazz promoting organizations, assisting musicians in obtaining engagements and answering general enquiries on jazz subjects. The JCS acts as a pressure group for jazz and organizes educational activities in association with ILEA. It also maintains lists of all available jazz films and works to preserve existing films and videotape material.

In the future the JCS hopes to secure premises which will serve as a permanent base for jazz in Britain. A branch has recently been opened in Manchester to serve the North and North West of England.

JUDAINE MUSIC LTD., Mountfield Court, Dormans Park, East Grinstead, Sussex. **T** Dormans Park 369. Robert Masters. Agency for US & British jazz musicians.

MAM AGENCY LTD, MAM House, 24/25 New Bond Street, London W1Y 9HD. **T** 01–629 9255. Harold Davidson. International artists.

TW ENTERPRISES, 19d Netherhall Gardens, London NW3 5RL. **T** 01–794 5154. **Managers** Michael Webber & Arthur Thompson. 3–10 concerts pa at venues such as RFH, Wigmore Hall, Fairfield Hall. Mainly mainstream.

LONDON AREA

ALBANY EMPIRE, Greek Road, Deptford, SE8. Wed. Modern–mainstream: John Curtis See Saw Band (Res).

ANCHOR, Church Square, Shepperton, Middx. **T** Walton-on-Thames 21618. Tues, Wed, Thurs, Fri, Sat, Sun evenings & Sun lunchtimes. Mostly resident groups, traditional & modern.

BATTERSEA TOWN HALL COMMUNITY ARTS CENTRE (Clapham Junction), Lavender Hill, SW11. **T** 01–223 5356. Sun afternoons. Open workshop led by Brett Hornby.

BIRKBECK COLLEGE STUDENTS UNION, Malet Street, WC1. **T** 01–580 6622 Ext 335. Regular jazz events.

'JAZZ AT THE BREWERY TAP', Brewery Tap, 2 Markhouse Road, Walthamstow, E17. **Organizers** John Reeve, 40 The Chiltons, Grove Hill, S Woodford, E18. **T** 01–580 6690 (day) & 01–989 2243 (weekend); Mike Brown, **T** 01–520 3754. Sundays. Broadly modern.

THE BRICKLAYERS ARMS, 67 Ealing Road, Brentford, Middx. **T** 01–560 7841. **Organizer** Nigel Palmer. Tues, Thurs, Sat. Traditional.

BULLS HEAD, Lonsdale Road, SW13. **T** 01–876 5241. **Organizer** Albert Tolley (licensee). Every evening & Sun lunchtimes: major visiting groups usually on Mon. All modern jazz, regulars include Tony Lee Trio, Peter King, Art Themen.

CAMBERLEY JAZZ CLUB, Cambridge Hotel, 121 London Road, Camberley, Surrey. **Organizer** Sheena Boddy. **T** 01–892 0133. Sun evenings. Mainly traditional, including major artists.

COCK TAVERN, 88 Green Lanes, Palmers Green, N13. **T** 01–888 6474 & 01–888 2000. Alan Elsdon Jazz Band (Res).

CENTRAL LONDON POLYTECHNIC, Bolsover Street, W1.
T 01–636 6271. Regular jazz events.

FLANAGANS FAMOUS RAILWAY PUB, Putney High Street,
SW15. **T** 01–788 1519. Regular jazz events, resident groups including
Gill Lyons' band.

GATEHOUSE, North Road, Highgate, N6. **T** 01–340 2154.
Resident groups: Sun evenings, Crouch End Allstars; Sun lunchtimes,
Gene Cottrell–Pete Chapman; Thurs, Doug Murray.

GREENWICH THEATRE (Bernards Bar), Crooms Hill, SE10.
T 01–858 7755. Sun lunchtimes. Ian Bird Quin (Res).

THE GUN, Church Street, Croydon. **T** 01–688 1046. Resident &
occasional visiting groups: Mon; Wed; Thurs, Equilibrium; Fri,
West London Line-up; Sun, Don Weller's Major Surgery & friends.

HACKNEY JAZZ SOCIETY. Chairman Ann Green, 30 Walford
Road, N16. **T** 01–254 2102. **Venues** Surrey Tavern, 107a Culford
Road, N1 & occasional concerts at other venues in Hackney area.
Mainly modern, avant-garde, mainstream.

HALF MOON, Lower Richmond Road, Putney, SW15. Thurs.
Mike Daniels Big Band (30's & 40's jazz).

HOPBINE, 86 East Lane, Wembley. **T** 01–904 8199. Tues evening &
Sun lunchtimes. Mainly mainstream & modern well-known groups.

JACKSON LANE COMMUNITY CENTRE, near Highgate Station,
Archway Road, N6. Tues. Improvised music, Maggie Nichols &
others.

KINGS HEAD THEATRE CLUB, 115 Upper Street, Islington N1.
T 01–226 2631 & 01–226 1916. Tues, George Khan Band (Res);
Thurs, trad & blues alternate weeks (Res groups); occasional jazz
on Mon.

LORD NAPIER, 111 Beulah Road, Thornton Heath, S. London.
T 01–653 2286. Every evening & Sun lunchtimes. Mainly traditional
jazz except Thurs, eg Sun & Wed, Blackbottom Stompers; Thurs
Peter Coe Big Band. (Res groups).

MITRE, 388 Tunnell Avenue, Greenwich SE10. **T** 01–858 0895.
Organizer Nick Sella. Thurs, Fri, Sat, Sun evenings & Sun lunchtimes.
Thurs & Sat for major artists. Mostly traditional.

NEW MERLINS CAVE, Margery Street, WC1. **T** 01–278 4068 &
01–837 2097. Fri evenings, John Picard (Res); Sun lunchtimes, John
Chilton Feetwarmers/Bruce Turner whenever touring commitments
allow.

100 CLUB, 100 Oxford Street, W1. **T** 01–636 0933. **Manager** Roger
Horton. Wed, Fri, Sat, Sun, mainly traditional & mainstream.

PEANUTS CLUB, Kings Arms, 213 Bishopsgate, EC2. **Organizer**
Ken May. **T** 01–539 6748. Fri. Mike Osborne, Harry Miller &

Friends (Res). Longest running pub jazz in London now in fourteenth year.

PINDAR OF WAKEFIELD, 328 Grays Inn Road, WC1.
T 01–837 1753. Tues, Keith Nichols Ragtime Band; Wed, traditional.
(Res groups).

PLOUGH, 90 Stockwell Road, SW9. **T** 01–274 3879. Wed, Thurs,
Fri, Sat. Modern jazz, eg Tony Lee, Dave Cliff – Ray Manderson
Quar, Bryan Spring Trio, Barbara Thompson, Brian Lemon.

RONNIE SCOTT'S, 47 Frith Street, London W1. **T** 01–439 0747.
Organizers Ronnie Scott & Pete King. Every night except Sunday,
late evening till 3 a.m. American & international artists. Agency.

SHIP INN, Jews Row, Wandsworth Bridge (South side). Tues &
Wed. Mainstream, traditional.

SIX BELLS, Kings Road, Chelsea, SW3. **T** 01–352 9255. Mon.

THAMES HOTEL, Hampton Court, Middlesex. Fridays. Traditional.
Max Collie.

THREE TUNS, Beckenham High Street, S London. Resident
groups: Tues, Squirrel; Thurs, Steam; Fri & Sun, West End
Stompers.

YE OLDE LEATHER BOTTLE, Kingston Road, Merton, SW19.
T 01–542 1977 & 01–542 7490. Sun, Mon, Thurs, Fri. Resident
groups, mainly traditional. Sun, Peter Coe Big Swing Band.

YE OLDE WHYTE HART, Drury Lane, WC2. Every evening.
Mainly modern.

SOUTH

SOUTH HILL PARK TRUST LTD, South Hill Park, *Bracknell*,
Berks. **T** Bracknell 27272. **Organizers** John D Cumming and Chris
Pettit. **Venues** South Hill Park (arts centre): modern jazz on
alternate Tuesdays, traditional jazz on alternate Wednesdays, jam
session on Mondays, annual jazz festival.

OXFORD JAZZ CLUB, Roebuck Inn, Market Street, *Oxford*.
T Oxford 48388. **Organizer** Jack St Clair. **Venues** Roebuck Inn,
Thursday evenings. Traditional jazz.

OXFORD UNIVERSITY JAZZ CLUB. Enquiries to The Senior
Member, Dr R Mallion, Christ Church, *Oxford*, 0X1 1DP. **Venues**
Roebuck Inn, Market Street, Oxford, Sundays during term-time. All
styles of jazz.

VICTORIA ARMS, Walton Street, *Oxford*. **Enquiries to** Alan

Pritchard, 39 Leckford Road, Oxford. **T** Oxford 54249. Tuesday evenings. Modern jazz.

READING JAZZ CIRCLE, 96 Elvaston Way, Tilehurst, *Reading*, Berks. RG3 4ND. **T** Reading 29383 (evenings). **Secretary** Ian Hills. **Venues** The Miller's Arms, Star Road, Caversham, monthly on Wednesdays.

CONCORDE, Old School, Stoneham Lane, North Stoneham, *Southampton*, Hants. **T** Eastleigh 3989. **Organizer** Cole Mathieson. **Venues** Old School, Fridays and Sundays. Occasional special presentations on other evenings. All styles of jazz.

SOUTHAMPTON CITY COUNCIL, Leisure Services Dept, Civic Centre, *Southampton* SO9 4XF. **T** Southampton 23855 ext 456. **Organizer** William Weston, City Arts Administrator. **Venues** Solent Suite, Guildhall, monthly.

SOUTHAMPTON JAZZ AND BLUES SOCIETY, Bridge Tavern, Six Dials, *Southampton*. **T** Chandlers Ford 66713 or Southampton 552782. **Secretary** 124 Kingsway, Chandlers Ford, Hants. **Venues** The Bridge Tavern alternate Tuesdays. All styles, emphasis on mainstream.

SWINDON JAZZ SOCIETY, Arts Centre, Devizes Road, *Swindon*, Wilts. **T** Swindon 26161. **Secretary** Tony Hazel, 7 Claremont Court, Whitworth Road, Swindon, Wilts. **Venues** Arts Centre, approx five times pa. Mostly traditional, New Orleans.

WYVERN THEATRE, Civic Centre, *Swindon*. **T** (Box Office) Swindon 24881. **Artistic Director** Tony Clayton. **Venues** Jolliffe Studio Theatre (fortnightly) and Main Auditorium (occasionally). All styles of jazz.

HERTFORDSHIRE AND THE SOUTH-EAST

BASILDON JAZZ SOCIETY, 57 Swallowdale, *Basildon*, Essex. **T** Basildon 23234. **Secretary** Mick Sexton. **Venues** Sweeney's, High Pavement, Basildon, Wednesday evenings. Contemporary/modern.

THE NORTHERN, 31 York Place, *Brighton*, Sussex. **T** Brighton 62519. **Organizer** B E Barton. **Venues** The Northern, Wednesday and Sunday evenings. New Orleans and mainstream.

CANTERBURY JAZZ APPRECIATION SOCIETY. Organizing secretary Pete I Webb, Empathy, 7 Glenside Avenue, *Canterbury*. **T** Canterbury 61812. **Venues** Occasional sessions at various venues.

ARTS CENTRE, New Metropole, The Leas, *Folkestone*, Kent. **T** Folkestone 55070. **Arts Director** John Eveleigh. 3 or 4 concerts pa.

ESCALATOR, 18 High Wickham, *Hastings*. **T** Hastings 430040.

Venues Palace Bars, sea front, Thursday evenings; Carlisle Hotel, Friday evenings; informal jam session at the Warriors Gate, St Leonards, Sunday evenings.

THE BELL INN JAZZ CLUB, The Bell Inn, Codicote, Nr *Hitchin*, Herts. **T** Stevenage 820 278. **Organizer** T R Young. Sunday evenings. Modern to mainstream.

THE GOAT INN, THE RED LION, THE SALISBURY, **Enquiries to** Ken Lindsay, 6 Alma Road, *St Albans*, Herts. **T** St Albans 53186. **Organizer** Ken Lindsay. **Venues** The Goat Inn, Sopwell Lane, *St Albans*, Sunday lunchtimes; The Red Lion Hotel, Great North Road, *Hatfield*, Herts, Monday evenings; The Salisbury Hotel, High Street, *Barnet*, Herts, Sunday evenings. Traditional and mainstream.

BLUE BOAR, Victoria Avenue, *Southend-on-Sea*. **T** Southend 43235. Tues. Trad.

MYRA'S BLUES CLUB, The Railway Hotel, Cliff Town Road, *Southend-on-Sea*. **Enquiries to** Myra Abbott, 50 Oakleigh Park Drive, Leigh-on-Sea, Essex. **T** Southend 73104. Tuesday evenings. Blues and traditional.

PUMPHOUSE THEATRE AND ARTS CENTRE TRUST LTD, 5/6 Local Board Road, *Watford*, Herts. **T** Watford 22792. **Organizer** Mick Cornwall. Thurs. Mainly trad.

WALES AND THE SOUTH-WEST

BBC CLUB, 118 Newport Street, *Cardiff*. Tuesday evenings. Modern jazz: Lionel Davies Trio.

QUEBEC HOTEL, Chrichton Street, *Cardiff*. Monday & Wednesday evenings. Vic Parker – Chris Hodgkins Duo. Most kinds of jazz except modern and avant garde.

NEW CONTINENTAL, Queen Street, *Cardiff* (Victoriana Suite). Thursday, Friday & Saturday evenings. Austin Davies Trio Mainstream & modern.

GREAT WESTERN HOTEL, St Mary Street, *Cardiff*. Sunday, Tuesday & Thursday evenings. New Orleans jazz.

UNIVERSITY COLLEGE, CARDIFF. Director Geoffrey Axworthy. **Manager** Branwen Iorwerth. **Venues** Sherman Theatre, Senghennyd Road, *Cardiff* and Sherman Arena. All styles of jazz.

THE BELL, Walcot Street, *Bath*. **T** Bath 25998. **Organizer** John Bradshaw. Thursday, Friday, Saturday evenings. Traditional and modern.

JAZZ AT THE ICEBOX, c/o 17 Tellcroft Close, *Corsham*, Wilts

SN13 9JH. **T** Corsham 712411. **Organizers** Jack Pennington and John Critchinson. **Venues** County Hotel, Pulteney Road, Bath, Avon, Friday evenings. Mainly modern jazz, guest stars and local trio.

ARNOLFINI MUSIC, Narrow Quay, *Bristol* 1. **T** Bristol 299191. **Music Co-ordinator** Jane Wells. **Venues** Arnolfini Music, evening concerts, approx twice pa; lunchtime, approx once per month. Progressive jazz.

PLYMOUTH ARTS CENTRE, 38 Looe Street, *Plymouth*. **T** Plymouth 60060. **Organizer** Bernard Samuels. **Venues** Various in Plymouth area, approx 4 concerts per season. Mainly avant-garde.

EAST MIDLANDS

LEICESTER JAZZ SOCIETY. Secretary Harry Walton, 128 Westcotes Drive, *Leicester* LE3 0QS. **T** Leicester 57600. **Venues** The County Arms, Blaby, *Leicester*, Monday evenings, and occasional concerts at local theatres. All styles of jazz.

BELL INN, Old Market Square, *Nottingham*. **T** Nottingham 45241. **Proprietors** Dorothy M and David R Jackson. Tuesday evenings and Sunday lunch-times. Traditional jazz.

NOTTINGHAM RHYTHM CLUB. Secretary B J Hagerty, 40 Geenwich Avenue, Basford, *Nottingham*. **T** Nottingham 77067. **Venues** Test Match Hotel, Gordon Road, West Bridgford, *Nottingham* monthly on Thursday evenings. New Orleans to mainstream.

NOTTINGHAM SWING SOCIETY, Federation House, Claremont Road, Sherwood Rise, *Nottingham*. **Organizer** Wilf Ashley, 28 Goathland Close, Bestwood Park, Nottingham. **T** Nottingham 267861. **Venues** Federation House on Wednesday evenings. Mainstream and modern jazz.

WEST MIDLANDS

BIRMINGHAM ARTS LABORATORY, Tower Street, Newtown, *Birmingham* 19. **T** 021–359 4192. **Music Director** Melvyn Poore. **Venues** Arts Lab once every 2 or 3 months. Experimental, avant garde, free jazz.

THE OPPOSITE LOCK CLUB, 52 Gas Street, *Birmingham* 1. **T** 021–643 2573/0691/1250. **Managing Director** Martin Hone. **Director** Ian Hone. **Venues** As above & The Engine House, London Lane, Tardebigge, Nr Bromsgrove. Every evening. All styles of jazz. **Agency** OLÉ sending bands out nationwide.

PROHIBITION CLUB, 3 Park Street, City Centre, *Birmingham* B55JD. **T** 021–643 3166/7. **Manager** Tony Richards. Modern, mainstream on Mon but jazz influenced policy every evening except Sun.

CLUB HARLEM – Dud Clews Jazz Orchestra, 190 Ashington Grove, Whitley, *Coventry* CV3 4DB. **T** Coventry 302339. **Organizer** Derek Habberjam. **Venues** The Fiesta, Longford, Coventry (on the A444). Saturday evenings. 20's & 30's big band jazz & swing.

YORKSHIRE

BRIDLINGTON JAZZ CLUB, 50 Marshall Avenue, *Bridlington,* North Humberside, YO15 2DS. **T** 0262–6566. **Secretary** Don Sellars. **Venues** Cock and Lion Hotel, Prince Street, Bridlington, alternate Friday evenings. All styles of jazz.

ROTHERHAM JAZZ CLUB, Cranworth Hotel, Fitzwilliam Road, *Rotherham.* **T** Rotherham 72122. **Organizer** Dave Brennan, Moorlands, 16 Hall Road, Moorgate, Rotherham S60 2BP. **T** Rotherham 70332. **Venues** Cranworth Hotel, Friday evenings. New Orleans jazz.

HURLFIELD ARTS, Hurlfield Campus, East Bank Road, *Sheffield* SZ 2AL. **T** Sheffield 392631. **Enquiries to** Fred Brown, address as above. **Venues** Hurlfield Arts, usually Thursday evenings. Local musicians and guests.

NORTH-WEST

BLUE MAGNOLIA JAZZ ORCHESTRA, The 'Coffee House', Church Road, Wavertree, *Liverpool* 15. **T** 051–733 2666 (Coffee House) and 051–428 3155 (Blue Magnolia Jazz Orchestra). **Organizer** Trevor Stent, 1 Gateacre Rise, Liverpool 25. **Venues** Coffee House, weekly on Tuesdays and monthly on Thursdays. Jazz of the 1920's.

SAVOY JAZZ CLUB. Organizer Tom Orrett, 20 Mayville Road, Mossley Hill, *Liverpool* L18 0HQ. **T** 051–733 2448. **Venues** Heath Hotel, Greenhill Road, Liverpool 19, Tuesday evenings. New Orleans to mainstream.

MANCHESTER CREATIVE MUSICIANS ASSOCIATION. Enquiries to Mike Farmer, 54 Highfield Road, Cheadle Hulme, *Cheadle,* Cheshire, SK8 6EP. **T** 061–485 3571. **Venues** Occasional sessions, Manchester area. Avant-garde, free-form jazz, etc.

MANCHESTER UNIVERSITY JAZZ CLUB AND UMIST JAZZ AND BLUES SOCIETY (The University and UMIST jazz clubs function as one club). **Enquiries to** the Secretary, Manchester University Union, Oxford Road, *Manchester* 13. **T** 061–273 5111 or UMIST, PO Box 88, Sackville Street, Manchester M60 1QD. **T** 061–236 1281. **Venues** Salem Bar, University Union (top floor) Monday evenings in term time. Main Debating Hall, University Union, on occasional Thursdays. Trad to avant garde jazz, mainly modern.

MIDLAND HOTEL, Lapwing Lane, West Didsbury, *Manchester.* **Venues** Midland Hotel every Monday. Big band with occasional guest.

PEACOCK CLUB, Hough End Hall, Mauldeth Road West, *Manchester* 21.

GRANGE ARTS CENTRE, Rochdale Road, *Oldham*, Lancashire. **T** 061–624 8012. **Organizer** Anthoy Allsop. **Venues** Infrequently at Grange Arts Centre.

BIRCH HALL HOTEL, Rhodes Hill, Lees, *Oldham*. **T** 061–624 8875. **Organizer** Ray Ibbotson. Thursdays. Mainstream, Dixieland.

WARREN BULKELEY JAZZ CELLAR, Warren Bulkeley Hotel, Warren Street, *Stockport*, Cheshire. **T** 061–480 3614. **Organizer** J A Jacobs. Thursday, Friday, Saturday and Sunday. All kinds of jazz except avant garde.

NORTH

KENDAL JAZZ CLUB, The Brewery Arts Centre, Highgate, *Kendal*, Cumbria. **T** Kendal 25133. **Organizer** Les Bull, 54 Bellingham Road, Kendal, Cumbria. **T** Kendal 22252. **Venues** Brewery Arts Centre Monday evenings. Mainly traditional, some modern jazz. (*Note:* Brewery Arts Centre also promotes jazz Sunday lunchtimes.)

THE 'ROYAL', *Keswick*, Cumbria. **Organizer** Nick Telford. **Venues** The 'Royal', Tuesday evenings.

JAZZ NORTH EAST. Secretary Chris Yates, 33 Newton Road, High Heaton, *Newcastle-upon-Tyne* 7. **T** 0632–813677. **Venues** Various, approximately monthly.

NEWCASTLE UNIVERSITY STUDENTS UNION, The Union Society, Kings Walk, The University, *Newcastle-upon-Tyne*. **T** 0632–28402. **Venues** Students' Union, approx alternate Wednesdays during term-time.

THE 'WHEATSHEAF', Wheatsheaf Inn, New York, *North Shields*, Tyne and Wear. **T** North Shields 70422. **Organizer** Bob Coulson, 63 Cauldwell Lane, Monkseaton, Whitley Bay, Tyne and Wear. **T** Whitley Bay 22085. **Venues** Wheatsheaf Inn every Thursday evening. Traditional jazz.

SCOTLAND

ABERDEEN STUDENTS CHARITIES CAMPAIGN, 151 King Street, *Aberdeen*. **T** Aberdeen 24963. Approx twice pa.

PLATFORM. *The following societies in Aberdeen, Edinburgh and Glasgow arrange events in their respective areas and co-operate in arranging tours.*

PLATFORM MUSIC SOCIETY, c/o 38 Balgownie Court, *Aberdeen* AB2 1XF. **T** Aberdeen 57580 or 30606. **Organizers** Chris Maughan/Bill Christie. **Venues** Aberdeen Art Gallery, Mitchell Hall and Arts Lecture Theatre, monthly. Mainly modern/avant-garde, some traditional jazz.

PLATFORM – Edinburgh. **Secretary** Bob Stewart, 20 Drum Street, Gilmerton, *Edinburgh*. **T** 031–664 1137. **Venues** The West End, 127 Princes Street. Weds. Modern, mainstream. Occasional concerts elsewhere.

PLATFORM – Glasgow. **Enquiries to** Bill Kyle, 15a Royal Terrace, *Glasgow* G3 7NY. **T** 041–332 3743. **Venues** Various, regular concerts. All styles of jazz.

MACROBERT CENTRE, University of Stirling, *Stirling*, Scotland. **T** Stirling 3171 ext 2301. **Director** J Dodgson. **Venues** MacRobert Centre Main Auditorium and Studio Theatre. All styles of jazz.

Jazz in print

A selected listing of books published since 1970. Unless otherwise stated they are British publications and many of them are available from the Bloomsbury Bookshop (see specialist shops section). International standard book numbers are given in brackets, together with publisher, date of publication, number of pages and approximate price.

ALBERTSON, Chris *Bessie – A Biography Of Bessie Smith*. Barrie & Jenkins 1973. 256pp. £2.95. (214 654 09 5).

BERTON, Ralph *Remembering Bix* – A Memoir Of The Jazz Age. W H Allen 1974. £4.95.

BLANDFORD, Ed L *Artie Shaw*. Blandford Studio Castle Press 1974. 123pp. £2.50.

BLESH, Rudi & Harriet JANIS *They All Played Ragtime*. Paperback rev ed. Quick Fox USA 1971. £2.50. (0 8256 0091 X).

BLESH, Rudi *Combo USA* – Eight Lives In Jazz. Chilton USA 1971 (0 8019 5250 6). Hayden p'back 1972 (0 8104 6104 8).

BLESH, Rudi *Classic Piano Rags*. Dover p'back USA 1973 (0 486 20469 3).

BUERKLE, Jack V & Danny BARKER *Bourbon Street Black* – New Orleans Black Jazzmen. OUP USA 1973. 254pp. £3.60. (19 501690 4). OUP p'back £1.75.

CARR, Ian *Music Outside* – Contemporary Jazz In Britain. Latimer New Dimensions 1973. 190pp. £3.00. (901539 25 2).

CHILTON, John *Who's Who Of Jazz* – Storyville To Swing Street. Bloomsbury Bookshop 1970. 460pp. £5.00. (9501290 0 3). Repr by Chilton USA.

CHILTON, John *Billie's Blues* – Billie Holiday. Quartet 1975. 264pp. £3.95.

COLE, Bill *Miles Davis* – A Musical Biography. Morrow USA 1974. £4.50. (0 688 00203 X).

COLLIER, Graham *Inside Jazz*. Quartet 1973. 144pp. P'back £1.50. (7043 3022 9).

COLLIER, Graham *Jazz*. Cambridge UP 1975. £4.00. (0 521 20561 1).

CONDON, Eddie & Hank O'NEAL *Eddie Condon's Scrapbook Of Jazz*. Robert Hale 1974. £4.80. (0 7091 4476 8).

COTTERRELL, Roger & Barry TEPPERMAN *Joe Harriott Memorial*. Jazz Centre Society 1974. 26pp. £0.40.

DANCE, Stanley *The World Of Duke Ellington*. Macmillan 1971. 301pp. £3.50. (333 13019 7).

DANCE, Stanley *The World Of Swing*. Scribner USA 1974. £7.00. (0 684 13778 X).

EASTON, Carol *Straight Ahead* – The Story Of Stan Kenton. Morrow USA. £4.50.

ELLINGTON, Duke *Music Is My Mistress*. W H Allen 1974. £6.00.

FEATHER, Leonard *The Pleasures Of Jazz*. Horizon USA 1974.

FEATHER, Leonard *From Satchmo To Miles*. Quartet 1974. 258pp. £2.95. Midway £1.50.

FOSTER, Pops *The Autobiography Of A New Orleans Jazzman As Told To Tom Stoddard*. Univ Calif Press USA 1973. P'back £1.75. (520 02355 2).

FOX, Charles *The Jazz Scene*. Photographs by Valerie Wilmer. Hamlyn 1972. 128pp. £1.75. (600 02119 X).

FREEMAN, Bud *You Don't Look Like A Musician*. Balamp USA 1974. (0 913642 05 3).

GAMMOND, Peter *Scott Joplin And The Ragtime Era*. Angus & Robertson 1975. Sphere p'back £1.25.

GERT ZUR HEIDE, Karl *Deep South Piano*. Studio Vista p'back 1970. 112pp. £0.65. (289 70027 2).

GITLER, Ira *Jazz Masters Of The Forties*. Collier Macmillan USA. New p'back ed 1975. 288pp. £1.80.

GREEN, Benny *Drums In My Ears*. Davis-Poynter 1973. P'back 188pp. £1.50. (0 7067 0067 8).

HADLOCK, Richard *Jazz Masters Of The Twenties*. Collier Macmillan USA. New p'back ed 1975. 256pp. £1.50.

HARVEY, Eddie *Jazz Piano*. English Univ Press Teach Yourself Series. P'back 161pp. £0.95.

HAWES, Hampton & Don ASHER *Raise Up Off Me*. Coward USA 1974. £4.50. (0 698 10590 7).

HENTOFF, Nat & Albert McCARTHY eds *Jazz*. Da Capo Music Reprint Series USA 1975. 387pp. £2.50. (0 306 70592 3).

HODEIR, André *Jazz* – Its Evolution And Essence. Da Capo Reprint USA 1975.

HOLIDAY, Billy with William DUFTY *Lady Sings The Blues*. Barrie & Jenkins rev ed 1973. 240pp. £2.95 (214 66872 X). Also in p'back £1.00.

HUGGINS, Nathan I *Harlem Renaissance*. OUP p'back USA 1973. £1.40. (0 19 501665 3).

JOANS, Ted *A Black Manifesto In Jazz Poetry And Prose*. Calder Signature Series 1971. 92pp. £1.50. (7145 0713 X). P'back £0.50. (7145 0714 8).

JONES, Max & John CHILTON *Louis* – The Louis Armstrong Story. Studio Vista 1971. 256pp. £3.20.

KAUFMANN, Helen L *From Jehovah To Jazz* – Music In America. Kennikat USA 1970. 303pp. £4.50. (8046 0565 3).

KENNINGTON, Donald *The Literature Of Jazz*. Library Assoc 1970. 142pp. £1.75. (85365 074 8).

LANGRIDGE, Derek *Your Jazz Collection*. Bingley 1970. 176pp. £2.00. (85157 100 X).

LEE, Edward, *Jazz* – An Introduction. Kahn & Averill 1972. 192pp. £2.50. (900707 119).

LOMAX, Alan *Mr Jelly Roll* – The Fortunes Of Jelly Roll Morton. Univ Calif Press USA 1974 (0 520 02237 8). P'back £1.75.

McCARTHY, Albert *The Dance Band Era* – Dancing Decades 1910-1950. Studio Vista 1971. 176pp. £4.20. (289 70218 6).

McCARTHY, Albert *Big Band Jazz*. Barrie & Jenkins 1974. 368pp. £5.00.

MINGUS, Charles *Beneath The Underdog*. Ed by Nel King. Redwood Press 1971. 366pp. £2.50. (0297 00446 8), Penguin p'back £0.75.

PANASSIÉ, Hugues & Madeleine GAUTIER *Guide To Jazz*. Greenwood USA 1973 repr of 1956 ed (0 8371 6766 3).

PANASSIÉ, Hugues *The Real Jazz*. Greenwood USA 1973 repr of 1960 ed (0 8371 7123 7).

PANASSIÉ, Hugues *Louis Armstrong*. Scribner USA 1974. P'back £1.75. (0 684 13689 9).

POSTGATE, John *Plain Man's Guide To Jazz*. Hanover 1973. 146pp. £1.50. (900994 05 3).

REISNER, Robert *Bird* – The Legend Of Charlie Parker. Quartet 1974. 256pp. £3.95. (0 704 32063 0). P'back £1.75. (0 704 31166 6).

ROSE, Al *Storyville New Orleans*. Univ Alabama Press USA 1974. 225pp. £9.00. (0 8173 4403 9).

RUSSELL, Ross *Jazz Style In Kansas City And The South West*. Univ Calif Press USA p'back 1973. 292pp. £1.75. (520 02363 3).

RUSSELL, Ross *Bird Lives* – The High Life And Hard Times Of Charlie Yardbird Parker. Quartet 1973. 404pp. £3.75. (0 704 32007 X). P'back £1.75. (0 704 33005 9).

RUSSO, William *Composing For The Jazz Orchestra*. Univ Chicago Press USA new p'back ed 1973. 90pp. £0.70. (226 73209 6).

RUST, Brian *The Dance Bands*. Ian Allan 1972. 160pp. £3.75. (7110 0341 6).

SARGEANT, Winthrop *Jazz* – Hot And Hybrid. Da Capo USA. New enlarged p'back ed 1975. £1.75.

SHACTER, James D *Piano Man* – The Story Of Ralph Sutton. Jaynar Press USA 1975. £4.00.

SIMON, George T *The Big Bands*. Macmillan rev ed USA (Robert Markel ed) 1971. Rev & enlarged p'back ed 1974.

SIMON, George T *Glenn Miller*. Crowell USA 1974. £4.95. (0 690 00470 2).

SIMOSKO, Vladimir & Barry TEPPERMAN *Eric Dolphy*. Smithsonian Instit USA 1974. 132pp. £5.00. (0 87474 142 4).

STEARNS, Marshall *The Story Of Jazz*. OUP USA new ed Galaxy p'back 1971. 392pp. £1.40. (19 501269 0).

STEWART, Rex *Jazz Masters Of The Thirties*. Collier Macmillan 1972. 223pp.

SUDHALTER, R M & P R EVANS with W Dean-Myatt *Bix* – Man And Legend. Quartet 1974. 512pp. £4.95. (0 704 32070 3). P'back £1.95. (0 704 31188 7).

WELLS, Dicky *Night People* – Reminiscences Of A Jazzman. Ed by Stanley Dance. Crescendo USA 1971. (0 87597 068 0).

WILLIAMS, Martin ed *The Art Of Jazz*. OUP new ed USA 1971. 256pp. £3.45. (19 500662 3).

WILLIAMS, Martin *The Jazz Tradition*. OUP USA 1970. 242pp. £4.80. (19 500664 X).

WILLIAMS, Martin *Jazz Masters In Transition 1957-69*. Collier Macmillan 1971, 288pp. £2.25. (02 629390 0).

Jazz in focus

Jazz and blues films currently available for hire from UK distributors. All the following films are available for public showing and can be hired direct from the distributors whose addresses are given at the end of this section. Distributors' listed hire prices current when this list was compiled are given as a guide. In most cases VAT, postage and packing costs and insurance will be added and, in any event, prices should be checked with the distributor before hire.

'Afro-American Worksongs in Texas Prison'　　　TCB £7.00
30 Mins B & W
Director: Pete Seeger 1956
An examination of the worksong tradition on a Texas Prison Farm

'Along The Old Man River'　　　TCB £15.00
50 Mins Colour
Director: Robert Manthoulis 1972
Country blues with Robert 'Pete' Williams, Bukka White, Furry Lewis, Roosevelt Sykes, Sonny Terry & Brownie McGee and others

'Louis Armstrong'　　　TCB £10.00
30 Mins B & W
Produced: Goodyear 1961
Studio concert also featuring Trummy Young, Joe Darensburg, Billy Kyle, Billy Kronk, Danny Barcelona and Jewel Brown. Titles include: *When its sleepy time down South, Nobody Knows the Trouble I've seen,* and *The Saints*

'A Way To Escape The Ghetto'　　　TCB £15.00
50 Mins Colour
Director: Robert Manthoulis 1972
Urban blues with Buddy Guy, Jr Wells, Willie Dixon, Arthur Crudup, Mance Lipscombe, Sonny Terry & Brownie McGee and B B King

'A Well-Spent Life'　　　FE & VPS £10.00
44 Mins Colour
Director: Les Blank 1970
A beautiful documentary on Mance Lipscombe, his music, his life and the rural Texas community in which he lives

'Chris Barber's Jazz Band'　　　Robert Kingston £1.00
16 Mins B & W
In Concert

'Big Ben' TCB £7.00
30 Mins B & W
Big Ben Webster filmed when he was living in Amsterdam. A
portrait of the man as well as his music, Don Byas also appears

'Big Bill's Blues' TCB £6.00
15 Mins B & W
Director: Jean Delire 1956
Big Bill Broonzy sings four numbers in a French club

'Black, White & Blues' Transatlantic £25.00
50 Mins Colour
Director: Revel Guest
Blues and rock with Muddy Waters, 'Champion' Jack DuPree,
Fleetwood Mac, Chicken Shack, Savoy Brown, Alexis Korner and
Duster Bennett

'Blues Accordin' To Lightnin' Hopkins' FE & VPS £5.00
31 Mins Colour
Director: Les Blank 1967
A documentary on one of the giants of the country blues

'Blues Like Showers Of Rain' TCB £7.00
30 Mins B & W
Filmed stills Music and speech from Otis Spann, J B Lenoir,
Speckled Red, James 'Butch' Cage, Willie Thomas, Wade Walton
and many others

'Blues Under The Skin' The Other Cinema £20.00
88 Mins Colour
Director: Robert Manthoulis 1972
A fictional story, set in Harlem, about the struggle of a Black couple
to survive and stay together, interwoven with performances from
B B King, Furry Lewis, Rossevelt Sykes, Sonny Terry & Brownie
McGee, Bukka White, Buddy Guy and Jr Wells. Most of the music
footage also appears in 'Along the Old Man River' or 'A Way to
Escape the Ghetto'

'Born to Swing' TCB £15.00
50 Mins Colour
Director: John Jeremy
An examination of Swing music and some of its surviving
practitioners with the Count Basie Band, Buddy Tate, Dicky Wells,
Earle Warren, Buck Clayton, Jo Jones and Gene Krupa

'Marion Brown' TCB £7.00 (B & W)
25 Mins B & W or Colour £10.00 (Colour)
Portrait of avant garde jazz musician, trumpet player Lee Smith
also appears

'Chicago Blues' Contemporary £14.00
50 Mins Colour
Director: Harley Cokliss 1970
A classic film which not only includes some of the best examples of
recorded Urban blues but which successfully examines the
environment from which it came, the ghetto, and the social, economic
and political exploitation of the people who live there.

Music by Johnnie Lewis, Muddy Waters, Floyd Jones, J B Hutte, Jr Wells & Buddy Guy. Interviews with Willie Dixon, Bob Koester, Dick Gregory and most of the above musicians

'Circle'   TCB £7.00 (B & W)
33 Mins Colour or B & W   £10.00 (Colour)
Free jazz from Chick Corea, Dave Holland and Barry Altschul

'Bill Coleman, In Paris'   TCB £4.00
10 Mins B & W
With French rhythm section, includes a version of *Colmanology*

'Eddie Condon'   TCB £7.00 (B & W)
30 Mins B & W Also 35 mm   £10.00 (Colour)
Produced: Goodyear 1961
Studio concert with Eddie Condon, 'Wild' Bill Davison, Cutty Cutshall, 'Peanuts' Hucko, Johnny Varre, Joe Williams and Buzzy Drootin
Numbers include *Muskrat Ramble, Stealin' Apples* and *Blue & Broken Hearted*

'Country Jazz'   Australian High
10 Mins Colour   Commission £1.00
Film of the 1971 Dubbo Jazz Festival

'Count Basie & His Band'   Watso £0.50
10 Mins B & W
Numbers include *Someone's Rockin' my Dreamboat* and *Count Basie Boogie*

'Lol Coxhill'   TCB £7.00
30 Mins B & W
Directed: Mick Audsley
A film about one of the best British contemporary jazz musicians. Steve Miller also appears

'Cry of Jazz'   Contemporary £2.75
35 Mins B & W
A reiteration of the old view that only the black man, with his background of racial oppression, can play good jazz. No actual musical performances on film but the soundtrack is excellent

'Blind Gary Davis'   VPS £4.00
11 Mins B & W
Director: Harold Becker 1964
The legendary blues and ragtime guitarist and singer. Includes performances of two numbers.

'De dans le Sud la Louisan (Within Southern Louisiana)'   FE £10.00
42 Mins Colour
Director: Jean Pierre Bruneau 1972
Cajun and Zydeco music from the Balfa Brother, Clifton Chenier, Nathan Abshire, Alphonse 'Bois Sec' Ardoin & Canray Fontenot, Bee & Ed Deshotels, Bee Fontenot, Dennis McGhee, Adam & Cypien Landreneau, Reven Reed

206

'Delta Blues Singer; James "Sonny Ford" Thomas'   FE £7.50
45 Mins B & W
Directors: Bill & Josette Ferris
Film on blues singer performing in local juke joints

'Dry Wood & Hot Pepper'   FE £20.00
91 Mins Colour
Director: Les Blank
A film in two parts. The first, 'Dry Wood' is about the people of a
rural Black community in south west Louisiana with a strong
musical content. The second, 'Hot Pepper', is about Clifton Chenier,
the famed king of the Zydeco blues and shows him touring and
playing clubs and bars with his band.

'Duke Ellington Orchestra, The'   Robert Kingston £0.75
10 Mins B & W
A short example of 'the Piano Player' and his band

'Duke Ellington and His Orchestra'   TCB £10.00
30 Mins Colour Also 35 mm
Produced: Goodyear 1961
Studio concert. Featured soloists include Paul Gonsalves, Ray Nance,
Harry Carney, Sam Woodyard, Johnny Hodges

'Duke Ellington in the 40's'   TCB £5.00
10 Mins B & W
Compilation of soundies. Ben Webster also appears

'Bill Evans'   FE £6.00
20 Mins B & W
Director: Leyland Wyler
Bill Evans and his trio filmed in the early sixties playing in a small
club

'Festival'   FE £20.00
90 Mins B & W Also 35 mm
Director: Murray Lerner
Highlights from the 1963 to 1966 Newport Festivals including Bob
Dylan, Fred McDowell, 'Mississippi' John Hurt, Ed Young's Fife
& Drum Band, The Swan Silvertones, The Staple Singers, 'Son'
House, Howlin' Wolf, Joan Baez, Johnny Cash and many others

'Follow that Music'   Robert Kingston £1.00
18 Mins B & W
Director: Arthur Dreifuss 1946
Featured are Gene Krupa with his trio and Orchestra with Marty
Napoleon, Anita O'Day, Red Rodney and Charlie Kennedy

'Dexter Gordon'   TCB £7.00
30 Mins B & W
Filmed at Montmarte Jazz Festival, Copenhagen, with Kenny Drew
and Nils Pedersen

'Bobby Hackett'   TCB £7.00 (B & W)
30 Mins B & W or Colour Also 35 mm   £10.00 (Colour)
Produced: Goodyear 1961
Studio concert with accompanying musicians, Urbie Green, Bob

Wilbur, Dave McKenna, Nabil Totah and Morey Field. Numbers include *Deed I do*, *When the saints . . .*, *Bill Bailey* and *Swing that Music*

'Harlem Jazz Festival'   Contemporary £4.00
50 Mins B & W   Watso £2.00
Director: Joseph Kohn 1955
A rare glimpse of what an early '50s R & B revue was like.
Featured are Nat 'King' Cole, Count Basie, Sarah Vaughan, Lionel Hampton, Dinah Washington. Amos Milburn, The Larks, Martha Davis, Herb Jeffries, Little Buck & The Clovers. Excellent music.

'Jack Johnson'   VPS £16.00
90 Mins B & W
Director: William Clayton
Documentary on the legendary Black Boxer with sound track music by Miles Davis

'Jazz is Our Religion'   TCB £12.00
50 Mins B & W Also 35 mm
Director: John Jeremy
Photographs by Valerie Wilmer, Poetry by Ted Joans. Music by Johnny Griffin, Jon Hendricks and others

'Jazz on a Summer's Day'   TCB £20.00
85 Mins Colour
Director: Bert Stern
Film of the 1958 Newport Festival, featuring Louis Armstrong, Jack Teagarden, Mahalia Jackson, Thelonious Monk, Gerry Mulligan, George Shearing, Sonny Stitt, Anita O'Day, Chuck Berry, Big Maybelle and others

'Larry Johnson'   TCB £6.00
20 Mins Colour
Director: John Hammond jr 1972
Straight film of musical performances by young Black blues guitarist and singer

'Mingus'   FE £7.50
50 Mins B & W
Director: Tom Reichman
Charles Mingus, filmed playing in a club with his band as well as shown at a period of crisis in his life, the 1966 eviction from his New York loft.

'Red Nichols'   FE £3.00
7 Mins B & W
Filmed in 1950, the leader of the famous Five Pennies performs *Three Blind Mice* and *Backroom Blues*

'Harry Parry'   FE £5.00
16 Mins B & W
Director: Horace Shepard 1943
1940's British jazz from Harry Parry and his Radio Rhythm Club Sextet. Numbers include *Rockin' Chair*, *Send In My Shoes* and *I Got it Bad and that Ain't Good*

'Django Reinhardt' French Institute £1.70
21 Mins B & W
Director: Paul Paviet
Compilation of stills and interviews with Reinhardt's contemporaries,
soundtrack by Reinhardt, but no film of his performances.
Commentary in French

'Sonny Rollins, Live at Laren 1973' TCB £15.00
40 Mins Colour Magnetic soundtrack only
With David Lee, Walter Bishop jr and Bob Cranshaw

'Shoutin' The Blues' FE £4.00
6 Mins Colour
Director: Jack Agins
Blues harmonica player Sonny Terry. A companion film to
'Whoopin the Blues'

'Bessie Smith' London Film
13 Mins B & W Makers Co-op £4.00
Director: Charles Levine
A cinematic tribute with an excerpt from 'St Louis Blues' and
commentary spoken by Joseph Marzano

'St Louis Blues' Vaughn £6.00
16 Mins B & W
Director: Dudley Murphy
Bessie Smith in 1928

'Sun's Gonna Shine, The' FE & VPS £4.00
10 Mins B & W
Director: Les Blank
Lightnin Hopkins

'Supershow' FE £30.00
93 Mins Colour
Director: John Crome
Filmed at the Lyceum in 1969, featured are Colosseum, Buddy Miles,
Modern Jazz Quartet, Buddy Guy, Roland Kirk Quartet, Led
Zeppelin, Eric Clapton, The Misunderstood and others

'Swing It' Robert Kingston £1.00
10 Mins B & W
1936 Short featuring the Louis Prima Orchestra with Pee Wee
Russell

'Cecil Taylor' 1 TCB £7.00
23 Mins Colour

'Cecil Taylor' 2 TCB £5.00
15 Mins Colour
Interviews plus music. Supporting musicians are Jimmy Lyons,
Andrew Cyrille and Alan Silva. Filmed in Paris 1968

'Jack Teagarden' FE £3.00
3 Mins B & W
1948 short of this great trombone player performing *Basin Street
Blues*

'That's Jazz'   C TVC £4.00
26 Mins Colour
Freddy Randall/Dave Shepherd Band with Danny Moss, Dave
Hewitt, Brian Lemon, Kenny Baldock and Johnny Richardson

'Til The Butcher cuts him down'   Contemporary £15.00
53 Mins Colour
Director: Phillip Spalding
Narration by William Russell, the New Orleans jazz historian.
Documentary on Punch Miller that includes performances at
Preservation Hall and the Louisiana Heritage Fair

'Toronto Jazz'   Welsh Office
26 Mins B & W   Film Library £1.50
Director: Donald Owen
Produced by the National Film Board of Canada
Lenny Breau Trio, Don Thompson Quintet and the Alf Jones
Quartet

'Mal Waldron'   TCB £6.00
20 Mins Colour
Jazz pianist filmed in concert in 1972

'Sonny Boy Williamson'   TCB £4.00
10 Mins B & W
Legendary blues harmonica player and singer in Denmark 1964

'Whoopin' the Blues'   FE £8.00
14 Mins Colour
Director: Jack Agins
Blues harmonica from Sonny Terry

DISTRIBUTORS

Australian Information Service.
Canberra House,
Maltravers Street,
Strand,
London WC2R 3EH
(01–836 2435)

BFI (British Film Institute)
42/3 Lower Marsh Street,
London SE1 7RG
(01–928 2986)

Central Film Library,
Government Building,
Bromyard Avenue,
Acton,
London W3 7JB
(01–743 5555)

Columbia-Warner (16 mm)
  Distributors,

135 Wardour Street,
London W1
(01–437 4321)

Churches Television & Radio
  Centre,
'Hillside'
Merry Hill Road,
Bushey,
Watford WD2 1DR
(01–950 4426/7 01–5944/6)

Contemporary Films Ltd,
55 Greek Street,
London W1V 6DB
(01–734 4901)

FE (Fair Enterprises)
57 Greek Street,
London W1.
(01–734 6981)

French Institute,

Queensbury Place,
London SW7
(01–589 6211)

Robert Kingston Ltd,
645/7 Uxbridge Road,
Hayes End,
Middlesex
(01–573 2940)

London Film Makers
  Co-Operative,
17/35 Prince of Wales Crescent,
London NW1.
(01–267 4907)

The Other Cinema,
12/13 Little Newport Street,
London WC2H 7JJ
(01–734 8508)

TCB,
The Mall House,
Brockham End,
Bath BA1 9BZ
(Bath 20877)

Transatlantic,
Albert House,
9 Holland Park,
London W11
(01–727 1416)

Vaughn Films Ltd,
12 Fouberts Place,
Regent Street,
London W1V 1HH
(01–437 1551   01–437 9433)

VPS Film Library,
645/7 Uxbridge Road,
Hayes End,
Middlesex
(01–573 2940)

Watso Ltd,
160 Holbrook Lane,
Coventry CV6 4BY
(Coventry 84735)

Welsh Office Film Library,
42 Park Place,
Cardiff CF1 3PY
Cardiff 28066)

Specialist book and record shops

Bloomsbury Book Shop (Jazz Literature), 31-5 Great Ormond Street, *London* WC1 (01–242 6780).

Collett's Record Shop, 108 Shaftesbury Avenue, *London* WC2 (01-240 3969).

Dave Carey's Swing Shop, 1B Mitcham Lane, Streatham, *London* SW16 (01–769 7345/01–668 3500).

Dobell's Jazz Record Shop, 77 Charing Cross Road, *London* WC2 (01–437 4197/3075).

HMV Shop, 363 Oxford Street, *London* W1R 2BJ (01–629 1240).

James Asman's Record Centre, 23 New Row, St Martin's Lane, *London* WC2 (01–240 1380).

James Asman's Record Centre, 63 Cannon Street, *London* EC4 (01–236 9274).

Flyright, 21 Wickham Avenue, *Bexhill-on-Sea*, Sussex.

The Diskery, 99 Bromsgrove Street, *Birmingham* B5 6QB (021–622 2219).

Express Record Service (Mail Order), PO Box 16, *Bradford* BD1 3QL, Yorkshire.

Bruce's, 79 Rose Street, *Edinburgh*.

Impact Music Centre, 49 High Street, *Gillingham*, Kent (Medway 50625).

Soundbox, 176 Allison Street, *Glasgow*.

Avgarde Gallery Ltd, King's House, King Street West, *Manchester* 3 (061–834 2178).

Barry's Record Rendezvous, Hime & Addison Ltd, 8 St James Square, *Manchester* 2 (061–834 8019).

Eric Rose's Music Inn, 32 Alfreton Road, *Nottingham* (Nottingham 74403).

Sunshine Records Ltd, 31 Little Clarendon Street, *Oxford* (0865–52930/52830). Mail Order, 56 Northbrook Street, *Newbury*, Berkshire (0635 45313).

Peter Russell's Hot Record Store Ltd, 22-24 Market Avenue, *Plymouth* PL1 1PJ (0752–60255).

Potter's Music Shop, 18 Hill Rise, *Richmond*, Surrey.
Wally Waring's, 7 Penelope Road, Irlams-o'-th'-Heights, *Salford*, Lancashire.
Derek Clarke, 211 Abbotsbury Road, *Weymouth* DT4 0LY.

Index to the Articles